BUSINESS WARFARE

This is a very important and rather rare book on Business Warfare. It offers a very rich and inspiring content on various military tactics and associated leadership styles and invites corporate managers to reflect on the lessons learned from these when formulating their business strategies.

Only someone like Paulo Amaral can write such a book! Indeed, his military genes (being the son and grandson of military officers) and studies at a military school in addition to his extensive teaching experience in business schools, makes him uniquely positioned to write on the applicability and benefits of military strategies to business corporations.

Dr. Tawfik Jelassi, Ph.D.
Professor and former Corporate Board Chair

Make no mistake, most current approaches to business strategy will not last forever; they come and go, like all fashions. The strategic ideas of Sun Tzu, Clausewitz, and Machiavelli, however, are forever; they have stood the test of time and have influenced generations of leaders, yet they remain absent in most business conversations. In this fascinating book, Paulo Amaral presents the ideas of these strategic masters in a way that makes them accessible to today's practicing managers. It's time to restore historically big thinkers to our strategy conversations.

Bill Fischer, Emeritus Professor
of Innovation Management, IMD,
Senior Lecturer, Sloan School of Management, MIT

Paulo Amaral's serendipitous encounter has yielded a fascinating read bristling with historical facts, business analogies, practical tools and a rich set of templates to equip executives to survey their business territory from a broad range of viewpoints which will undoubtedly yield fresh insights and new routes to success.

Paul Hunter, Director of Programs and Learning Design, IMD Business School

This book is monumental in terms of content. The ability to bring together Clausewitz's Trinity, Sun Tzu's enduring principles, and General Foch's Economy of Forces, and then to correlate all of these in Chapter 23, is truly magnificent. The added value of referencing the ever-controversial Machiavelli at the end of the book further enhances its usefulness. I fully commend the author for this outstanding achievement!

António Gameiro Marques, Admiral of the Portuguese Navy (Ret), President of the Portuguese National Security Cabinet

Paulo Amaral has masterfully bridged the gap between the timeless principles of military strategy and the dynamic demands of modern business. Amaral's ability to translate historical insights into modern applications is unparalleled, making 'Business Warfare' not just a book, but a strategic companion for leaders committed to innovation and collaboration.

Patricia Santos, ZOME Group Chairwomen, Portugal

Brilliantly crafted and deeply engaging, this book will stay with you long after you've finished reading.

Alberto Amaral, Flexdeal CEO

BUSINESS
WARFARE

A framework for business strategy based on
Clausewitz, Sun Tzu, Foch and Machiavelli

PAULO CARDOSO DO AMARAL

BUSINESS WARFARE

Business Warfare
Copyright © 2024 by Paulo Cardoso do Amaral

All rights reserved under the Pan-American and International Copyright Conventions. This book may not be reproduced in whole or in part, except for brief quotations embodied in critical articles or reviews, in any form or by any means, electronic or mechanical, including photocopying, recording, or by any information storage and retrieval system now known or hereinafter invented, without written permission of the publisher.

Library of Congress Control Number: 2024939518

ISBN Paperback: 978-1-963271-20-1
ISBN Hardcover: 978-1-963271-21-8
ISBN Ebook 978-1-963271-22-5

Published by Armin Lear Press, Inc.
215 W Riverside Drive, #4362
Estes Park, CO 80517

CONTENTS

Introduction   1

PART I: Clausewitz on Strategy   7

1   Total War Or Not—That Is The Question   13

2   Clausewitz's Trinity   19

3   The World Today As A "Total Phenomenon"   25

4   On Economic and Information Warfare   29
     On Cyberwarfare   35
     Social Networks' Warfare   38
     Perception's management at its best?   43

5   Culture as a Weapon   49

6   The Emergence of Natural Monopolies   53
     Natural monopolies as platforms   55
     Playing on network effects   59

7   The Financial Infrastructure   67

8   Other Strategic Factors to consider   75
     Regulations as strategy   75
     Energy and transportation as strategy   77

9   Trinity's First Pole — The Political Power at Stake   81
     Explaining pure reason, chance, and violence   83
     Political level powers   84
     Regulation, trade deals and unwritten rules
     of the game   86
     Political/economic alliances   89
     Political influences coming from the outside   90
     Law applied to politics   91
     Media and social networking influences   92
     Direct influences from the other two dimensions   95
     Trinity's First pole -The Political framework in action   98

10 Trinity's Second Pole — The Armed Forces, And Chance — 102
- Companies — 103
- Players in the ICT infrastructure — 104
- Players in the payment infrastructure — 107
- Business level regulators — 113
- Players in the legal infrastructure — 115
- Players in the energy infrastructure — 116
- Players in Transportation — 117
- Players in the media and social networking — 118
- Direct influences from the other two dimensions — 120
- Trinity's Second pole - The armed forces' framework in action — 121

11 Trinity's Third Pole - The People — 124
- People's behavior — 124
- Social context — 125
- Company behavior — 127
- Special organizations' behavior — 129
- Technology and communications and media available — 133
- Energy, transportation and the sharing economy — 135
- Direct influences from the other two dimensions — 136
- Trinity's Third pole - The people's framework — 139

12 Clausewitz Complete Framework — 142

PART II: Sun Tzu on Engagement — 145

13 Sun Tzu's 10 Command and Control Leadership Virtues — 151
- Leadership Virtue #1 - Wisdom — 153
- Leadership Virtue #2 – Strictness (rewards and punishments) — 153
- Leadership Virtue #3 – Humanity or benevolence — 156
- Leadership Virtue #4 – Courage, engagement — 157
- Leadership Virtue #5 - Sincerity — 158
- Leadership Virtue #6 -Serene and self-controlled — 159
- Leadership Virtue #7 – Inscrutable — 160
- Leadership Virtue #8 – Impartial — 162
- Leadership Virtue #9 – Open to learn and adapt — 163
- Leadership Virtue #10 - Humble — 163
- The Virtues Framework — 165

14 The Nine Combat Grounds — 167
- Combat ground #1 - Dispersive (feudal) — 168
- Combat ground #2 - Frontier ground (shallow penetration) — 169
- Combat ground #3 - Key ground (equally advantageous) — 170
- Combat ground #4 – Communicating ground (open, not key) — 172
- Combat ground #5 - Focal ground (enclosed and critical) — 173
- Combat ground #6 - Serious or deep ground — 174
- Combat ground #7 - difficult ground — 175
- Combat ground #8 and #9 - Encircled/death ground — 176
- The Nine-Combat Grounds Framework — 178

15 The 6 Factors of Situational Awareness — 179
- Situational awareness factor #1 - Terrain — 181
- Situational awareness factor #2 - Adversaries — 183
- Situational awareness factor #3 - Weather — 186
- Situational awareness factor #4 - Doctrine and resources — 189
- Situational awareness factor #5 - Command — 190
- Situational awareness factor #6 - Moral influence (the harmony with leadership) — 191

16 Sun Tzu's Ten Tactics — 193
- Political-level tactics — 195
  - Tactic #1 - subdue the enemy without fighting by attacking his strategy — 196
  - Tactic #2 - disrupt alliances and the armies only after — 197
- Ground-level tactics — 199
  - Tactic #3 - Bring the enemy to the field of battle — 199
  - Tactic #4 - Create a position not to be defeated and grab every opportunity — 203
  - Tactic #5 - Create momentum — 206
  - Tactic #6 - Conserve your strength and maintain your freedom — 207
  - Tactic #7 - Prevent the enemy from concentrating — 209
- Support-level tactics — 211
  - Tactic #8 - Use extraordinary (special) forces ("Infinite as the heavens on earth") — 211
  - Tactic #9 - Capture enemy resources — 213
  - Tactic #10 - Throw your troops to prepare to die (throw the army into a desperate position) — 214

17 General Foch's Economy of Forces — 223
- Economy of Forces factor #1 - Concentration of forces — 229
- Economy of Forces factor #2 - Freedom of action — 234
- Economy of Forces factor #3 - Economy of effort — 241

Foch's superior principle in action	244
Foch's Economy of Forces framework – Assessing tactics' strategic power	248

18 Examples of Sun Tzu's Ten Tactics Using Foch's *Economy of Forces* — 251

- Political-level tactics — 252
- Ground-level tactics — 256
- Support-level tactics — 271

19 Sun Tzu's Dynamic Engagement Checklist — 277

20 Sun Tzu's Tactical Health Checks — 281

- The Five Command Losing Factors — 282
- Factor #1 - Recklessness — 282
- Factor #2 - Cowardice — 283
- Factor #3 - Short-temper — 284
- Factor #4 - Irascibility — 284
- Factor #5 - Excessive Compassion — 285

21 The 6 Tactical Losing Conditions — 287

- Losing condition #1 - Insubordinate troops — 287
- Losing condition #2 - Strong troops with weak officers — 288
- Losing condition #3 - Valiant officers with ineffective troops — 289
- Losing condition #4 - Angry and insubordinate officers — 289
- Losing condition #5 - Morally weak general without a strict discipline — 290
- Losing condition #6 - Unable to estimate the enemy's forces — 290

22 Sun Tzu's Strategy In Action — The Route Map — 291

- Start with Clausewitz Trinity to define strategic objectives — 292
- Explore Situational Awareness for Tactical Planning — 293
- Explore Sun Tzu's tactics — 295
- Define the strategic route map with a sequence of tactics — 296
- Test the strategy against Foch's Economy of Forces — 298
- Perform a tactical health check — 300

23 Putting It All Together: Sun Tzu's Strategic Checklist	301
24 Afterthought	303

PART III: Capitalizing on Machiavelli's Virtù — 305

25 Virtù – The Six Prince's Qualities	311
Quality #1: Free-spending and generous	314
Quality #2: Merciful	315
Quality #3: Word-keeping and socially chaste	318
Quality #4: Friendly	320
Quality #5: Decision-making: brave, straightforward, firm, and grave	322
Quality #6: Believing	323
26 The Four Business Dimensions of *Virtù*	327
Dimension #1 - Emotions	330
Dimension #2 - Social rewards	335
Dimension #3 - Convenience	338
Dimension #4 - Greed	345
Combining *Virtù* qualities	349
27 Value Capturing Chords	351
Towards price discrimination	352
On price discrimination and price matching	354
Revenue models (RM)	357
Playing melodies with Value Capturing Chords	362
Aligning Value Capturing Chords with Strategy	364
Why profitability is a consequence of strategic sustainability	369
About the Author	371
Appendix I: Frameworks	373

INTRODUCTION

Like many things in life, an element of chance helped shape this book.

Targeting a business audience, I address military strategy, an unplanned yet intense interest of mine. My passion for grasping it didn't come out of nowhere, though.

My grandfather was an infantry captain in WWI, my father was also a captain in the Portuguese colonial wars in the 1960s, and I was brought up in a military boarding school in the 1970s. Yes, I have the military running my veins, and I started reading and reflecting on military strategy in 1992 after earning my Ph.D. in technology. In 1996, I started lecturing on business strategy with technological roots on what later came to be known as digital transformation and disruption.

In the decades since then, I have been experimenting with military strategy elements in the world of business. After writing a book on competitive intelligence, together with the discussions with the military in my classes on information warfare, I increasingly discerned the benefits of military strategy for business. For example, the military go to battle on a bedrock of situational awareness, both for planning and execution. I believe this also makes sense for business strategy because markets are becoming more unpredictable than ever, with the management of surprise a priority concern. Besides, our moves entail adversaries' responses, sometimes jeopardizing our plans from day one.

In summary, handling businesses like military warfare has as justifiable appeal. However, the relevant military concepts, authors, and examples had not taken shape into a cohesive narrative or how-to manual in my mind. I needed a spark to initiate a "chemical reaction" if you will. It happened by chance.

In the middle of a discussion with my good friend Nuno Rolo at *CatólicaLisbon*, an insight came to mind and struck me like lightning. Nuno asked my opinion about the applicability of Sun Tzu's teachings to business, and, out of the blue, my immediate answer was, "Well, yes, if we add Carl von Clausewitz and Niccolò Machiavelli to the lot."

I decided to write this book on the spot. During subsequent writing and research, the new perspective was complemented with the insights of a fourth military genius, Ferdinand Foch, to create a complete, comprehensive, and actionable methodology around an architecture of frameworks.

But why all this excitement?

Sun Tzu already provides great teachings for battleground struggles, so why do we need more authors and insights? Because Sun Tzu deals essentially with confrontation, and nowadays, the business environment is living a more encompassing scope. There are currently more factors influencing any entity's strategic positioning than just fighting for consumers, customers, and clients—unexpected factors beyond eyesight at battleground level, like regulations and political moves unleashed by unsuspected stakeholders. So, I sensed the need to use Clausewitz for a broad inclusion of the factors currently influencing business because that is what I learned from reading his unfinished book, *On War*. The most cited Clausewitz quote, "War is politics by other means," or "with other means," depending on the translation, invites the strategist to contemplate political level actions besides war, something not so extensively covered by Sun Tzu. Moreover, the wisdom in Clausewitz's Trinity concept is a bedrock for a solid, encompassing, and enlightened strategic appraisal, well beyond traditional methodologies like PESTLE (Political, Economic, Social, Technological, Legal and Environmental) factors in marketing and Porter's Five Forces in competitive analysis, among others. Inspired by the French revolution, Clausewitz was right when mentioning the Absolute War.

My flashing insight also encompassed Sun Tzu's dynamic approach to struggle, on a substratum of situational awareness, which previous authors primarily missed when analyzing *The Art of War*. Situational awareness is paramount for benefiting business strategy. Moreover, Sun Tzu's strategic vision is bottom-up, which is refreshing because traditional strategic planning has been primarily top-down. Following his teachings, battleground moves intend to gain strategic leverage, just like in a chess game. In other words, strategy emerges from recurring tactical appraisal followed by subsequent actions. So, building a bottom-up strategy around situational awareness became immediately appealing.

Moreover, having worked with traditional strategic business strategy tools, I found outstanding comprehensiveness and dynamics with Sun Tzu's approach. We can still use Design Thinking for the value proposition, the BMC (Business Model Canvas) for strategic management, and Porter's Five Forces for rivalry assessment, to name just a few, although embedded in Sun Tzu's tactics in motion, all rising from good situational awareness. It's powerful and exciting.

Sun Tzu's situational awareness is different from the current competitive intelligence approach. For him, strategy unfolds from a sequence of tactical moves, requiring real-time decision-making before each maneuver. Where strategic planning is closer to traditional Plan-Do-Check-Act (PDCA), in my view, Sun Tzu defends Observe-Orient-Decide-Act (OODA) for tactical execution, and the difference is enormous because the latter starts with situational awareness upfront. Where PDCA thrives in exploitation and incremental improvements, OODA is exploration itself. The former is efficient for stable environments, and the latter is effective for turbulent ones. Then with the Clausewitz Trinity in the mix, my idea was to build another tool as a set of frameworks, capturing the entirety of Sun Tzu's approach, with situational awareness and OODA in mind.

Then came Ferdinand Foch—a mandatory add-on for developing Sun Tzu's framework. While examining Sun Tzu's methods, I realized the need to measure tactical effectiveness. Otherwise, how could we choose among different tactical choices? The goal is a dynamic and evolutive approach to strategy. More than a plan, we want a decision-making framework capable of following the competitive environment the best way possible; plans get outdated and PDCA is not fast enough. Sun Tzu's approach is OODA if we can appraise the strategic power of each tactical move. So, I got help from General Ferdinand Foch's principles. They are straightforward. Even if the tactical appraisal is also included in Sun Tzu's teachings, Foch devised a superior principle to guide our tactical decisions, which fits marvelously for externalizing the needed steps for the complete OODA approach. So, it would be only fair to mention Foch as well.

At this point, it seems that we already have everything we need to proceed with strategy through tactics, but Machiavelli popped up. Whereas Sun Tzu deals with battle, Machiavelli specializes in what to do with victory. For businesses, that means profit. And how do we make a profit nowadays? By winning everybody's hearts, and that is Machiavelli's specialty.

When we talk about Machiavelli, we talk about *The Prince*, his most well-known book. Our Machiavellian approach has two facets. The first one is getting an individual's acceptance, recognition, admiration, or any other positive feeling somehow bonding our relationship. It's Machiavellian because we create value, and people appreciate it, only to find their pockets emptier. The second facet addresses the latter, capturing value from customers' good intentions of all sorts. It's a tactic creating value for both sides, which is its magic because increasing revenues is a consequence of buyers' yearning. We also develop an OODA-like framework, synchronized with Sun Tzu's dynamics, continually aligning value capturing with business strategy, thus maximizing profit.

If you live in a predictable and stable competitive environment, this book is not for you. If not, and you need strategic thinking, the practical frameworks put forward will foster your insights.

PART I
CLAUSEWITZ ON STRATEGY

"...war is not merely an act of policy but a true political instrument, a continuation of political intercourse, carried on with other means."
CARL VON CLAUSEWITZ, ON WAR, 1832[1]

Classical business strategy is not enough anymore.

Environmental surprises, such as unexpected government regulations, attacks from giant technology companies, or disruptive fintech start-ups, have become the norm. And daily the consequences of the COVID-19 pandemic were here to remind us that nothing can be taken for granted.

In this interconnected world, the ruthless business environment has engendered natural monopolies, some at the global

---

[1] Carl von Clausewitz, trans. Michael Howard and Peter Paret, *On War*, (New Jersey: Princeton University Press, 1976), page 87

level, to which we have become accustomed in this new digitized parallel universe. Individuals, as well as companies, struggle for victory; "business as usual" is an outdated concept. We are now obliged to consider all possible actors influencing an enlarged competing landscape, even global for some industries. At the worldwide level, we also have to scrutinize governments, political thrusts, regulations, and other less apparent bodies, institutions, or authorities, whoever they may be. The most dangerous surprises generally emerge from the unexpected. Amid globalization, even bats on the other side of the world can play their part in large-scale disruption.

Besides, our economies value scarcity above all things because all unparalleled assets are effectively worthy, whereas commodities and public goods are not. These are unsurmountable facets of any strategic balance today, anywhere on earth, shaping economies everywhere. Just consider today's most invaluable worldwide companies when compared with the previous decade's front-runners. Now, the most prosperous are technology-based. Besides, because technology has been abundantly available for decades, technology alone hardly explains victories. Strategy does—military-style strategy deciphering and prescribing the business environment.

The more we understand today's complex web of relationships, the better we will choose the most effective course of action. Today, business strategy is no longer self-reliant and will be ineffective if we just consider the prominent traditional strategic stakeholders' immediacy. The web of actors effectively sustaining our business in all its forms has a life of its own, originating opportunities and threats by itself, which we should investigate.

In a dynamic and non-linear complex world, chaotic strategic balances naturally emerge. The traditional and static SWOT (strengths, weaknesses, opportunities, and threats) analysis, for instance, is no longer enough. For better or for worse, its facets do not unveil themselves just by planning anymore. Nor traditional external PESTLE (Political, Economic, Social, Technological and Environmental) analysis, for that matter. So, in this work, we are going to put all conventional business strategy frameworks aside and deploy, in its place, a complete architecture of military strategy concepts.

Only by understanding the strategic objectives of the various contenders, at all economic levels, as companies, non-profit organizations, ordinary citizens, and even governments, together with their balance within the interconnected web of influence, will we be able to grasp even a minimal vision about any meaningful scenarios onwards. Without it, we will continue blindfolded to compelling transitions ahead, with the Big Short[2] and the 2020 pandemics being two notable examples.

The same is true when trying to picture different foreign business environments. As an example, I am pretty sure that, when moving East, both eBay and Uber went through their market's due diligence process, together with a most developed strategic plan. So, why did they both lose shortly after entering the Chinese market? Some may say it was for political reasons and that both companies should not have even tried to compete in that different and probably politically adverse market in the first place. But that would hide a most magnificent and insightful interpretation because we usually learn more from losses than

---

2   Adam McKay, dir., *The Big Short* (2015; United States of America: Universal Pictures,2016).

from victories. But why do we hardly hear about these losses? It's only reasonable that, as in politics, companies always try to foster a positive and winning image, even when it's not the case. Like most bad things in life, losses are intentionally forgotten.

The Asian market is challenging and different because network effects have disparate rules. In China, network effects generate the peculiar balance of mobile social networking and a different flavor provided by the financial infrastructure and Super Apps like Alipay and WeChat (Note: WeChat is much more than a social networking app). Super Apps are related to the Chinese regulations, having political roots in the geopolitical objectives regarding the worldwide economic warfare. When a business strategy is blind to all these and other factors, it will significantly miss that environment's real opportunities while under-valuating its threats. Businesses risk falling into the first environmental trap along the way due to major blind spots. So, without carefully considering all actors and the emerging relationships in the globalized environment, we will always face significant pitfalls, as well as missed opportunities beyond our line of sight. In a nutshell, both Uber and eBay could probably have gotten it right by looking at the business environment in its entirety and not only by using the traditional business-level strategy recipes that had brought them success in other parts of the world.

Never take things for granted. Despite globalization, the world seems stubborn in maintaining geostrategic powers prescribing specific and unwritten rules in their vicinity. Even natural monopolies have their limits, which is maybe not so bad after all. We must take all these macro-factors into account when dealing with business strategy and with no previous assumptions. Every strategic analysis should consider all meaningful scenarios, even when strange and unusual.

I think I know what you are thinking now. And the answer is no! PESTLE analysis, in all its variants, is not enough. First, the PESTLE misses the various actors, their level of visibility in the value chain, and their mutual influences. And we need it all. Each actor is important for the final strategic balance of all relevant elements in the value chain and should be duly spotted. That is particularly true for platforms, which are a significant invention of the 21st century, forever changing the world.

Also, we need to scrutinize the dynamic relationships between all these actors, which prescribes the balances we should now be browsing, and we will achieve it by deploying Clausewitz's macro-level approach. Instead of looking for disparate tendencies at various dimensions, Clausewitz invites us to consider a route map of entities and relationships, identifying their roles, objectives, and practices. The strategic balance will emerge within all this practical information labyrinth, appropriate for this crazy and ever more globalized and interconnected world.

Welcome to the beautiful world of Clausewitz's grand strategy!

ONE
TOTAL WAR OR NOT—
THAT IS THE QUESTION

Clausewitz's concept of war has been a matter of much debate. On the one hand, reference authors like John Keegan[3] and Jan Honig[4] consider, without any room for doubt, *total war* to be the concept that Clausewitz meant when referring *absolute war*.

Clausewitz never mentions *total war* in his book, though. He uses various other terms referring to the encompassing nature of war throughout the book. Concepts like absolute war and ideal war are not the same, and probably written about by him at different times. According to Clausewitz's wife, *On War* was an unfinished project because her husband died before finishing it. That version got published a few years after her husband's death.

Clausewitz worked on this masterpiece of military literature during his appointment to the Prussian War College for fifteen years, just before going on assignment as chief of staff

---

3   John Keegan, *A History of Warfare*, (Pimlico, 2004).
4   Jan Willem Honig, *The Idea of Total War: From Clausewitz to Ludendorff*, March 2012, In book: The Pacific War as Total War: Proceedings of the 2011 International Forum on War History, Publisher: Tokyo: National Institute for Defense Studies, pp.29-41

of the Prussian army during the Polish November Uprising in November 1830. He would die one year afterward, touched by the second European cholera pandemic spread, which happened to break out exactly where he was fighting.

When publishing Clausewitz's work in 1832, the preface written by his wife confirms the unfinished status of *On War* which was going through revisions at the time of his death. That should be the reason for controversy about the *absolute* and *ideal* concepts of war, together with the reference of war being a *total phenomenon*, also mentioned in the book. These are crucial concepts for Clausewitz's strategic vision.

In the first chapter of the book, Clausewitz talks about *ideal war*, a conflict that "will seem increasingly political in character."[5] Then, at the end of the book, Clausewitz discusses *Absolute War and Real War*, so, "two different concepts of success arise."[6] Still, he does not leave any room for doubt regarding war's *absolute form*, which is "indivisible, and its parts (the individual victories) are of value only in their relation to the whole."[7]

With absolute war, each tactical action has to be deservedly considered in its global strategic context. But absolute war is effectively different from *total war*.

The term *total* is our focus. It appears when Clausewitz puts forward his important Trinity concept, calling the war a total phenomenon with dominant tendencies that make it a trinity. This concept is the basis for Part I because the strategic model proposed is entirely based on its interpretation and details.

---

5   Clausewitz, On War, 1976, page 88
6   Clausewitz, On War, 1976, page 582
7   Clausewitz, *On War*, 1976, page 582

Throughout his book, Clausewitz interpreted Napoleon's victories because the French military genius initiated a different and unrestricted way of fighting, which explains his incredible successes. R.R. Palmer explains:

> Before the French Revolution, the war was mostly a conflict between rulers. After the French Revolution, it's important to remember that France engaged in wars abroad because the surrounding European countries were concerned about Napoleon's expansionist policies and growing dominance in Europe.[8]

After the French Revolution, we should recall that France only went abroad fighting after having defeated three international coalitions in their own territory between 1792 and 1806. These conflicts emerged when the international coalitions of surrounding countries tried to reinstate monarchy after its abolishment by the French revolution in favor of a Republic. When Napoleon took his campaigns abroad during the French Revolutionary Wars, which began in 1796, he initially achieved significant success. However, he began losing everything after his major mistake of attacking Russia and capturing Moscow in 1812, in an attempt to enforce the Continental Blockade against the British Empire. That victory, which some deem Pyrrhic, did not serve Napoleon's strategic intent well, as it failed to defeat Tsar Alexander's army. After one month of waiting in Moscow for some kind of negotiation, Napoleon's army left the city in harsh logistic conditions, increasing the casualty rate to an astonishing 80 percent of the

---

8   Edward Mead Earle, ed., *Makers of Modern Strategy*, (Princeton: Princeton University Press, 1943)

initial attacking force. That marks the beginning of Napoleon's final defeat, which happened three years afterward at Waterloo.

Clausewitz's thoughts about Napoleon are essential and may have led him to write *On War* in the first place. Napoleon's genius and successes inspired several other military strategists, including General Ferdinand Foch, whose fundamental ideas are the basis for strategic assessment and discussed in Part II. All these authors refer to Napoleon's battles with examples of strategy and tactics to justify their theoretical interpretation.

Clausewitz's thoughts rely on more than thirty years of practical military experience. Starting to serve in the German army' at age twelve, Clausewitz engaged against the French in 1793, with just months of training, only to taste the bitterness of defeat. After Napoleon's overwhelming victory against the 4th international coalition in 1805, he occupied Prussia in 1806 with the battles of Jena and Auerstedt. These two battles took place in less than one month, resuming in a mesmerizing final victory. One single month to defeat and occupy the overwhelming Prussian empire with all its rigor and training. And it was not even Napoleon himself that grabbed the primary piece of glory, but General Louis-Nicolas Davout. With a smaller army of around 27,000 men, this general defeated a 65,000-man strong Prussian army lead by the Prussian King himself. Napoleon did not want to believe he was being overshadowed; he was commanding a bigger army of 40,000 men at Jena. Clausewitz witnessed the dismantling of the Prussian army first-hand because he became one of the prisoners again. How could an apparently less organized band of mostly non-professional army men be able to trounce

Prussia, a well-organized nation forged by Frederick the Great's tactical discipline just years before?

That dramatic experience was probably a cornerstone for coining *On War*. He then went fighting for the Russians, and against the French again, in the Russian-German Legion in 1813, only to experience defeat anew in Borodino's battle, because Napoleon did enter Moscow after all. But then, he also witnessed Napoleon's subsequent collapse, also helping it with some intelligence in coordination with the Prussian army when a multitude of frozen, hungry, and dying French men were trying just to survive and get back home. Moscow's victory did not serve Napoleon at all, because "the successful stage was not only wasted but led to disaster"[9].

Reading *On War* is also a history lesson. Napoleon's examples pop up everywhere in the book. Clausewitz explains the various happenings while putting in place a structured vision to encompass both military strategy and politics, considering war a broader concept, well in line with the already referred *total phenomenon*.[10]

Clausewitz's broader vision about war, where politics is involved, is prone to controversy because the German word politics can also mean policy, which is an entirely different concept. Still, in Clausewitz's book, and according to the chosen translation,[11] "the political object is the goal"[12], so, "war is, therefore, an

---

9   Clausewitz, *On War*, 1976, page 582
10   Clausewitz, *On War*, 1976, page 582
11   Clausewitz, *On War*, 1976
12   Clausewitz, *On War*, 1976, page 87

act of policy"[13] and "a true political instrument, a continuation of political intercourse, carried on with other means."[14]

Clausewitz thus saw conflict in a comprehensive sense, which is the focus of interest. His Trinity summarizes all concerned components of conflict in a practical manner, and our job now is to fully understand this concept and interpret it in today's business and geopolitical contexts. The following discussion's objective is to transform all this knowledge into a practical and easily actionable framework for business strategy.

---

13   Clausewitz, *On War*, 1976, page 86
14   Clausewitz, *On War*, 1976, page 87

TWO
CLAUSEWITZ'S TRINITY

The unfinished nature of *On War* turns out to be fascinating, giving rise to multiple interpretations. Maybe that is why so many different and contradictory schools of thought proliferated, in the strategic debate,[15] from utter totalitarianism to democracy and pacifism. The previously discussed Clausewitz's *total* approach may justify the importance of considering every facet of what could influence the competitive environment, much beyond the traditional battleground level strategy approach. Even if this *total* aspect of warfare, as practiced in the twentieth century, could not exist in Clausewitz's mind, he captured an enduring concept when proposing his *Trinity*. The Trinity model represents his way of incorporating the strategic levels involved during any conflict. In this text, we use his inspired model for assessing the globality of the multiple dimensions and contenders involved in any dispute, which is the best way we know to bootstrap any strategic reasoning.

---

15 E. Alterman, The uses and abuses of Clausewitz, *The Military Espectator*, n. 157, 1988, page 416-424

Clausewitz's defines his Trinity[16] as a total phenomenon, concerning the three following elements:

- government
    - subordination as an instrument of policy (that is, pure reason);

- commander and his army
    - the creative spirit playing chance and probability;

- people
    - natural forces, acting through violence, hatred, and enmity.

Clausewitz develops a useful model with his remarkable Trinity, encompassing all the concepts he considers necessary for strategy in action. It's a trinity because these three concepts interconnect as a triangle, that is, each one has a dynamic and evolving relationship with the other two.

Another crucial concept for understanding Clausewitz's model of the world is the notion of *center of gravity*, which appears in Chapter 9 of *On War*'s *Fourth Book*, and it's engaging. For Clausewitz, "a center of gravity is always found where the mass concentrates most densely,"[17] and he also considers that "the battle must always be considered as the true center of gravity of the war."[18]

---

16   Clausewitz, *On War*, 1976, page 89; note that translators initially used the word paradoxical to describe the Trinity, but that has since been revised.
17   Clausewitz, *On War*, 1976, page 485
18   Clausewitz, *On War*, 1976, page 248

Clausewitz thus defines a battle as a massive deployment of armed forces and an act of human violence. War happens with an arbitrary number of struggles, a sequence of undisciplined episodes in a complex environment. In such a dynamic environment, planning is not enough. Human nature and luck are also part of the game, much in contradiction with significant contemporary thinkers, including the Swiss Baron Antoine-Henri de Jomini[19] and the Prussian General von Bulow. Interestingly enough, chance resides in the second dimension of the *Trinity*.

The ancient, traditional, and somehow narrow definition of war started to change in practice with Napoleon due to the encompassing nature of his approach to disputes, the total phenomenon, as Clausewitz calls it. Besides, Napoleon and Clausewitz witnessed the Russian victory "by other means,"[20] other than with battleground combat, and involving different actors than just soldiers. Like the French have been doing since their revolution, the Russian used the entire population for the war effort to accomplish the scorched earth' tactics.

The total phenomenon of conflict naturally evolved for the last two centuries, not only in waging any physical and violent war but also because the confrontation also happens by other means, including information and economic warfare. We just need to identify the new "spheres of effectiveness"[21], keeping in mind his Trinity's dynamics, because that is how battles unfold.

---

19 We should bear in mind that Henri de Jomini outlived Carl von Clausewitz and we are mentioning Jomini's early writings, well at the beginning of the nineteenth century. Jomini's reference books, *Traité de Grande Tactique*, and *Precis de l'Art de la Guèrre*, were published after Clausowitz's death and subsequent publishing of *On War*.
20 Clausewitz, *On War*, 1976, page 87
21 Clausewitz, *On War*, 1976, page 486

Therefore, using Clausewitz's Trinity to identify centers of gravity in a conflict is a way to transform strategy into something concrete by identifying the various forces underneath struggle at all decision-making levels, from high-level strategy to applied tactics on the field. This is one of this work's own centers of gravity, a major important one, and the objective of Part I. We aim to detail meaningful centers of gravity of each Trinity's element, offering a tool and a methodology to perform a complete high-level strategic analysis and cope with the current *total* competitive landscape across its current complex and unpredictable facets.

Battles happen at all three levels of the Trinity, that is, between governments, between armed force, and between people. All these entities are related to one another.

Companies are the new armed forces in the age of economic warfare. Clausewitz grasped this multitude of actors and relationships and theorized it before anyone else. During conflict and struggle, multiple interacting centers of gravity will exist at these levels, and his Trinity concept considers them all in an integrated manner. Clausewitz's Trinity is, thus, a handy analytical tool.

Countries do battle with one another. That may happen with diplomacy, public news in the media, or high-level alliances. In the worst case, armed forces can also engage in battles.

People—citizens—relate to their governments, depending on each political system. Consequently, governments reflect people's will in the same way that governments will also reflect on people's actions. It goes both ways.

The resources of armed forces comprise people and companies, among others, some of which are intangible. Fortunately, economic warfare has become a preferred battleground in many environments after WWII. It's fortunate because if a conflict must exist, it's better to keep it in the context of other means, leaving physical violence aside.

However, regulations set the rules of the competitive environment, which, in turn, are set by governments. Additionally, governments may also instruct companies regarding their common strategic objectives, which means that it also goes both ways.

Thus, the three dimensions of the Trinity are directionally connected in a triangle because each entity is capable of influencing the other two. As we are talking about decision making, the center of gravity will move towards the factor with more relevance at each point in time. Clausewitz calls it magnets[22]. We will call them poles.

Christopher Brassford[23] proposes a magnetic pendulum analogy to foresee war's evolutive nature, naturally balancing among the three poles. This author refers to this type of movement as "deterministic chaos." According to the Trinity, chances and probabilities are also part of the game, alongside reason and will. The result will be a dynamic and evolving balance between all three poles, keeping in mind that our adversaries also try to influence the same factors to their own advantage.

We want to look closer to each of the poles to develop a detailed route map about all centers of gravity under consideration in the current competitive landscape. We first discuss several vital

---

22   Clausewitz, *On War*, 1976, page 89
23   Christopher Bassford, "Teaching the Clausewitzian Trinity" 1995-2022, http://www.clausewitz.com/readings/Bassford/Trinity/TrinityTeachingNote.htm

layers of the actual competitive environment, detailing afterward, its interpretation in face of Clausewitz's Trinity. It's my interpretation upon which you may develop your own.

THREE
THE WORLD TODAY AS A "TOTAL PHENOMENON"

Clausewitz's Trinity in today's world requires a model to unveil the fundamental environmental characteristics at stake today. It's all about power. In a world of scarce resources, there is an underlying belief that power leads to well-being. Power underneath everything else. For companies, power means increased profits. For governments, it will depend on their political agenda. Still, even for those less close to capitalism, it will be difficult to conceive well-being without economic success, with access to critical resources taking the stage instead of capital. That is true even for the most radical movements, with oil amid most conflicts. Consequently, we consider economic warfare to be a reality, with companies part of the governments' armed forces, maybe even the most critical weapons for some. Still, there are other dimensions to consider. What drives power? What are the most critical aspects dominating the world's conflicts today? The next four chapters examine the new normal, discussing a vision about today's most pressing challenges, all beyond the previous boring usual. We thus summarize and discuss the most recent weapons, resources, and methods, when considering the societal impact of information technology, seemingly the current main disruptive thrust.

Seeing economic warfare as the baseline of today's conflicts, we start by discussing how information warfare and cybersecurity contribute to constant rivalry, quite far away from the previous landscape of conventional and incidental conflict. Social networks and perception management have been powerful tools in today's asymmetric struggles, which is as new as surprising. Take, for example, the assault on the United States Capitol Building just before the inauguration of Joe Biden as the 46th president. How accurate was the attackers' perception of reality? How did that perception contribute to belief and subsequent actions?

The discussion continues by focusing on how platforms create a whole new advantageous battleground for Big Techs, spawning new and surprising natural monopolies, with tremendous impacts witnessed everywhere on earth. Indeed, platforms are so much more than just a shared set of virtual services and functionalities, seeing the network effects they create. Network effects are effectively fostering a new breed of ecosystems, thus shaping the rules of every competitive environment at arm's length.

We end the discussion in chapters 7 and 8 with the financial ecosystem as an example of how platforms' dynamics depict a new strategic balance, including payments. We also discuss regulations, a most potent tool in government hands in prescribing the economic warfare strategic balance to their own advantage.

Any resource or tactics deemed necessary in the current global strategic landscape may also be part of the lot. Consequently, like oil, water, nuclear resources of any kind, traditional armed forces, intelligence, and the like, the usual ones will be under consideration as well.

Our objective here is to devise an actionable framework issued from the interpretation of Clausewitz's Trinity to discuss details afterward in chapters 9 to 12.

FOUR
ON ECONOMIC AND INFORMATION WARFARE

Economic warfare is not part of just the big companies' agenda anymore.

Wars were the ancient normal for everybody. Most wars, if not all, always had economic objectives in one way or another. According to Sir Michael Howard, only for roughly the last two centuries did societies start to believe in peace; war was just a means to attain it, although with a new, more favorable, economic balance than before. The same author also defends that "peace is a far more complex affair than war."[24]

Even with peace in mind, the world experienced two devastating global conflicts in the twentieth century, and war is still part of the daily news in the twenty-first. Even when conflicts happen between some minor economic contenders, the struggles may part of proxy wars between major ones. For our proposes, we only need to consider the existence of conflict in any of its forms.

---

24   Sir Michael Howard, *The Invention of Peace*, (Yale University Press, 2001), page 1R

We should also remember that, for engaging in traditional warfare, someone has to build and sell weapons, which also justifies some of the conflicts. General Eisenhower's farewell address in 1961[25] as the 34th US president about the potential influence in politics of the military-industrial complex comes to mind. Moreover, social and economic unbalances foster political turnovers, and, in the context of international political alliances, there is always some country interested in a political twist within another country. Maybe this justifies yet other conflicts.

After the Cold War, and with the advent of globalization, economic warfare became the focal point for many countries. With decreasing economic borders, economies become interdependent and can be attacked. Even if everybody is better-off amid these agreements, in the long run, what counts is the balance between coopetitors, that is, competitors who choose to collaborate in the hope of reaping mutually beneficial results. Coopetition effectively allows more fragmented economic struggles. Directly attacking economies in any way possible is even more compelling than going through expensive and regrettable traditional warfare. All types of relationships underpin economic warfare, including energy, information, goods, people, services, and the list goes on and on. In particular, global communications are a cornerstone of economic warfare's tremendous opportunities.

Global interconnected relationships among everybody are increasing the world's entropy and social networks. Jointly, instant multimedia communications at zero marginal costs, are fostering it fast. It's the first time on earth where real-time international interactions are possible without apparent cost—I am referring

---

25 Military-Industrial Complex Speech, Dwight D. Eisenhower, 1961", Avalon Project. 2008, http://avalon.law.yale.edu/20th_century/eisenhower001.asp

to multimedia on top of traditional voice and messages. Short messages are a reality of the twenty-first century, and these also carried a price before the existence of certain platforms and cross-platform messaging services such as WhatsApp, Telegram, and Signal. On the other hand, emails were always free and around since the 1970s, but only for an almost insignificant small group of people until the emancipation of the Internet, which happened almost three decades afterward.

Furthermore, the communications landscape totally changed when the above met mobility, which materialized after 2010. We can now communicate freely, or at least by providing just our own data, anywhere in the world, as long as we are within the same politically permitted communication space: for example we cannot communicate with most social networking platforms when located in China.

Nowadays, everybody is using Over the Top (OTT) services virtually everywhere. This is new and is altering the social landscape, for better and worse. On the one hand, we do have easy and free access to information and knowledge, both in the form of news or more straightforward personal communications, sometimes within groups. We use it with all sorts of groups, whether personal, business, professional, or family. It has become so influential and so important that we cannot imagine our life without it anymore. On the other hand, social networks have also been prone to manipulation and other less-than-ethical objectives in a way that our personal information can also be used against us—Facebook's role in Brexit is an excellent example of this. A new world has come up, although not easy to keep pace with when the environment keeps itself progressively and continuously changing. At this time of writing, 5G promises to increase communications' bandwidth tenfold while decreasing its latency to instant near-real-time availability, which will accelerate disruption even more at all levels. And 5G has been the stage of economic warfare even before its practical release.

This near zero-cost communication environment fosters a new social landscape, with all powers capable of leveraging it do so for their own benefit. Besides, even traditional media can fully exploit it for building common social perceptions. We see it daily in the news and everywhere else. It's called information warfare, and it's pervasive.

In his prominent book, Clausewitz devises ways to "to compel our enemy to do our will,"[26] because what truly matters is what people think and believe. Fear and weapons may do the trick, which is unfortunately used by some to gain power, with populism being perhaps the best current example yet. Today, both the economy and information are tools to achieve the same goal, with much more effectiveness than conventional battles. With information warfare, attackers' costs are slim compared to conventional war, so it can become asymmetric, at the reach of small actors. After all, the nature of information warfare is to exercise power by directly affecting the thinking of people.

Moreover, virtually anyone can perpetrate information warfare, which opens the field to every other contender besides significant powers, hence the asymmetric attribute to this type of conflict. It's being used more and more, not only with political intent but also for economic leverage between companies in

---

26 Clausewitz, *On War*, 1976, page 75

several civic spaces, with cyberwarfare, including espionage, being current mainstream examples.

It is time to think about the meaning of economic leverage on high-level strategy and the difference between economic and information warfare. Information warfare may instill our will in our opponents' minds, even without their awareness, most probably by making them believe they are not our opponents in the first place. On the other hand, economic warfare works much like conventional wars, only "by other means," part of today's hybrid warfare. The economy is a different way to deal with peoples' beliefs and is also closely linked with information warfare due to the same necessity of entering peoples' minds, even if indirectly.

A country with influential companies and a sound economy is undoubtedly powerful. For example, Germany's permanent surplus of 5 to 6 percent regarding its European counterparts has been a clear example of such power in the first two decades of the century.

Moreover, today's social interaction is prone to populism and information warfare in all its forms. From traditional social networking to more recent and powerful mobile networking, anything goes. Disinformation disguised as information has never been so widespread; it's falsehoods told deliberately with malicious intent. This so-called fake or fabricated "news" when passed around by trustful people, becomes the rumors and innuendo with the somewhat more benign characterization of misinformation. More often than not, we tend to believe in misinformation due to the sender's implicit communication signature, hence its power and danger.

Weakening economies of a foe is also a way to gain leverage over their will, thus fulfilling Clausewitz's requirements. Economic warfare is here to stay! Furthermore, whereas traditional war only happened at specific and limited points in time, both information and economic warfare take place concurrently.

The current type of war deploying all different types of aggressions, all those already referred and all possible others, has been named the 4th generation warfare by William Lind and others.[27] The first generation happened in the period immediately after the Westphalia treaty in 1648-1650, when the religious wars officially disappeared from the face of Europe (actually, more formally than in practical terms during the following century). The second and the third generations are more commonly associated with conventional warfare, which is limited to the type of forces at stake, as well as limited scope along with clearly defined time boundaries.

At the end of the Cold War, we have been increasingly living in a 4th generation warfare environment, where anything goes. Today, we live in a continuous conflict mode, characterized to be complex and employing all possible available aggression methods on top of conventional warfare, including asymmetric warfare, cyberwarfare, regulations, information warfare in all its forms—perception management comes again to mind—economic warfare, and even cultural warfare with decentralized, sometimes distributed and transnational forces, involved in apparent low-intensity permanent conflicts.

Current warfare could probably not be more total or absolute than it already is. Thus, companies must consider that

---
[27] William S. Lind, Keith Nightengale, John F. Schmitt, Joseph W. Sutton, Gary Wilson, "The Changing Face of War: Into the Fourth Generation.," *Marine Corps Gazette*, October 1989

the geographical span of such warfare has strong roots in the underlying economic balance. Several contributing factors should be seriously taken into account. We start with cyberwarfare in offering an overview.

On Cyberwarfare

Cyberwarfare is part of the current asymmetric conflict, where the small can also take advantage of this fertile hostility ground to try disrupting the big. It's here to stay for several reasons.

The first is technical. With the simple operating systems we have been using—all too simple and all too flawed—hostile forces find it increasingly easy to turn them against their users, namely us. That has been particularly true for Microsoft Windows, but also for Unix and Linux.

We can sum up the technical insecurity, both at the operating and communication levels, with the following image. Because systems and communications are insecure by nature, the solution has been to surround everything with protection layers. Still, current protection strategies will always be an inglorious job because the bad guys will always find ways to hide and circumvent its protections, both in the communication protocols and on arrival in our computers–all coming from the insecurity-by-design nature of both computing and communication technology due to their origins and backward compatibility needs. This vision contrasts with what technical evolution has led us to believe.

A second reason comes from politics. Because everybody on earth uses the same operating systems and the corresponding Internet protocols, its flaws can be broadly exploited. In this regard, a good example of the inventiveness of intelligence agencies appears in the documents disclosed by Edward Snowden, the computer intelligence consultant who leaked highly classified data from the National Security Agency in 2013 and then fled to Russia.

All in all, the current technical environment is a mess, and most people are not even aware of what they are up against, including the company's technologists. The bad guys will probably always know more!

Solutions are coming, but no one knows if they will ever be adopted. I am referring to a proper technical architecture in place, namely by using cryptography by design. George Gilder has compelling arguments towards this reasoning in the first three chapters of his book about the Blockchain Economy.[28] Until then, we have to live with what we have.

Some of the most technologically powerful companies on earth should not be too interested in it because, if the cryptography revolution takes place, everything will change, including the information they possess about their users/consumers. With such a revolution, Self Sovereign Identity[29] will allow users/consumers to control their personal information again, instead of checking "read and accept" boxes without paying attention all the time. Therefore, without free access to information and knowledge about consumers, most Big Techs would experience a significant decrease in their profits. This change would be highly disruptive and would largely decrease their power, which will surely hinder their offering to in evolve distributed secure computing environments with cryptography-based security by design. On the other

---

28 George Gilder, Life After Google: *The Fall of Big Data and the Rise of the Blockchain Economy*, Regnery Gateway , 2018
29 Alex Preukschat and Drummond Reed, Self-Sovereign Identity Decentralized digital identity and verifiable credentials, New York, Manning Publications, 2021

hand, the possible increase of crime-as-a-service will be on the horizon and should be addressed. SSI may happen, but Big Techs will undoubtedly struggle against it. And Big Techs are powerful, politically powerful.

Maybe there is a third technical cybersecurity weakness coming from hardware threats, potentially involving its manufacturers. We can hardly imagine that a hardware manufacturer will ever include some additional malware in the form of unnoticeable harmful hardware specifically designed to fit intelligence or espionage purposes. Or can we? Out-of-band IP communication with hypervisors in Intel chips when the operating system is halted (means shutdown but connected to the mains) comes to mind. The computer will behave like the movie *Matrix* because, for the attacker, everything is stopped, including the operating system and all security systems. Yet, the attacker can communicate with the central processing unit and probably browse inside the concerned computer without raising any suspicion whatsoever.

Consequently, cyberwarfare is here for good. It's being used for intelligence, as well as for supporting traditional warfare and network-centric operations. But maybe the most impactful usage of cyberwarfare is felt at the economic level, by crippling companies' operations, stealing their secrets and disrupting critical infrastructures. The disruption of Critical Infrastructures has, undoubtedly, an economic impact. However, ot has a evermore social impact, in the security perception of the people (the third of Clausewitz Trinity Elements), which then may trigger economic instability. There is no economic development without security, and history proves it. Some companies disclose their breaches, but, most probably, the results of the most successful attacks remain in secrecy. Computer Incidents Response Teams are available, but these are more "monitoring services" than anything else because there is really not much they can do after damage erupts if the right precautions are not in place.

So, what should we do? We will consider cyberwarfare as part of the terrain and a strategic weapon as well. After all, attacking has been the best defense, at least since the Romans – "*si vis pacem, para bellum.*"[30]

Social Networks' Warfare

There is a close and increasing relationship between information warfare and social networks. On September 11, 2001, TV was king at the time, and the most significant impact of the Twin Tower attack happened in peoples' minds. That was seemingly the attackers' objective.

Media companies' bedrock lies in broadcasting content highly relevant to its targeted audiences everywhere. Even with the emergence of new communication paradigms, like customization and personalization through the Web, media remains highly relevant today and will continue to significantly influence the minds of the recipients. Television is often a social act, replacing the old conversations at the fireplace. There is a social aspect involved in broadcasting TV content, not only upon reception but also with the common meaning and interpretation discussed by everybody afterward. That is probably one of the main reasons for the success of reality shows. Broadcasting content also carries the social aspect of raising shared awareness, creating a common ground, sometimes even bonds between audience members. Only

---
30   "If you want peace, prepare for war", attributed to Publius Renatus, 4th century AD.

that today, on top of media, we also have social networks together with the Web, where people tend to be much more participative, pushing forward media's social impact to unimaginable heights. That is called synergy.

But whereas media broadcasts convey the sense that everybody is watching the same thing, the Web is another matter. With the Web, each recipient can receive personalized content depending on the sender's knowledge about recipients. The importance of this knowledge is revealed when some of the wealthiest and most influential companies on earth are generating rents precisely on the value created by personalization.

Thus, social networks are a different battleground. Instead of receiving standard broadcasts, all communications include the sender's tacit signature, which makes all the difference. For example, suppose someone we know, by mistake or ingenuity, forwards a false message. In that case, we tend to believe the information simply because we naturally trust the sender. This is the classic case of misinformation, which often spreads in the form of disinformation. Misinformation is what many refer to as fake news, even if it's actually fabricated news. The news is real but may include misleading content, or misinformation. But when people spread misinformation, it takes on a life of its own and turns into disinformation. Most of us are simply not trained to confirm all information fragments, just as intelligence officers theoretically would. Unfortunately, this property of social networks has been extensively used by some of the world's darkest forces with seeming success. And the most frightening is the negative being always so much more powerful and easy to get through. Consider the role of social media in the attack on the US Capitol on January 6, 2021.

We are all living in this harsh, disinformation environment, therefore companies cannot escape using it for their own advantage.

But social environments are different everywhere. Where major social networks were simple Web portals at first,[31] they now are mostly mobile. Where multimedia content was relevant at the beginning of the World Wide Web, relationships have now evolved much with the value of immediacy and ubiquitous multicast communication, that is, automatic and instant one-to-many broadcasts. As long as different spoken languages are spoken, there is also a place for a multitude of OTT services. Given the presence of distinct web ecosystems coexisting over the same internet, it's unlikely that a single communications provider will dominate the entire market. That is why different OTT services exist, operating in disparate parts of the world, and governed by their own set of rules, a situation meriting seriously consideration.

Want to go to China? WeChat Chinese is mandatory. Unlike WhatsApp, it's a Super App encompassing mini-apps from hundreds of thousands of different companies. This creates a different environment with its own ecosystem. The rules of this ecosystem, for instance, led to Uber being compelled to sell its operations in China to Didi in 2016. This occurred because Uber was unprepared to compete against rivals that thrived withing the single sign-on environment of the Super App. A similar scenario unfolded in Singapore when Uber sold its operations to Grab

---

31   We have to say that social networks appeared long before the Web, with private bulletin board systems (BSS) and the first fora with the news on the Internet. The French Minitel and America On-line are also good examples.

in 2018, meaning its permanent exit from Southeast Asia and retreating from eight countries in a single blow. Something was not right for Uber's business model in the East, likely due to the different social networking environments in those regions.

eBay's disaster in China also comes to mind. It happened in a different era when mobility was not widespread in China. Alibaba's TaoBao emerged as the winner, once again due to the particular of that ecosystem. TaoBao turned out to be a master in dealing with local network effects, and eBay was simply unable to cope with it, even with its fortunate experience in the West. The rules in the East were already different even when the Web started to expand there. What counts, then, is not the political environment but the rules of the ecosystem.

However, regulations also have an impact on the ecosystem's rules, including social networking. Which functionalities are allowed? What about financial transactions? What about data protection? In this regard, the East, the West, and Africa have entirely different approaches to all these matters.

Companies need a license to operate in finance, from simple payments to full-fledged banking capabilities. In India, WhatsApp started to roll out its payment functionality in December 2018, only to encounter regulation hurdles. Apple Pay is effectively working in many countries and always as an outlet of traditional banking payments, including Visa and others. In Africa non-financial companies handle payment processing, as seen with telecommunication companies like Vodafone in Kenya's with their M-PESA service. This is an exciting example of how technology is being used to include unbanked citizens in the payment system using technology, a trend that has been spreading accross Africa since 2008. Therefore, each government, or economic region, craves to foster its economy through the set of local rules imposing their specific balance. We will tackle this subject further when discussing the economic infrastructure.

Companies should consider the possible properties of the social network's environment in each geographical scope for their intended operations before assessing the competitive landscape at the business level. Which OTT services are accessible? Which functionalities are or can be incorporated? What are their usage patterns? In a nutshell, what are the characteristics of the social networking ecosystem at stake?

Due to political reasons, we can never wholly separate a social network environment from its regulations. However, governments cannot control everything, and the proof lies in the very nature of the internet itself when bending the rules in Europe back in the early 1990s. In Europe, telecommunications were initially dominated by monopolists. Opening up communications to the internet involved accepting several protocols originally conceived in the US and developed by its military. An unnatural happening, I believe. Network effects of natural monopolies explain this transition, a topic we will explore further, along with the strategic relevance of regulations. Europe had to open its regulations to US protocols, allowing its incumbent monopolists and newcomers to offer Internet services at the expense of all other local protocols. In France, the Minitel was the most successful one in the 1980s. Its interface was raw text interaction, called videotext, and could not compete with the World Wide Web's hypertext in the nineties. Even if a newer version of videotext emerged incorporating hypertext, it would not stand a chance compared with the global network already established by Internet two decades beforehand. US protocols won, and Europe's own protocols and regulations were all left behind. The power of network effects is immense.

Thus, there is a close link between communications' availability, social networks' effectiveness, and economic warfare. Network effects are part of the game in all these confrontation layers. It's only natural that a strategic view of the world, through Clausewitz's eyes employing his Trinity, ought to consider them all.

But there is still one additional upper layer to consider: perception due to social networks and personalized communication. Yes, people's perceptions can be manipulated!

Perception's management at its best?

Perception management is not new. Let's go for a compelling military example.

In 1870, the German Chancellor Otto von Bismarck intended to enter into war with France. After the victory in the Bruederkrieg with the Austrian Empire three years before, a war with France would be an excellent excuse to proceed with the Prussian Empire's unification because, when under attack, it's only natural to convene against the common enemy. Bismarck's idea was getting together with all still independent south German states against France—a magnificent strategic move with unification in mind. That same strategy had already worked, in part, three years before, in the previous eastbound war against the Austrian Empire, and it would work again westbound against the French. Although initiating hostilities with a direct attack could build on the surprise element, it would also entail a significant risk of rightfully provoking the French and other possible allies, namely Britain. Instead, the clever Bismarck undermined English public opinion upfront, through the British media,[32] thus breaking up any possible subsequent alliance between the two states at the French-Prussian war outbreak. Bismarck used *The Times* in London to reveal a secret, ancient and outrageous French proposal to remain neutral regarding the Bruederkrieg as long as Prussia agreed with Belgium's annexation and Luxemburg by France. The inflamed British public opinion would compel British neutrality in the war to come because, for the British, it would be better to foster a feud between France and Prussia than to risk seeing the Low Countries united with France just across the channel. Moreover, that revelation meant that France had scandalously been violating the previous Treaty of London in 1839 and would not merit British help if hostilities eventually broke up.

Only after Bismarck manipulated the British public opinion would the aggravation against the French take place, still at perception level again, with complete success. Provoking the French with just words was an opportunity for Bismarck to create a concrete French response with much more than words, intending to fabricate an image of victimization, both internationally and in the head of all German states' citizens. So, what was Bismarck's next strategic move?

In 1870, the Spanish Cortes were still seeking a successor to the throne, and the Spanish did not like to see a German Hohenzollern candidacy apply, risking the same ruling family, both to the East and the West. So, the French government sent

---

32   Fenton Bresler, *Napoleon III: A Life* (Carol & Graf, 1999)

an ambassador to ask the Prussian emperor to guarantee that a Prussian ruler would never again apply to the Spanish throne. However, Bismarck was a propaganda master.[33] The news about this meeting was an opportunity for Bismarck to attack the French public opinion[34] by editing the text of a telegram to be sent to the French government so that its content was subliminally offensive to the French citizens, that is, a question of public perception. Bismarck sent the tweaked telegram from the town of Ems, which came to be known as the Ems Dispatch. This telegram effectively offended the French, who immediately took the initiative to attack Prussia, hence complying with Bismarck's original intentions. The attack on these grounds depicted a state of affairs that looked like the Prussian Empire was under unjustified attack, seemingly generating two strategic advantages. On the one hand, the questionable attack was somehow easy to sustain regarding possible alliances between the French and other countries because the conflict's crux became exclusively bound to French animosity. On the other hand, all still independent southern German states would have an incentive to join forces against the common aggression.

The French lost the war, which was probably Bismarck's inner belief and strategic assumption. He knew he could count on the exceptional leadership and know-how on General von Moltke's (the Elder[35]) tactics and operations. Von Moltke's outstanding new tactical maneuverings had already been tested successfully in the previous war against the powerful Austrian

---

33   Bismarck, propaganda and public relations, Linda Senne, Simon Moore, Public Relations Review nº 41, 2015
34   French Public Opinion on War with Prussia in 1870, The American Historical Review, vol 31, nº 4, Oxford University Press, 1926
35   Günter Roth, *Field Marshal von Moltke the Elder His Importance Then and Now*, Army History, U.S. Army Center of Military History, No. 23, Summer 1992, page 1-10

adversary and Bismarck believed it would prevail again. The historian, John Keegan[36] states that Von Moltke attributed his own victories to Clausewitz's *On War* readings. Keegan argues that this seemingly brought Clausewitz's book under the spotlight since then. And the rest is history.

Bismarck used perception management via the media to weaken France's alliances and provoke a conflict with France, all while avoiding being the public initiator of any aggression. Perception management can thus be instrumental and effective, right in the midst of disputes. It has always been a crucial element in the arsenal and the battleground of conflicts, indicating that struggles can occur solely at the management of perceptions. This is even more evident today, due to the democratization of communication channels, an argument superbly discussed by John Mattox.[37]

We live in an era of constant 4th Generation Warfare conflicts, where economic warfare plays a significant role and perception management is an integral part of the conflict's fabric in one way or another. If we must become a shark to successfully swim and compete in a sea of sharks. And remember that oceans will hardly be blue when sharks are around. How useful and essential was propaganda for governments with political objectives and their armed forces for engaging throughout the twentieth century in all major conflicts? Was Archduke Franz Ferdinand's assassination in Serbia, in June 1914, the real reason for the outbreak of WWI? Was the existence of mass destruction weapons in Iraq the real reason for allies' invasion in 2003?

---

36   John Keegan, *A History of Warfare*, Random House, 1993
37   John Mark Mattox, *The Clausewitzian Trinity in the Information Age: a just war approach*, Journal of Military Ethics, Vol 7, nº3, 2008

Perception management is thus in the realm of information warfare. The military call it Effects-Based Operations, considering the media as part of the arsenal. Therefore, social networks and the media have an effective means to spread an advantageous contextual understanding about something or someone, which is essentially perception management. In this context, today's harsh reality has shown that real facts aren't always necessary to alter people's perceptions, as any convenient facts can be fabricated or manipulated as needed. Again, this is often mistakenly referred to a *fake* news due to its fabricated content. It's real news all right, although with phony content. The accurate term for this is disinformation.[38] Perhaps Machiavelli was right as increasingly it appears that the ends are being used to justify the means! For example, how hard is it to pay several people to act publicly in a certain way to fuel disinformation and spread it rapidly, much like a virus?

Today, the most critical tools for perception management are naturally available in the form of social networks. How can these be used in our competitive space, either by companies, governments, or other organizations? What are their intentions? How can we play this game? How can we also be a shark?

Perceptions' management lucidity is key. It's part of today's Trinity.

---

38   Petite Histoire de la désinformation, Vladimir Volkoff, Édition du Rocker, 1999

FIVE
CULTURE AS A WEAPON

Culture is an essential, often disregarded, and challenging dimension of business. We cannot imagine messing up directly with culture, so we presume, by definition, its natural stability in time, assuming our strong dependence on it.

Social networks, the media, and perception management techniques can indeed influence culture in due time, so we must be vigilant as well. But above all, we should deeply study culture beforehand and devise the probable reactions to our own actions, always learning from the outcome of every input we can identify. One of the best cultural identification frameworks I have seen throughout the years is Geert Hofstede's five-dimensional space.[39] While we can utilize various methods to discern expectations about cultural meanings within a specific geographical scope, using social networks and media is both powerful and convenient. Authentic cultural experiences are tacit by nature and should be the best source of inspiration. However, in practice, we

---

39 Gert Hofstede, *Cultures and Organizations: Software of the Mind: Intercultural Cooperation and Its Importance for Survival*, McGraw-Hill, 1991

don't have the time to learn from every required geography, as this would necessitate experiencing them all across multiple parallel lifetimes. Therefore, our learning about each culture is likely to be limited to its explicit characterization, a type of understanding that requires considerably less time, by several orders of magnitude. Instead of living a culture from the inside, we just need the correct description conveying its meaningful traits. Hofstede's tool is most convenient to explicit each culture's main characteristics.

When eBay opened in China, it missed understanding that consumer-to-consumer (C2C) interactions are eminently different from those in the West. In China's particular culture, the friendly connection between buyer and seller is crucial for trading because transactions largely assume friendship. Therefore, unlike eBay, when Taobao launched its operations, fees were abolished, thus freeing buyers and sellers to interact before any transactions whatsoever, disregarding if actual transactions were going to occur within Taobao's environment or not. To compensate, the Chinese company uncovered some other revenue streams, like advertisements and listing priority. And it worked. In just three years, the former uncontested leader, eBay, completely vanished from the map. Taobao was thus smart in leveraging eBay's network effects to its advantage, and eBay found itself unable to respond. We can just try to guess why. But one thing is for sure: culture was behind these two different ways of approaching the market. Taobao won, and eBay lost.

Never take things for granted and carefully study which cultural characteristics may be an advantage, or precisely the opposite, and then process the results. Besides, only companies with substantial resources may invest in their own transformation with new routines, with new perceptions in mind, eventually leading to cultural evolution. For example, that is Uber's case, leading the way for other companies to take advantage of the recent habits they helped create, already spanning various other businesses in different geographies. Remember to verify if the cost of creating these new habits, or market(s), is compensated with leverage regarding every other upcoming contender; otherwise, you will just be creating the demand for everybody else.

In the new platform environments, network effects are essential, and are the major hint for understanding the developing strategic balance. Therefore, by beginning with these upper-level dimensions, we can reveal a likely scenario leading to network effects. In this context, we will next explore natural monopolies to introduce a discussion about the significant and often overlooked concept of network effects.

SIX
THE EMERGENCE OF NATURAL MONOPOLIES

The rise of the Web has increased competition by creating more accessible, cheaper, and more abundant communications for everybody, which is true for companies as well as for customers and consumers.[40] It became more comfortable for the consumer to contact, get additional information, compare, and negotiate with many companies, and that has increased competition for every business present in this new competitive environment.

When information is involved, and transportation costs are not an issue, any company can supply contents and services virtually, and potentially to the whole world.[41] For example, Google can provide emails wherever its service access is not blocked. And when there are unstoppable economies of scale involved, meaning that the cost increase is smaller than the revenue increase with

---
40 Michael Porter, Strategy and the Internet, Harvard Business Review, March 2001.
41 For an interesting discussion on this, please refer to Thomas Friedman, The world is flat, Farrar, Straus, and Giroux, 2005

scale, a monopoly will naturally emerge in the long run.[42] Of course, for this to happen, economies of scale can never plateau with size. That is how Big Techs make their living out of consumer knowledge. Even more so when consumers can use the services for free and only need to view advertisements in exchange. Does this ring a bell? Consumers are an audience consuming free services, just like a public good. The real clients for Big Techs are the advertisers. In a monopolistic environment, platforms can only thrive, so everybody rushes to be the one.

Is there a place for more than one in Netflix's space? Amazon Prime, HBO, and Disney are taking their chances. The fact is that Netflix is not yet making money despite its size and growth.[43] The crucial lesson is: We closely examine both the economic balance underpinning natural monopolies and any governmental support for platform companies, particularly in terms of regulations, when applicable. These are crucial strategic dimensions to consider in the context of Clausewitz's Trinity.

In the case of natural monopolies, our focus should be on understanding the underlying economic principles that determine the final balance in the market. Grasping such balance provides a powerful hint to disclose the end state of the game beforehand.

And what is the significance of all this? Because major platforms behave like natural monopolies and shape everybody's business environment in every region of the globe, both regulations and the economy's rules underpin the fate of platforms. Governments may even be available to support particular com-

---

[42] On the origins of the concept of natural monopoly: Manuela Mosca, Economies of scale and competition, The European Journal of the History of Economic Thought, Vol. 15, 2008

[43] Trefis Team, Netflix One Question: Is It Losing Money Or Making Money?, Forbes, May 1, 2020

panies in creating natural monopolies, to take advantage of their taxes and need for human resources. Suppose such a monopoly is likely to exist in some economic area. In that case, it's only natural that each geopolitical power will dream about occupying that same space through one of its companies, with the monopolistic powers dictating that particular industry's rules. Just remember that monopoly prices maximize the company's returns, completely disregarding consumer surplus.

Therefore, global natural monopolies are particularly appealing, both for the companies exploiting them and for the governments of the economic spaces benefiting from those monopolies in the context of economic warfare. In this regard, maybe "quantitative easing"[44] rings a bell. This strategy, among others, has helped the West in such endeavors, especially when governments are incline to in subsidize the economy, including Big Tech companies, if it means gaining economic leverage over the competitors.

In other parts of the world, governments appear to have a more direct influence on companies, based on the government's ruling capabilities. The objective? The goal is to expand platforms everyone uses, thereby occupying the space of that natural monopoly, also mandating their use and learning from it.

Natural monopolies as platforms

Students attending the first hours of any microeconomy course know that governments tend not to foster monopolies in their geographical scope. That is one relevant reason for regulators' existence, so there is always a minimum threshold on consumer

---

44 Jonathan Ashworth, *Quantitative Easing, The Great Central Bank Experiment*, Columbia University Press, 2020

surplus versus profits for each industry's supplying companies. A monopolist, or a relatively small number of suppliers, leads to a non-competitive environment. In this scenario they tend to focus on their balance sheet from a position of dominant power, rather than concentrating on creating value for the consumer. So, regulators do their job to prevent concentration.

For example, in the US, the creation of the five Baby Bells was the result of the breakup of the telecommunication's monopolist in 1984, the disaggregation of the Bell System, which was under the control of AT&T at the time. On another note, in Europe, communications monopolists flourished at the country-level until the 2000s, with a good reason for it. Without monopolies only large cities would have access to phone lines, as the investment needed to extend these lines to rural areas would not have been offset by the corresponding revenues. A monopoly with social objectives was a natural choice to ensure fulfilling the basic needs, liberalizing the industry just afterward.[45]

We already noted that governments do not tend to facilitate monopolies because the latter, as a supplier, tend to favor their own gains over service. Regulators do care about consumer surplus and monitor competition accordingly. On the other hand, companies do not like competitors due to the negative impact on their margins, especially monopolists in the making. Thus, the business world naturally oscillates between these forces: (i) the market and its inherent dynamics, (ii) regulatory policies, and (iii) company strategies aimed at maximizing their returns. And that is how platforms establish their place in the global market, by leveraging their inherent strengths, eliminating potential

---

[45] Some telecommunication services as mobile communications started earlier in some European countries.

competitors, overcoming regulatory concerns, sometimes internationally, and offering sufficient value to consumers. Like PayPal, some platforms have maintained their value proposition throughout the years because there is no real reason to evolve. However, the risk is high because, as the competitive landscape evolves, a new contender may develop a sharper platform, much like eBay's loss in China.

You may argue that these are the rules of any business, so why should platforms be considered differently? Well, precisely because there is a legitimate tendency to become a natural monopoly in their case. For incumbents, the existence of competitors is the norm. However, when users experience significant benefits from sharing a platform's services with one another, which applies to both suppliers and consumers, they typically prefer the platform with more users on board. Over time, the platform with more users is likely to prevail by creating more value for each individual user than any other platform, acting as a powerful attractor, like a magnet. This balance resembles economies of scale, therefore reinforcing the path towards a natural monopoly.

Some believe that apps or platforms compete by offering functionalities. However, relying solely on software for positioning can be weak, as competitors can easily replicate it. Platforms naturally tend imitate each other, so, offering the same features is not the same as creating unique value. In the long term, network effects, rather than the functionality or specific features provided by a platform, are what truly matter. While initial differentiation may exist, sustaining it without network effects is unattainable. Features are explicit and can be copied, whereas relationships and interactions between users are tacit and cannot. It's as simple as that. How hard was it to copy Skype? How hard would it be for Skype to copy the Zoom platform that experienced extraordinary growth through worldwide pandemic confinement? Would Adobe Connect or Cisco WebEx find difficulties in replicating the same functionalities as well? Why did so many people choose Zoom despite bad publicity regarding security concerns during its growth period? The answers to these questions should guide our thinking about platforms in the right direction. In the world of platforms, software and functionalities are far away from sustainable success.

Platforms result from network effects and are a consequence of social networking and the advent of cloud computing in the 2000s. Remember Altavista? It did not survive Google's value proposition with its simplicity and marvelous data orchestration. In reality, platforms such as these are knowledge engines. It's unlikely anyone could copy Google anymore because the relevant knowledge is generated by consumers' experience when searching. Competitors struggle to attract these same consumers due to a lack of the first mover's advantage—the same for Facebook or any other platform for social knowledge, for precisely the same reason. The difference lies just in the type of expertise sustaining each platform's value proposition.

Recently, platforms further evolved with mobile technology and OTT services. Eastern platforms in the form of Super Apps are more advanced and sustainable than their western counterparts due to their enhanced ability to gather insights and foster social connections. This a phenomenon will be analyzed in more detail in the next section. Additionally, platforms based on web3 technology promise a significant disruption ahead. It's a never-ending story poised to change the world.

For all the reasons above, many entrepreneurs dream of creating the next big hit, searching for the next disruption. Today, there are platforms for literary everything, from pet care to restaurant evaluation and discovery.

The importance of platforms is thus twofold. On the one hand, the obvious concern is finding the next successful concept and being a recognized disruptor or entrepreneur. And on the other hand, we can take platforms as a given, and ride the new networked environment to our value proposition's advantage. More on this below, when discussing the crucial payment's infrastructure.

Platforms have been shaping the competitive environment for good. Promoting them to a mainstream strategic dimension has been, unfortunately, disregarded by many. Only this time, we will duly consider platforms by finding their right place in Clausewitz's Trinity. While we may not all be competing with platforms, we will certainly be using them. Platforms have become an essential facet of competitive terrain and part of everybody's tactics with the corresponding strategic impact. Absolutely crucial!

Since platforms rely on network effects for success, we next explore this concept. Ultimately, victory depends on how well each contender leverages network effects, recognizing that there is only top spot on the podium.

Playing on network effects

At first glance, platforms appear to be mere technology tools, offering appealing functionalities for communication and content. However, platforms are changing the world's competitive landscape everywhere. Platforms come in various forms, aggregating knowledge, content, services, and communications. Its network effects explain ecosystem balance, which has been a most disregarded concept in business strategy. Let's unveil its strategic power.

There are two main strategies for a platform to build strong network effects, (i) on the demand side and (ii) on the supply side.

By definition, platforms support stakeholders' ecosystems. Consumers on the demand-side use the platform for services, communication, or content, sometimes paying for it. The presence of consumers sharing content, communication, or even benefiting from a platform's knowledge originated by other consumers, creates the infamous network effects. In other words, any consumer using the platform will feel the value created by other consumers' presence, and the more, the better. Why do many people in the West prefer WhatsApp to Viber or Facetime? Because they will find most people in their contact list in WhatsApp. This type of convenience is an attractor and an excellent example of the value of network effects. Thus, for stakeholders, network effects are a measure of value. Once a user has established his network of friends on a platform, it becomes sticky in a way that discourages switching to another platform, even if a competitor emerges with the same or better functionalities. That is, for instance, why Google+ failed in Facebook's playing field, despite having a more compelling value proposition in terms of functionality.

Among all kinds of network effects, social networks have become most prominent for organizations and individuals alike. Their value is unquestionable, with stunning examples like Facebook, which brings over three billion users together to share multimedia content worldwide, or Wikipedia, where crowdsourcers cooperate to build a knowledge base available to all. Concentrating all content in a single platform increases the value of each contribution because it's cumulative. So, when a challenger platform tries to provide the same features, no contributor will move because each interaction has more value on the previously existing platform. Thus, the platform's knowledge base and the user's community habits become sticky, and that is how Wikipedia became one of the mentioned natural monopolists.

Studying the growth of a platform in terms of the number of nodes is crucial, both on the supply and demand sides, to understand their contribution to value creation. The value proposition is the primary ingredient for attracting consumers. Nonetheless, factors such as regulation, availability of capital for marketing or expansion, and political intent significantly influence this growth. In the beginning of this century, Amazon was investing a lot without foreseeable profits, and business analysts found it outrageous. But now we have seen companies investing several billion per quarter, a practice that has become generally accepted. Even well-known companies like Spotify and Netflix still have to prove their future profitability. And Uber invested an absurd amount of money for so many quarters in a row, with no profitability in sight until 2021. The argument here is not Uber's non-profitability situation for so long, but the fact that there were venture capitalists available for that investment intensity. So, is the world flat in this sense? Can this happen everywhere? Or are these investments attainable only in some regions of the globe, becoming today's economic warfare's preferred weapons? As we shall see below, multiple factors involving platform's success make them a perfect candidate to be part of the enlightening Clausewitz's Trinity.

Uber's network effects are a case study themselves deserving a few additional words. For network effects, we ask the following question: what happens to value when users get on board, both on the supply and demand sides? In Uber's case, consumers compete with other consumers for transportation, and then prices go temporarily up. Not good. Even if prices are stable, a consumer gains no advantage if many other consumers are also requesting the service in the same area at the same time, as this increases waiting times. The only real benefit for consumers comes from the existence of suppliers, seeing that drivers agree to be working with a minimum number of consumers available. Therefore, a critical mass of consumers is needed for the service to be available in the first place, otherwise, drivers will not have any incentive to join in. That is why prices have to increase when users surge, functioning as incentives for suppliers, effectively regulating the market. But that's it. For consumers, price surges diminish Uber's service value. So, after reaching the consumers' critical mass, which allows drivers to be sufficiently interested in going down the street, from the consumers' point of view, there is no benefit for having even more consumers on board. A decrease in value with an increasing number of users is precisely the opposite of what constitutes healthy and value-creating platform. But there is more.

Uber's supplier side is also not particularly healthy and curiously mirrors the demand side. Achieving a critical mass of drivers is essential to attract consumers. Each new supplier (driver) competes for rides with all other drivers in the vicinity and does not perceive the benefit of having even more drivers join the platform. Quite the opposite, because these drivers will share the same available market, diminishing their share of rides with direct negative impacts on their revenues. So much for network effects on the supply side as well! Thus, Uber's platform is less than perfect on scale, which totally undermines the advantage of a platform business model and will never attain the natural monopoly status they probably aspire. Maybe Uber's investors know better and took all this into account, probably possessing additional information that will make me eat these words when attaining complete success in the long run. But tomorrow is probably not the eve of the day.

All in all, Uber's platform has some network effects, although weak in the long run on both sides of the market. They are relatively high at the beginning of market formation, but then they just plateau. These are known asymptotic network effects. When they occur, there is room for more than one supplier as the market matures, meaning a natural monopoly is unlikely to develop.

On another note, the negative scaling on the supply-side network effects also happens in exchanges. In such platforms, every new supplier will be competing with the others. Therefore, when the portal grows in the number of suppliers, the supply-side network effects diminish. Not good again because increased competition reduces margins. It's dangerous because, if suppliers flee, there will be no one to make consumers happy, and without consumers, a platform has no value at all. What a challenging game this is.

The negative examples cited above, such as those involving Uber and exchanges, are difficult to overcome. However, this does not imply there is no room for success. Evidence of potential for success an be seen in the numerous positive examples provided by Big Tech companies, some of which are part of our daily lives. Still, we should expect significant difficulties. For example, how many years did X/Twitter pray for revenues? Why is WhatsApp still not a money maker in 2024? Maybe WhatsApp Business will do the trick, maybe not. Meta is trying to monetize on WhatsApp's data, although risks losing users to alternatives like Signal and Telegram, as users generally dislike feeling threatened.[46]

Google is a prime example of a well-established platform, or ecosystem of platforms. Its success is achieved even without a focus on social networking, which is remarkable. The primary success of these companies lies in robust demand-side network effects, centered around data orchestration involving consumers who don't pay. Leveraging this captive audience, companies like Google then target their clients, who act as suppliers of advertisements for these consumers. Google does not need to actively foster network effects on the supply side because its ecosystem naturally positioned atop the demand side. For Google's clients, it's the audience that counts, whereas, for consumers, it's the knowledge created by everybody else's presence. Only positives in both cases.

And this is how we analyze network effects. It's quite simple, and maybe should be mandatory for current business strategy analysis. We examine the scaling of nodes within the ecosystem on all sides in a multi-sided platform to understand

---

[46] In 2021, Facebook forced WhatsApp consumers to accept data sharing with Facebook, threatening to erase their accounts.

how it affects the value for each type of stakeholder. Positives on all stakeholders always win.

Consequently, investors and analysts of any platform should look at network effects upfront, on all sides. Capital may be essential for growth, but clearly not enough. Additionally, when network effects do not act as entry barriers for the first mover, there is a risk of inadvertently creating market opportunities for followers, thus going in the opposite direction of natural monopolies. For example, with Uber in place, and users' culture already adapted to this new way to benefiting from transportation services, what hinders drivers from simultaneously subscribing to another service?

Capital is essential today because nothing appears to be happening in the world of platforms without tremendous amounts of cash burn. We do like to see all these start-ups and all these Web Summits in Europe. Still, we should also be aware that even if some unicorns are appearing in places other than the US, European companies seem particularly weak when compared with the restricted set of the most valuable companies in the world. These companies are all deploying technology, all somehow platform-based, and all originating in geographies outside Europe, that is, the US and China. The reason? Maybe the investment underneath. Maybe the size of original markets permitting sizable network effects working towards the first mover's advantage. Maybe both. These platforms could perhaps have flourished in Europe, as long as sufficient cash burn-out rates were duly available, raising another point for strategic consideration. One thing is sure: network effects have a place of excellence in Clausewitz's Trinity.

SEVEN
THE FINANCIAL INFRASTRUCTURE

The financial infrastructure is essential for a sound economy, and I am not sure if the differences between the various geopolitical spaces are duly considered for strategy nowadays. I suspect that some governments and most regulators are simply dormant about this. And there are multiple dimensions to consider. Let's go bottom-up this time.

Payments appear at the bottom side of the financial industry's ladder. I do not believe we pay much attention to payments, although essential for business-to-consumer (B2C), and even for consumer-to-consumer (C2C).

Cash works well for face-to-face transactions, and, in many countries, it's still the preferred payment system for cultural reasons. In some cases, the lack of technological infrastructure explains the high usage of cash, as in Africa, although not always, as in Germany. But Africa is also a most incredible example in advanced mobile payment systems. Kenya's M-PESA is the best and most widely known example since 2008, reaching around 60 million users in 12 countries in 2024. The same happens in

China, both with WeChat and Alipay. Not in Europe, nor the US. Why? Mobile payments exist in the West, but they are scattered throughout many different applications, each with limited network effects.

Using different apps for mobile payments has been the norm in the West where users subscribe to each payment channel separately. In China, everybody can pay almost anything to anyone quite easily if that person or business is part of the same Super App environment. Convenience fosters payment ecosystems to be natural monopolies of some kind.

Surprisingly, the West has relied much on payment systems supported wire transfers and the on-line version of old card processing networks. Wire transfers are typically batched-based, that is, they lag on average 24 hours and have relatively high fees. Card processing networks are real-time but cumbersome and have fees for merchants. Just keep in mind that cards only provide a form of identification enabling authorization and transfer processes to proceed effectively. Merchants started using analogic phone calls a long time ago, which was duly substituted by their digital counterparts such as POSs (Point of Sales), Payment Processors, Acquirers, and everything else needed to make payments work automatically in real-time. The financial ecosystem built a dedicated network to handle all this data, similar to wire transfers. But with mobile phones we no longer need this infrastructure. Moreover, all these ancient networks have fees, and it seems that banks are not ready to let them go.

Some geographies leapfrogged their financial data networks into something more advanced. African countries do not have enough people with sufficient resources to pay for the traditional banking system with all its complexities. Therefore, these countries had to go for another solution, and they found it in mobile phones by transforming mobile telecommunications accounts into cash accounts. In Kenya, local merchants started to play the role of banking agencies for liquidity, now spanning other African countries. ATMs became superfluous. The question is: was this possible in the West? Yes, but politicians, legislators and regulators would have to allow it. And what about those banking fees? Incumbents rarely disrupt themselves.

The financial environment is becoming complex with the fintech wave. Fintech refers to software, mobile apps, and other technologies created to automate traditional forms of finance for businesses and consumers. They are popping up everywhere with remarkable features, but they still must stick to current regulations and build their functionality on the extant infrastructure, preferably with backward compatibility. That is precisely why Revolut, for instance, has been sufficiently successful, building on the EMV network (Europay, MasterCard, and Visa). Their advantage lies in their reduced fees when compared to their incumbent counterparts.

Revolut is a notable example of a developing person-to-person (P2P) ecosystem. For broader reach, their payment service should incorporate B2C, just like in China, with QR-codes or other convenient technologies. POS integrations are all that is needed, but they have been lagging. For a significant shift in POS technologies in the West, there likely needs to be widespread consumer adoption of a payment network, such as Revolut's peer-to-peer (P2P) payments. This mass adoption could drive POS technologies to integrate directly with these types of accounts. No one knows if the current network effects of the Revolut payment system are strong enough to achieve it.

With fintechs in mind, the world is becoming insane with the rise of web3. The craziness flourished when Facebook promised a globalized wallet based on their cryptocurrency, the Libra. Even VISA and PayPal were initially part of the project, which surprised many, but they withdrew shortly thereafter. The project became highly controversial; its objectives were redefined, and Libra became Diem. Facebook attempted to convert their initial proposal into a payment system but persisted in using a proprietary cryptocurrency for transactions. This approach essentially mirrored that of any regulated monetary aggregate. Consequently, central banks would block any rollout tentative in the regulated economy. Another mess. Our salvation? Network effects again, not forgetting regulations, of course. Only a solution that satisfies both will ever work.

With the Clausewitz's Trinity, we deal with all environmental factors, and network effects explaining the financial industry's competitive balance. Here is another factor.

The current Western payment infrastructure has been reducing network effects because it's scattered. One should remember that an economy consists of all contributing transactions and anything that fosters every single one can have a meaningful impact. The payment system is an aspect that should be carefully considered, as its evolution can have significant economic repercussions.

Coming from the East, Alipay is already present in Europe. But will it spread? What about WeChat, which is already used by many of us for social networking? Note that WeChat is already part of an internationalization process in other countries in Asia. And what about wallets and tokenization? Why is China so keen about the Blockchain, already releasing its state-owned cryptocurrency in seven different cities, and even internationally for trade finance? What is its meaning in the context of the new Chinese One Belt, One Road Initiative?[47] Is the dollar at stake in future transactions for this international business segment?

These are some of the concerns that we should be careful about in this critical dimension, never to be ignored with a Clausewitz-style view on strategy because it may influence our perceived strategic positioning.

Payments are just the first layer of very sophisticated financial surroundings. The number of financial products sustaining the economy is complicated, from wire transfers to an ever-growing set of credit options, escrow mechanisms like Stand-by Letters of Credit, and collateralization, to name just a few.

We are witnessing an unprecedented acceleration of information technology advances with new impressive capabilities during the last decade. Artificial Intelligence and analytics, including Machine Learning, Deep Learning and Generative Learning, Big Data, mobility, social networks, web3 and Quantum Computing, are among the most promising technologies. The financial industry is all about information and has been a preferred target for technological novelties. The innovative examples have been immense, and some are already revamping the financial industry at its core. For instance, in China, credit and debit cards have their days numbered because mobility already converted every smartphone into a payment's terminal, with tre-

---

47 China's new Silk Road, David Tweed, April 6, 2019, Bloomberg

mendous impact on all other sectors, and much beyond simple financial features. Just imagine this type of liquidity spanning other financial products or assets. Envision just for one moment asset tokenization becoming a reality for all financial assets and services, which is not hard in technical terms.

The hardest part will be the regulatory environment. But imagine, just for the sake of this scenario, that *financial prospects* have already been tokenized with success. Can you guess the size of this atomic bomb and what it would mean, not only for the financial industry but for all other sectors as well, with commerce and trading upfront? Is this part of China's strategy in the context of the new Chinese silk road? Is this related to China's Blockchain Service Network (BSN)[48] and the already referred new crypto-Yuan?[49] The regulatory authorities underpin the execution of all these innovative ideas, and that is why China is taking the lead once again.[50]

We should pay close attention to the financial industry in the years to come because, if any critical innovation disrupts like asset tokenization or Central Bank Digital Currencies, an earthquake of significant proportions might occur.

We'd better prepare to get on board this technological train establishing the new world's order. Or we can create a new order ourselves because change is the only certitude, and if we participate in its evolution, maybe the new balance will favor our strategic positioning.

---

48 Wolfie Zhao and David Pan, Inside China's Plan to Power Global Blockchain Adoption, Coindesk, April 14, 2020
49 Karen Yeung, What is China's cryptocurrency alternative sovereign digital currency and why is it not like bitcoin?, South China Morning Post, May 13, 2020
50 David Pan, China Announces New Regulatory Authority to Certify Digital Payments, Blockchain Products, Coindesk, October 29, 2019

Another dimension to take care of within the financial infrastructure is funding because nothing happens without liquidity. In today's world, the frequency and intensity of cash burn examples seem quite astonishing. An increasingly interconnected and globalized world requires a comprehensive approach, accompanied by the necessary availability of funding. It seems that the United States is leading here, not only because there is venture capital available beyond belief but also because the banking system has a different way to deal with collateralization. The result is a venture US culture favoring test and fail, whereas failure in Europe has a general negative allure. More often than not, one defeat in Europe may be enough to rip apart, for good, the entrepreneur's financial health, whereas in the USA, it can be considered an act of courage. A harsh lending environment does not leave space for failure, and thus for exploration. How are companies supposed to explore new ventures without it?

We should consider differences in cultures and regulations without any assumptions regarding the competitive environment's geographical scope. Central banks and capital market regulators play a significant role, alongside the influence of legislators in each geopolitical region. All in all, the financial infrastructure, ranging from simple payment systems to the availability of capital, is strategically vital and should be considered at the level of Clausewitz's Trinity.

EIGHT
OTHER STRATEGIC FACTORS TO CONSIDER

The financial infrastructure goes hand in hand with regulations, explaining the differences between the different geopolitical regions. Regulations are that important and span all areas of the economy. In addition to all factors already discussed, more traditional ones will continue to shape competitive environments, and our high-level strategic analysis should naturally consider them all. The classic factors for strategic leverage come in access to scarce resources, both tangible and intangible. Let's summarize a few important ones.

Regulations as strategy
The law sets a good part of the competitive landscape. For example, it's no secret that one of the arguments for Brexit was exactly the regulatory harness imposed by Brussels. US President Donald Trump also started to dismantle parts of the regulatory framework quickly after stepping into office in 2016. This move was as

bold as getting out of the already negotiated Paris environmental agreement.

A good many of us believe in environmental concerns as a direct consequence of the way we live. Jeremy Rifkin, for example, is quite clear about this in his conferences and writings. Changing the balance towards new energy sources and new transportation technologies requires investment and hard measures. The ordinary citizen has difficulties understanding that his small actions contribute to environmental balance, in one way or another. Regulations are thus mandatory, both for the individual, for companies, as for entire countries.

Most countries believe something must be done about the environment and are keen on supporting these costs. But what happens to those that do not agree? Companies outside agreements will be more profitable and thus more competitive at the expense of everybody else. A compromise among all must occur. Otherwise, agreements fall apart, with probable devasting results for everyone, some already even in the short term. Abandoning such treaties feels like treason and can be particularly severe when the most powerful country on earth sets the worst example. The country with the most exceptional economy, where energy consumption per capita is higher and the greatest polluter, almost stepped down from the Paris agreement to argue that climate change is a Chinese invention. The same Chinese are investing much above average in renewable energies.[51]

The previous environmental example, where regulations support the political intent, could almost be funny, if not a terri-

---

51 China Is Set To Become The World's Renewable Energy Superpower, According To New Report, Forbes, January 11, 2019

ble and sad example of unethical behavior, with conflict in mind. Profitability is not the same thing as greed.

Considering that business struggles happen in the geopolitical arena, a strategy should see regulations from two perspectives. The first one is compliance, and the other is the possibility of influencing regulations for someone's advantage, including ours.

The regulatory arenas of the main geopolitical landscapes worldwide are quite different from each other. There is a tendency for *de jure* standards in the European Union, broadcasted by Brussels upfront, and then specifically within each country. In the United States, *de facto* standards are the norm, and lobbying is a professional activity, a practice strictly forbidden in Europe. China and Russia are yet a completely different reality due to their peculiar and particularly effective political systems. Once again, financial market regualtors play a pivotal role in this regard.

Regulations ought to be on our radar, with those pertaining to the 2020 pandemic being notable examples. The law took the lead in controlling economic activity with substantial negative impact everywhere to contain the new deadly virus. It will stay forever in our collective memory.

Energy and transportation as strategy

Energy has become either an asset or a liability for all countries, sometimes both. For example, oil is probably the primary cause for the unrest we have been living in the Middle East after WWII, with no solution in sight. However, climate change has engendered investment in alternative energy sources, which also entail dependencies on their own. Even if some countries are still betting on coal,[52] others are dismantling nuclear power,[53] and yet others have been fostering renewable energies.[54] Because energy is a critical resource, any unbalance may have significant strategic consequences on either side of the fence.

The same happens with transportation, which is also highly dependent on energy. Despite the digital transformation of all businesses, transportation is still a significant factor for most economies' health. The proof comes from the confinement originated by the 2020 pandemic. Health reasons forced the ecosystem's demand-side to stop, entailing major transportation business disruption for all players. The bombshell also impacted all industries related to hospitality, tourism, and events. Transportation of both people and goods, including supply chains, is a strategic resource in one way or another due to our dependence on it, which is true for all organizations, whole countries included. Supply chains' effectiveness underpins the profitability of many businesses. What happens when significant disruptions affect the supply chain? How can companies control back after disruption when they depend simultaneously on so many players, sometimes scattered on several continents?

Still, we should also examine other less conspicuous strategic factors other than energy and transportation, including actual and potential actors on the battlefield. For all entities playing the strategic chess game, the ends may justify the means. After thoroughly analyzing the constraints of each battleground, which

---

52 Alleen Brown, Donald Trump Rewards Fossil Fuel Industry By Signing Climate Denial Executive Order, The Intercept, March 28 2017, https://theintercept.com/2017/03/28/donald-trump-rewards-fossil-fuel-industry-by-signing-climate-denial-executive-order/
53 Germany shuts down atomic plant as nuclear phase-out enters final stretch, Deutsche Welle, December 31, 2019, https://www.dw.com/en/germany-shuts-down-atomic-plant-as-nuclear-phase-out-enters-final-stretch/a-51845616
54 11 Countries Leading The Charge On Renewable Energy, Climate Council, January 1, 2019, https://www.climatecouncil.org.au/11-countries-leading-the-charge-on-renewable-energy/

inspires a clarified vision of each distinct ecosystem, we aim to identify the key players involved and their possible actions, as well as their underlying intentions.

Therefore, after discussing all strategic dimensions above, the time has come to delve deeper into examining Clausewitz's prominent Trinity with the intent of developing a comprehensive analytical framework, which should be the first to be deployed in our proposed methodology for business strategy. The framework offers a set of distinct entities for each Trinity's pole, although not exhaustive, and helps to revise all referred entities, leaving room for interpreting the degree of freedom of each model's dimension when considering the dynamics of all factors discussed above. The framework is an open checklist with the aggregated interpretation of all high-level actors, and all these factors will enable us to start thinking about possible future strategic scenarios. Anything less will represent a short-sighted vision on strategy, entailing enormous risks. Let's thus hope for the best.

NINE
TRINITY'S FIRST POLE —
THE POLITICAL POWER AT STAKE

According to Peter Paret and Michael Howard's translation of *On War*, Clausewitz puts forward his Trinity right at the beginning of his almost 600-page book. Having experienced war so young and witnessing Napoleon's way of battling, Clausewitz realized that there are more elements in war than just the correct disposal of available resources. For Clausewitz, both the underlying reason for confrontation, namely politics, and the emotions experienced by those involved in violence, emerged as crucial elements in his analysis.

Napoleon's probably most famous victory happened in the battle of Austerlitz, late 1805, more than 1000 km away from home, and with a smaller army when compared to its opponents of the third international coalition against the French Revolution. Napoleon even offered the best terrain to its opponents just before the battle, luring them into a position that reduced their freedom of action and subsequent defeat. An option that dictated his victory even before the Alliance had time to mobilize its reserves, meaning that there are times where having more resources is just not enough. Napoleon displayed an excellent example of engaging resources for battle in the right way.

But Clausewitz saw much beyond. In his view, three interdependent forces set up the victory.

First, he observed the importance of political disputes underneath all wars, justifying the need for battles and, at the same time, being influenced by its outcome.

Second, Clausewitz was indeed astounded with French peasants transformed into soldiers passionately protecting their republican beliefs, not wanting to return to monarchy anymore. Their emotional engagement was thus much above average. Armed forces competencies, including soldiers' behavior, played their own part in the tactical success and had to be duly considered.

Third, at Austerlitz, Napoleon was seen on the battlefield just before the battle, riding his horse and inflaming his soldiers' passions. He increased hatred and enmity, and the resulting violence on the field naturally favored his highly motivated soldiers. Therefore, in Clausewitz's view, victory highly depends on the superposition of all these three dimensions, which form an interdependent Trinity. Certainly not what theorists, like Von Bulow and others, were considering at the time, relying just on science for troops' disposition.

Napoleon's example is one of many witnessed by Clausewitz that probably forged his vision and willingness to put his insight in writing. His outstandingly, and still relevant concept, coherently joins the three above dimensions and considers the cross cause-effect relationships between them all. Ingenious, to say the least.

We now look at Clausewitz's Trinity in detail to develop a framework encompassing the same elements for the actual competitive environment, including economic warfare and all others introduced above, hence its intrinsic value for business strategy overall.

Explaining pure reason, chance, and violence

The government appears at the upper-level dimension of Clausewitz's Trinity. Instead of dimension, we prefer to call it pole because of its dynamic nature regarding the other two dimensions, an allusion Clausewitz made himself when referring to these elements as "magnet poles."[55]

This first pole has become more complicated in today's globalized world with a scope beyond pure political forces. Presently, we also must consider all entities able to deploy their political intent in the context of confrontation (that is, the war in its various forms) utilizing their (armed) forces. In the context of economic warfare, companies possessing political-level capabilities, meaning those with independence or free will and operating in a commercial space, may wield this type of political-level power. Big techs, as already referred to above, are a glaring illustration of this. The proof? Facebook could influence Brexit[56] and is promised to wage economic warfare worldwide utilizing its own cryptocurrency.[57]

At this level, decisions follow pure political purposes. We are able to identify two instances of this magnet: first, who has power in the geopolitical arena and second, exactly which degrees

---

55   Clausewitz, *On War*, Page 89
56   Jame Wakefield, Facebook challenged to give TED talk on political ads, BBC News, 16 April 2019
57   Libra White Paper, the Blockchain Association, https://libra.org/en-US/white-paper/

of freedom are attainable, that is, which instruments are actionable for direct political purposes. Note that the latter is different from the weapons deployed by armies when in confrontation, which are part of the next pole.

We carry out this Trinity's pole analysis by considering the various available ingredients to reach politically enlightened decisions. The diverse aspects of the world today inspire the following subdimensions, which I previously introduced and are my interpretation of Clausewitz's concept of the "total phenomenon." This framework is a work in progress, expected to evolve in response to the shifting balance among global entities.

The world will probably change again due to Artificial Intelligence, 5G, the Blockchain, the sharing economy, the circular economy, the renewable energy movement, the new transportation infrastructure, and so forth. These, and any other tendencies, may mature to identify new scenarios and pinpoint possible new subdimensions to consider in this Trinity's pole analysis.

Political level powers

Political level powers are the first mandatory subdimensions of this pole because Clausewitz explicitly names them. Still, politics is becoming foggy. For example, governments are not single straightforward entities anymore. In the United States, the White House (executive branch) has adequate power, but the House of Representatives and the Senate (legislative branch) can have their own agendas—and so can those serving in the judicial system. On the opposite side of the Atlantic, Brussels can extend its influence beyond each country's borders in many areas. And what to say about the clashes that occurred between the house of commons and the British government concerning Brexit? Thus, we should duly contextualize governments' degree of freedom regarding their deals, alliances, and dependencies in the concerned geographical space of action.

A government exerts its influence within its own geopolitical territory but can also extend its power internationally. This is especially true in the case of alliances and trade deals.

Military alliances are the most developed mutual influence between political allies. And the alliances' landscape is not easy to grasp. In Europe, for example, a country may be part of an arbitrary set of agreements, including the European Union, the Euro Zone, the Schengen Treaty, the EU Customs Union, the Central European Free Trade Agreement, the European Economic Area, the European Council, and the European Free Trade Organization. And this list is not exhaustive. Not easy at all.

As with all other subdimensions of this framework, we should identify in detail which entities are relevant for the geographic space, their discernible actions, and their probable defined strategic objectives. These objectives should be inferred in the face of the political situation, as the identified maneuvers often unveil underlying intentions. It's like chess.

Identifying sources of power is a compelling way to look for political level acting entities. We have been mentioning sources related to political belief in one way or another, but there is another utterly exciting way to grasp it by analyzing access to resources.

Everybody needs resources, so any entity capable of commanding "armies" controlling or influencing access to resources, can have a significant political impact. Current environmental organizations are particularly powerful nowadays because various energy industries are under attack, and we all depend on them for our daily lives. It's not just nuclear energy anymore. Environmental organizations are targeting transportation as well, which is also critical for citizens as for countries. For example, during the last century, oil-related struggles have been popping up continuously, mainly in the Middle East. Access to potable water may follow in this century. On another note, access to technology can also be paramount, including communications and platforms, as already discussed. The list can thus be endless, but it is what it is: (i) we first identify assets' dependency and, (ii) next, the forces behind political moves around it, both of internal and external origins regarding the concerned geopolitical space.

Remember that any of these entities can be organizations playing directly at political power levels. As we saw with the above examples, this may include actors other than the government, governmental agencies, or other organizations, or powers operating in that geopolitical space. Therefore, the first proposed subdimensions are the following:

- Official political level entities like governments and governmental agencies.
- Companies with lobbying capabilities.
- Any other forces with political influence, with the media at the forefront.

Regulation, trade deals and unwritten rules of the game
Regulation, trade deals, and unwritten rules of the game are the most critical subdimensions of this Trinity's high-level pole.

In Clausewitz's own time, the actual confrontation ultimately happened through acts of real human violence. However, in the current asymmetric world of information and economic warfare there are alternative options for compelling opponents to align with our intentions. Regulation, in particular, is a most conspicuous one and the examples already put forward above are quite evident in this respect.

First, we must verify the laws dominating the target geographic region and then the unwritten rules. Sometimes the law seems to be the norm, but unwritten rules always exist, can be overwhelming and make all the difference.

In a state of law, regulations set the rules of the game, and we are particularly interested in provisions influencing economic balance, which may be as critical inside borders as outside. Regulating inside borders certainly favors the region's companies. We continue employing the term region because these regulations may occur either within countries or within alliances like the EU. It's no secret, for example, that one of the arguments sustained by Brexiteers was UK's dependence on Brussels' legislation.

The current critical aspect of the regulatory system comes from everything related to the environment. Judging on the public negotiation difficulties between country representatives, year after year, this international regulatory arena promises to be a perennial headache for nations, companies, and agencies. Reaching consensus usually requires a considerable amount of time, and the final outcome often appears to be unsatisfactory to all parties involved. Thus, the current balance in environmental negotiations is still faint, which promises a continuing debate and probably more demonstrations and clashes in the streets. Still, environmental regulations are essential for everybody because of their direct impact on every region's underlying energy and transportation layers. We should keep an eye on environmental regulations looking for threats, as well as opportunities.

But regulations also have repercussions outside borders, both directly and indirectly. Foreign companies endure it when crossing borders. For example, the "Brussels effect," coined by Professor Anu Bradford of Columbia Law School and describing unilateral regulatory globalization triggered by EU law, is an excellent example of out-of-borders' indirect effect, impacting chemicals, airplane emissions, data protection, and boat emissions, among others. If corporations want to operate in the European market, they must comply with the rules. Have you ever tried to import a European car from another geographical area? It does not work because, while the vehicle is the same, its Certificate of Conformity does not comply. The reason? Just to prevent arbitrage.

Other examples of written rules and regulations are the important international trade agreements. Just look at the number of trade deals in place for each country or each economic region and the time and effort it takes to negotiate each one. We are talking about dozens of deals per country here, some taking decades to settle due to the ever more globalized international trade nature. Also, the negotiation effort must be sustained to keep these deals up to date. We expect a significant impact of environmental issues on many, if not most, trade deals.

And then, there are totally unwritten rules, and that is the unique challenge! When going abroad, a company cannot assume the market to accept its operations. Cultural difficulties may occur just because the company is foreign or just perceived as foreign, and these difficulties may come at an operational level backstage when trying to get the correct set of conditions to operate in the first place. Still, sometimes, the unwritten rules may be favorable, as is the case with German technology, Swiss clocks, French wine, Italian marble, Spanish ham, or Portuguese fish.

On a more political level, when going international in African countries, including Northern Africa, entering the market will probably not even be possible without a good connection with high-level members of the ruling elite, whatever form it may take. Want to internationalize to Brazil? Be prepared for the most amazing bureaucratic and workforce-related legal difficulties firsthand. The United States? Have you heard about the power of labor unions in many states?

In summary, we need a vision about the meaning of regulations for the strategic environment in place, including the actors, their actions, and their probable objectives. When analyzing this Trinity's pole, several possible strategic paths emerge for a government or an equally relevant entity, that is, one having sufficient power to force or somehow influence any regulatory decision. Unwritten rules must be taken seriously.

Political/economic alliances

Political/economic alliances form another major subdimension. Partnerships have always been in place since conflicts and happen at the enlightened purely political decision-making level, with a direct strategic outcome every time. In today's world, the web of influences can be tricky to read. Alliances exist in some regions between the same entities that may be harsh contenders elsewhere, which is particularly true with foreign politics but is also happening more and more in the business environment. Coopetition,[58] the strange cooperative competition concept, has been happening on several distinct occasions and locations during the whole twentieth century and has been fostered by globalization.

For this Trinity's pole, we consider all possible political alliances, even if not between direct political actors, like the Big Techs, because companies operating at the global level can be blunt political instruments. Facebook allowed meddling directly in several elections, including Brexit, the Trump presidency,[59] and elsewhere.[60]

Additionally, all significant entities influencing the geographical space should be pointed out, as well as their objectives and actions, both past and possible future ones.

Political influences coming from the outside

We also should recognize possible external influences at the political level due to the direct impact on strategy makers acting in our own environment. This includes everything personal connections to atypical economic interests and even less obvious forces of influence – all of which should be identified and considered.

Dealing with political influences originating from external sources is a particularly challenging subdimension, often due to their clandestine nature. Effectively addressing these influences may rely heavily on intelligence gathering and analysis. Certainly, a country with excellent intelligence services will find it easier

---

[58] Giovanni Dagnino & Giovanna Padula, Coopetition Strategy: Towards a New Kind of Interfirm Dynamics for Value Creation, , EURAM 2nd Annual Conference, Stockholm School of Entrepreneurship, 2002
[59] Carole Cadwalladr's speech on Ted Talk: Facebook's role in Brexit and the threat to democracy
[60] "The Great Hack", Netflix's documentary on Cambridge Analytica.

to be aware of these matters. Less so for companies, seeing the cost of intelligence services as well as their tricky and grey nature. Companies do not usually have the means to buy exquisite intelligence resources.

We conduct this exercise thoroughly, utilizing all information available, and open-source intelligence from the Web can do wonders. Most of the time, there is no need for the mentioned exquisite and sometimes risky intelligence services.

The maze influence will always be challenging to unveil, although crucial. We may grasp it scrutinizing regulatory measures, investments, acquisitions, and all measures with strategic impact, deducing their foreseeable objectives.

One particular example of external influences occurs through the legal environment, which we discuss next.

Law applied to politics

Law applied to politics is usually an entirely overlooked subdimension.

The law sets the rules for the business environment and is supposedly independent of every other force. But what happens when it's not always the case?

After elections, governments abide by the law. Still, if for some reason the law is used against the governmental status quo, or if the law itself is a weakness, we must be attentive about its use as a weapon. That is true for every political space we operate in or intend to serve.

Moreover, is there complete independence between politics and the rule of law? How independent are the judges themselves? How many examples do we know about a dreadful court decision influenced by silent, anonymous networks or more uncomplicated and straightforward corruption? More often than not, there is politics involved in legal decisions at the highest level. We certainly have seen evidence of this since the United States Supreme Court became dominated by blatantly conservative judges.

As usual, we should consider this subdimension in both ways, internal and external.

We start with our surroundings. Are there weaknesses, and can these be exploited? By whom, with which intent and possible consequences? Also, do we have enough influence to play the game?

The other possibility is to consider going abroad and asking precisely the same questions, a mandatory analysis for any government. Influencing governments or governmental agencies has the potential of directly influencing our operations as well, and that justifies its analysis. For example, when WhatsApp announced going live with Facebook Pay in Brazil, the local competition authority immediately suspended the payments.[61] Why? Are Facebook's executives not cautious enough to invest and deploy a complete and new service without consulting with regulators? Or are there any other unwritten rules to consider, or any other obscure entity to negotiate with in the first place?

Media and social networking influences

Ubiquitous communications are evolving fast, year after year, which is true both for broadcasting and for more personal interactions, including the Web and social networking. Digital

---

[61] Mario Sergio Lima and Kurt Wagner, Brazilian Authorities Suspend WhatsApp Payments, Bloomberg, 24 June 2020, https://www.bloomberg.com/news/articles/2020-06-23/brazil-s-central-bank-suspends-whatsapp-payments

marketing is already as old as companies started using the Web to reach consumers in the 1990s.

In this subdimension, we are interested in how major political contenders use communications to their own advantage. This trend has been flourishing nowadays with no foreseen tendency whatsoever to slow down.

The media, in all its forms, influences peoples' minds. For instance, in 1871, the already mentioned Ems dispatch is a phenomenal proof of the British and the French public opinion manipulation using newspapers to make the right conditions for confrontation, leading to the subsequent second and final German unification. As for radio and television examples, these just started to pop up throughout the whole twentieth century and are still utterly relevant today. Politics has been heavily relying on media everywhere.

On the other hand, social networking is new in this business, at least with its global impact worldwide, as already debated before. Social networking examples of political influence happened as soon as the early 1990s, even before the Web, and its power increased exponentially with ubiquitous mobile communication. For example, some say that disinformation spread though social networks may have played a role in Jair Bolsonaro's election in Brazil[62], as well in January 6, 2021, assault on the United States Capitol Building.[63]

Consequently, both the media and social networking are benefiting from cross-synergies. Who is using them? How?

---

62 Clara Long, Did Coordinated Misinformation Campaigns On Social Media Affect The Brazilian Presidential Elections?, Pacific Standard, November 2, 2018; Jair Bolsonaro accused of creating 'criminal network' to spread fake news in Brazil election, The Telegraph, October 18, 2018
63 Nicholas Iacobuzio, A Breeding Ground for Conspiracies: How QAnon Helped Bring About the U.S. Capitol Assault, American University, Washington D.C., January 7, 2021

With which intent? Besides, these can also be powerful tools in our hands.

Consumers tend to find the media more convenient to follow because it's omnipresent. In contrast, to witness social network communications, one needs to be part of each particular transmission-chain, which can be exceptionally challenging. In this regard, to fully benefit from social networks, much like media, the communication chain has to be enlarged as much as possible, which is the objective of the well-known viral effect.[64] But there are risks because, in social networking, each communication is inherently personal. That is why Cambridge Analytica used Facebook to address only potentially vulnerable voters with fabricated news with so much success to induce Brexit.[65]

We add cyberwarfare to our current reasoning. Cyberwarfare is a combination of social networking and media techniques with covert intelligence operations on the Web. Some say that, in 2016, Russia interfered with the US presidential election, and maybe there was intelligence involved to get unlawful information. Still, one thing is for sure: the central manipulation of public opinion happened through WikiLeaks (that is, social networking) and its news rebounded in the media. The synergistic combination of various communication means can be a bombshell.

Together, media and social networking are particularly significant now, directly addressing public opinion manipulation in a world of permanent unrest. Politicians have difficulty pursuing their agendas independently from what their bases are led to

---

[64] Jure Leskovec, Lada A. Adamic, Bernardo A. Huberman, The Dynamics of Viral Marketing, ACM Transactions on the Web, Vol. 1, No. 1, May 2007

[65] You may also see Netflix's documentary on Cambridge Analytica called "The Great Hack." it's also commented on TechCrunch: "The Great Hack: Netflix doc unpacks Cambridge Analytica, Trump, Brexit and democracy's death" by Mike Butcher July 24, 2019

think. Public opinion has always been important, but it's getting even more critical because, in a world of asymmetric warfare, even ordinary people have found ways to make themselves heard.

Consequently, we should carefully analyze the communication environment in all its forms, looking for hints unveiling direct political meddling in the social surroundings. Also, other innovative uses of communication technology will always be possible, meaning that, if we have the power to move forward and fit our objectives, we must deploy everything at hand, rationally and effectively. The ends supposedly justify the means.

It seems that the political forces have been learning how to use these new tools to their advantage and not always following ethical conduct, as we would naturally expect from our nominated representatives.[66]

Direct influences from the other two dimensions

Because all Clausewitz Trinity's poles are interconnected, it's only natural to assess the impact the other two poles have on this one. Playing with Clausewitz's own words, we will be grasping the influence that chance and hatred may have on reason. The power that the armed forces and people may have on governments is another way to state this assessment.

A current, frequent, and overwhelming example is the influence that environmental demonstrations are having on governments. All current social weapons are involved, including social networking, all types of media, political moves, you name it. So, people's influence on governments does not happen solely with elections; it can also occur through demonstrations of any

---

66 . Politicians are embracing disinformation in the UK election, Quartz, 12 Dec 2019, https://qz.com/1766968/uk-election-politicians-embrace-fake-news-disinformation/

kind. Remember the Gillet Jaunes in France? Gillet Jaunes means yellow vests and refers to the demonstrations that have been storming many countries around the world, with a particular focus in France, the country where the concept was coined and put into practice in November 2018.[67] In these demonstrations, sometimes riots, participants wear yellow vests to recognize themselves when in action and arouse interest. The movement has been considered a form of direct or participative democracy, as opposed to representative democracy.[68]

Demonstrations are not new. The nineteenth century was fertile for uprisings all over Europe. Even centuries before, the French Revolution bases its ideals primarily on ordinary people, which eventually shaped the face of a good part of Europe by spreading out the *liberté, égalité, fraternité* belief. Today, uprisings seem to be spreading all over again, increasing in frequency and granularity at the same time. Deploying media and social networking to manipulate the crowds, and subsequently, governments, has become much more straightforward and effective. That does not mean that uprisings always succeed in their intents. Still, uprisings can provide a method of pressure to negotiate at the highest level, among other intentions, such as creating economic attrition. But the danger is always there. The unrest can have consequences, ranging from overthrowing governments to different types of political crisis.

We should carefully study the direct impact people may have on political entities, including governments. A paramount assessment, not only because it can be part of the arsenal of the

---

67 Peter Wilkin Fear of a Yellow Vest Planet, Lexington Books, 2021
68 Benjamin Tinturier, To Explain to Understand or to tell the Gillet Jaunes?, Europe Now, https://www.europenowjournal.org/2020/01/15/11569/

contenders at risings stake, but also because we also need to understand the high-level strategic balance upon which to develop any strategy. That is the Clausewitz-style view on business strategy. We will use it in Part II to define the applied business strategy methodology with frameworks summarizing Sun Tzu's teachings.

The other influence on this Trinity's pole comes from the "armed forces" and chance, which is an apparent significant risk, as well as a threat, just by looking at the number of governments controlled by the military throughout the twentieth century.

One of the most horrifying examples originated from Weimar Republic in post-WWI Germany, during what Helmut Schmidt referred to as the second Thirty Years' War.[69] The German military backed the Nazi's uprising, leading to long-lasting disgusting consequences that history still echoes.

More recently, General Dwight Eisenhower's farewell speech as a former president in 1961 mentions the possible influences of the military-industrial complex on public policy and the risk it represents. In particular, Eisenhower said, "We must guard against the acquisition of unwarranted influence, whether sought or unsought, by the military-industrial complex."[70] The term *unwarranted influences* should be sufficiently clear, seeing that Eisenhower was an admirable armed forces element. For example, he was the commander of WWII's Normandy invasion and the 34th president of the United States for eight years.

The two above examples are clear regarding the importance of the two other Trinity's poles' influences on current one. More

---

[69] The horrific nature of what happened in the Weimar Republic is that it creates the conditions for the uprising of the nationalism that ended in the disaster of WWII, claiming around 60 million lives.

[70] Public Papers of the Presidents of the United States, Dwight D. Eisenhower, 1960-61: Containing the Public Messages, Speeches, and Statements of the President, January 1, 1960 to January 20, 1961, University of Michigan Library, 2005, page 1038

recently, we can ask, for instance, if the most prestigious companies on earth have any impact on their governments and legislation—the same regarding banking and finance. We should recall that economic activity tends to be regulated. So, with economic warfare in mind, governments are interested in creating conditions for successful companies to pay taxes under their umbrella. Taxes only come after business success, and governments define the former while championing the latter, which means that influence of the "armed forces" at a political level is a must.

Even if, when leading, there is really nothing much we can do regarding the influences the other two Trinity's poles have on this one, we should nevertheless not overlook these influences in the global political arena. Understanding the direct relationship between the three dimensions of the Trinity is key to comprehending the complexity of the competitive landscape and establishing probable future trends.

What matters now is to develop an understanding of their influence on the specific aspect under scrutiny, namely the dimension of reason at the government level. If any strategy is to be enlightened, we should consider the effects governments have on every entity playing in the competitive landscape, both at the armed forces and citizen levels. So, we also discuss the influences this pole has on the two other poles further down.

Trinity's 1st pole -The Political framework in action

The several subdimensions of this first upper-level Trinity's pole serve to deepen and detail its comprehension. After reviewing all discussed subdimensions, we create a global picture of all high-level forces around. The more insight we have about everything happening underneath the blatant and often misleading layer of appearances, the better prepared we will be to define a fruitful vision about everything at stake. Thus, we may find possible successes through all the continuously increasing surrounding noise, and more and more on a ubiquitous and real-time basis.

We develop comprehension by creating a scenario where all subdimensions are coherently laid-up. And it has to make sense. If we find a piece out of place, the scenario is probably wrong, and we need additional research.

We are living in a complicated and complex world. For example, we may argue that, for the past decades, the challenging environment in the Middle East is probably an outcome of external influences, alliances, media, social networking, and other factors. These should be all considered together to comprehend the picture in its entirety. In this particular case, we will merely scratch the surface by looking at power struggles as they are portrayed in the media. Most probably, the direct and indirect economic impacts of the confrontations at stake have much more to do with global economic warfare than anything else. Would it be the same if the Middle East was oil-dry, thus only basing conflict solely on religious grounds?

We believe this reasoning is meaningful for every political space.

The outcome of this Trinity's pole final analysis is a strategic scenario pointing out its significant facets and the meaning of all partakers' actions taken from the interaction of all subdimensions. Insight is what counts, which is what we should be desperately searching for. The strategic scenario provides that insight.

TEN
TRINITY'S SECOND POLE — THE ARMED FORCES, AND CHANCE

The commander and the armed forces are the cornerstones of the second pole in Clausewitz Trinity, where, according to his theory, the element of chance also plays a significant place. Not that everything is left to chance because Clausewitz's book provides myriad details for engagement rules, thus leaving as little to chance as possible. But chance is part of the game, and we also contemplate it here. We start moving to the battleground with this pole, considering all the needed elements for attaining victory. Furthermore, we should concentrate on identifying all external forces, recognizing their vital contribution to the final outcome.

In the current analysis, we consider decision-making and chance at the armed forces engagement level to assess the global strategic playfield. Still, contrasting with the unpredictability of chance, Part II details the best way to deploy the armed forces with Sun Tzu's frameworks. So, chance is there, but only when there is no escape.

For the armed forces, we thus consider:
- our own forces,
- independent entities not under our own control, operating in the same geopolitical space,
- entities under governmental authority in the same geopolitical space,
- entities under foreign political control also working in the concerned space, and
- the particular case of powerful entities such as Big Techs.

Also, because we cannot assume that armed forces are restricted to any particular terrain, we must consider all the possible conditions embracing the competitive landscape. In today's world, the way these entities are interconnected is of utmost importance, as it amplifies the potential value of smaller genetic structures. The confrontation environment is also the consequence of the strategic moves perpetrated by anybody acting in the previous Trinity's pole, deploying strategies issued by pure reason and using the tools (or weapons) already discussed above.

The next discussion summarizes all main subdimensions of this second model's component, corresponding to Clausewitz's armed forces pole. The complete proposed framework's structure for the three Trinity's poles can be found in Appendix I.

Companies

In today's business context, armed forces are all entities with enough power to make a difference in the international competitive arena, whether in the scope of a country or an entire region encompassing several countries. The first subdimension of this pole is thus relatively straightforward. We contemplate companies as the main instruments of economic warfare because companies all abide by regulations. Governments directly or indirectly control most. Companies are thus part of the arsenal of any political cause.

The most dangerous contenders are those not yet operating in the market, which are particularly perilous because they can appear suddenly. But there is a way to circumvent this risk. No company can operate without resources, and these are generally hard to set up. And we are not just talking about financial support, but everything else needed to have the business up and running. Therefore, we can verify which possible contenders are prepared to attack by identifying these needed critical resources.

Consequently, we should scrutinize all companies with relevant tangible or intangible assets for engaging in the competition. The same for well-funded start-ups because investors are willing to allow completely unheard-of cash burn rates. Access to almost unlimited financial resources enables a growth pace out of the ordinary with the added benefits of (i) possibly thriving in markets previously created by others or (ii) having the resources needed to be first movers, sometimes worldwide.

In conclusion, this subdimension deals with all exciting companies, their actions, both current and possible, as well as their probable strategic and tactical intentions. We can only go to war after detailed recognition of armies. After this analysis, we revisit the previous pole's evaluation.

Players in the ICT infrastructure

No words are sufficiently strong to describe what has happened and what will happen to society overall due to information technology in all its forms. Information technology is an obvious subdimension for this second Trinity's pole, so overwhelming that it's particularly challenging to discuss all its possible outcomes. However, the latest developments in distributed technologies are too significant not to be mentioned here, just as an example. Players in the Technological arena influence this pole, as information technology is a powerful weapon.

Web3 is promising to change the world and is based on Distributed Ledger Technologies (DLT) like the Blockchain. DLT's (i) make great use of cryptography, (ii) distribute secure and persistent information autonomously, and (iii) are programmable and self-executable.

DLTs autonomously execute programmed transaction sequences in a distributed environment, known as Smart Contracts, and operate without the need for trust between parties. Since trust is a crucial element in business relationships, any disruption to it can significantly affect the strategic balance throughout the value chain.

Cryptocurrencies are implemented with DLTs, but the link between both ends there. As with any other technology, DLTs can be used wisely or be the stage of the worst nightmares. Erroneous uses, abuses, and biased opinions everywhere should not hinder the promise of increased economic effectiveness for virtually all industries.

DLT's are supported by a network of computers behaving like a single operating system running in a single machine. That is new and makes all the difference because it creates an operational trustless layer that did not exist before! Why trustless? Because the distributed system runs autonomously on a redundant web of machines, and all information is persistent and safeguarded with cryptography. Most interestingly, security is so strong that we do not have to rely on demilitarized zones protected with firewalls and such. Cryptography ensures low-level security by design.

Numerous countries are formulating strategies for web3 and Smart Legal Contracts, marking the beginning of DLT use cases extending into the regulated economy. Web3 is significant as it promises to reduce transaction costs in the regulated economy to extents previously unimaginable, potentially leading to profound impacts across all industries. For example, in the EU, the Pilot DLT regime supports, since April 2023, the tokenization of shares, bonds, and UCITS funds (Undertakings for the Collective Investment in Transferable Securities).

DLTs are just a minor yet vital example of this significant subdimension, given their potential and sometimes unforeseen impact on all businesses, possibly including Big Techs. Other technologies, like generative AI, with chatGPT as its most notorious example, are also pushing the world forward, creating disruptions, opportunities, and all the proper characteristics of an exciting and revolutionary environment.

Digital technologies have been significantly influencing the evolution of the market balance. Natural monopolies at regional level have popped up in several industries, including transportation and vacation rentals. Monopolies create a take-it-or-leave-it situation for their clients, because they rely on these platforms to keep selling.

The meager marginal costs for operating platforms promise high profitability. With abundant and free public access to content, consumers are less prepared to pay for the value proposition, which explains the difficulty in having profitable e-business operations. DLTs can help here. For example, in streaming companies like Netflix or Spotify, what if content and services were tokenized and then published in web3? The platform would concentrate on digital marketing without needing to acquire content's rights because the consumer would automatically remunerate all other stakeholders.[71]

5G promises to increase bandwidth by one order of magnitude in the mobile arena, and IoT will finally flourish in the next decade. Which meaningful players will appear on the market? What is the foreseeable strategic impact?

What to say about AI, including Machine Learning, Deep Learning, Generative Learning and Quantum Computing augmented analytics? Who will exploit these technologies to compete, and how will it shape the competitive environment?

The same for platform-based Big Techs. Will platforms continue to grow worldwide, only to encompass even more services, maybe entire industries?

Once again, we should carefully follow this subdimension due to its direct impact on this second Trinity's pole subdimensions, both on the positive and negative sides. Even if chance is part of this game, do not leave it to chance alone.

Players in the payment infrastructure

The financial payment is sometimes taken for granted, like a utility, although it can significantly influence businesses. In this

---

[71] Christopher Woodrow On Blockchain Technology For The Film Industry, Rachel Wolfson, Forbes, September 17, 2018

subdimension, we discuss its relationship to the other economic activities and measure its power as a weapon for economic warfare.

In the past, cash was universally used for transactions. Subsequently, banker's drafts were introduced, and later, with the advent of the telegraph, wire transfers became a method for making payments. The arrival of computers unfolded a significant disruption in the banking service, highly increasing the whole industry's efficiency, starting with payments. Currently, we have myriad different payment options, depending on the geographical region at stake, with debit and credit cards taking the lead in the West.

The emerging landscape of payments is not getting simpler. Quite the opposite; start-ups and fintechs have been innovating just because it's possible. Bear in mind that a financial transaction, like a payment for example, is just a data job when not performed in cash. Even cash is data, although not always digital because possessing banknotes only reflects the amount of fiduciary money in the hands of whoever is holding these fungible assets. So, cash is exceptionally efficient to manage in the distributed environment and inexpensive while maintaining complete distributed coherency. We call it distributed because everybody can exchange money with everybody else without any central coordination. However, there are alternative digital methods for managing the same information carried by a banknote, which has been transforming the economy.

The significant, yet often overlooked, evolutionary step in financial infrastructure is the cost of data processing. Prior to the advent of computers, the highly decentralized financial fabric relied solely human intervention to maintain its coherence. The introduction of computers revolutionized everything, introducing automation and efficiency to all processing nodes, including banks. This evolution was furthered by advancements in communications, initially facilitating inter-bank connectivity, then expanding to include consumers via home banking, and most recently, achieving a widespread presence through mobile technologies. Web3 also carries the promise of digitally transforming large chunks of the financial value chain. Knowing the cornerstone importance of the financial infrastructure for every other sector, stakes are becoming high.

However, wire transfers are still quite costly to process because we must pay for the technological infrastructure and communications in place. That is one reason why payment terminals, together with dedicated networks, have seen the light of day in the first place. However, that is not the case anymore. In today's world, ubiquitous data transfers have become abundant, and individuals can use payment systems without any high marginal costs. It's like everybody is carrying their own payment terminal in their smartphones. Square even went as far as developing a hardware version of a complete payment terminal for mobile phones, reading traditional credit cards' magnetic stripes.

On a more encompassing vision, mobile banking sits precisely on top of the mobile phone's cheap communications and processing capabilities. It would be possible to move towards a cashless society, and fast, if the cost of data was the only factor involved. Unfortunately, it's not.

Computer revolutionized the financial industry's back offices, and the user interface was the next big thing. Whereas, in the old days, wire transfers were somehow cumbersome and always needed to identify the entities involved and the corresponding clearance. Today, with QR codes, face recognition, RFID, or Short Messages to simple phone numbers, P2P payments have grown to be even more convenient than cash. All that is required for mobile payments is already present in the most inexpensive smartphones and cheap communication bandwidth. The marginal cost of handling the few bytes necessary for payments has fallen very close to zero for everyone, true for both consumers and merchants. Countries like China have been taking advantage of this, building additional economic strength.

The zero-marginal cost of payment communications leads to the natural expansion of digital payments' ecosystems. Such ecosystems entail network effects, that is, the more nodes, the better, which is a most delicate and strategically important facet. In this challenge, China is leading the pack, leapfrogging to a new convenient and integrated payment environment, targeting its outstandingly large society. In China, we now have close to 1 billion people using WeChat and Alipay for payments in both P2P and B2C environments. Can you imagine the value of the network effects involved?

In the West, payment solutions are popping up daily in its scattered financial environment, not favoring the creation of network effects. Moreover, the legacy payment infrastructure and all the revenues generated by its fees have proved to be difficult to surmount. We should follow the promise of E-Monkey Tokens created by the MiCA (Markets in Crypto Assets) applied in July 2024 in the EU.

In summary, when attacking a particular market, the underlying payment system is crucial for dealing with the final consumer due to the convenience involved and the creation of network effects. It all depends on the suppliers of payment systems in the region at stake and its regulations. For example, when WhatsApp partnered with NuBank in Brazil to move forward with Facebook Pay in its social network, it was immediately suspended by the Brazilian Competition Authority, probably due to its negative impact on local payment service providers. In any case, Facebook Pay was not a disruptive proposal due to the 3.99 percent fees merchants would have to pay.

Managing payments in web3 marks another notable technical evolution. While previously centralized entities such as banks and clearinghouses were necessary for handling financial information, with the advent of web3, the convenience of QR Code-based transactions is poised to thrive. For example, in the EU, banks and other financial institutions are licensed to coin tokenized Euros as a regulated monetary aggregate since July 2024[72]. That can decrease transaction fees for payments by several orders of magnitude, increase settlement speed, and build a trustless environment, thus disrupting the current EU payment infrastructure. Moreover, the infamous network effects are again at stake here, and this time at a global scale, which can be as advantageous as dangerous.

Payment systems deal with consumer information beyond financial transactions. Payment systems must be convenient and trustful, and we can extend this trust to everything dealing with digital marketing. For example, telecommunications companies have used customers' calling records to develop end-of-the-month invoices. Web3 can self-execute invoicing calculations while simultaneously activating several other digital marketing

---

[72] Issam Hallak, *Markets in Crypto-Assets (MiCA)*, European Parliamentary Research Service, Belgium, April 2023

functionalities, all bundled in the same service. The service provider does not even need the current expensive invoice systems anymore, reducing operational costs.

On another note, China's mobile digital environment that some call O2O (Online to Off-line) is virtually years ahead of what is going on in the West—just look to the PinDuoDuo example.[73] Their mobile payment infrastructure is integrated into their social networks, fostering the whole economy. Imagine WhatsApp with a wallet just like Revolut or N26. Imagine that we could quickly pay anyone, or anything, as long as that person or company had a WhatsApp account. No logins, no subscriptions, no fees. Now, imagine that any business could be part of that ecosystem. For starters, companies would not pay fees to debit card issuers or payment processors, nor to any other entity in the payment system anymore. Maybe that is a reason why this type of environment has failed to thrive in the West.

Moreover, envision a scenario where companies on WhatsApp can receive bookings or conduct other transactions without needing to switch to a different app. This means that consumers wouldn't have to install numerous apps to interact with various companies. The concept is straightforward to grasp, as it mirrors out experience with the Web. Just as browsers allow us to interact with any company's website without the need to install specific apps, a similar principle applies here. Although, on the Web, clients still have to rely on the traditional payment systems. In the proposed scenario, anyone would be able to pay anything, as simple as reading a QR-code or Apple Pay double click. Welcome to Super Apps and their mini-sites.

---

73   China Has an Ecommerce Giant You've Never Heard Of, *Wired*, 9 September 2019

The described scenario is fostering a whole new economy without precedents in the East with the appropriate regulations, and is creating a tremendous convenience for both consumers and companies, handling all needed information for transactions in the same simple locus.

There is consequently more power coming from the payment infrastructure than just payments. It depends on the geographical region, its regulations, the companies involved, and the latter's evolving culture because of network effects. This sub-dimension has much to offer. Never leave it to chance.

Business level regulators

As we saw when discussing the first Trinity's pole, political level entities usually use regulation to influence the market according to their political agendas. Regulation is thus a preferred tool for economic warfare. But how clear is this? Who can affect the governmental scheduling of laws and directives? How hard is it to lobby, convince, or even buy politicians? It depends on the local environment, and these are questions in the scope of the first Trinity's pole. Still, regulations can have dramatic strategic consequences on the field. In other words, regulations' competitive landscape influence armies' capabilities by setting market boundaries, thus defining the competitive terrain, seeing regulators' objectives.

For example, there has been much discussion about the regulation of asset tokenization.[74] Let's focus on the concrete case of securities.

---

[74] Asset tokenization means their representation exists in the context of a blockchain's Smart Contracts instead of traditional contracts safeguarded by conventional custodians.

The definition of securities differs significantly from region to region. In the United States, securities are anything abiding by the 1949 Howey test[75] and can be tokenized either as security or utility tokens. But that is not the case in the EU. Unlike the US, the European Union defines transferable securities by classes[76] and has considered utility tokens a form of crowdsourcing. This limits much the regulatory freedom in Europe for these types of financial instruments, with the corresponding negative consequences on the economy. In the EU, more straightforward crowdsourcing rules have been applied to utility tokens, which left investors reasonably unprotected in most cases when compared to the United States. Furthermore, the regulation of traditional securities in Europe varies much from country to country. The EU finally regulated utility tokens with the Markets in Crypto Assets Regulation (MiCAR[77]), maybe because it has become clear that the crowdsourcing classification of utility tokens was simply not protective enough, and still leaving securities out of scope. The tokenization of securities in the EU was finally adresseed with the Pilot DLT Regulation[78] in April 2023, a sandbox experiment limited to simple shares, bonds and mutual funds until 2029. Are all other types of financial instruments waiting to be tokenized only in the next decade?

Regulations could foster asset liquidity, more than just increasing operational efficiency when handling tokenized assets

---

75 Defining An "Investment Contract": The Commonality Requirement of The Howey Test, 43 Washington Lee and Law Review, 1986, https://scholarlycommons.law.wlu.edu/wlulr/vol43/iss3/11
76 Commission Delegated Directive (EU) 2017/593, Official Journal of the European Union, L87/500, March 2017
77 Hallak, Markets in Crypto-Assets (MiCA), 2023
78 Regulation (EU) 2022/858 Of The European Parliament And Of The Council of 30 May 2022 on a pilot regime for market infrastructures based on distributed ledger technology, and amending Regulations (EU) No 600/2014 and (EU) No 909/2014 and Directive 2014/65/EU, Official Journal of the European Union, L151/1-33, 2 June 2022

for all types of transactions. For the last twenty years, we have seen what can happen to the economy when transaction costs decrease by orders of magnitude; I am referring to web3's impact. Regulating asset tokenization can positively disrupt the market's supporting financial infrastructure, and the argument here is that, without regulation, nothing will happen. That is why the United States is more advanced than the EU, and China follows the same superior path when state-backed tokenized cash or CBDCs is already a reality since 2022. In this environment, one where crypto tokens also represent monetary aggregates, other assets may be tokenized according to regulations. Note that increasing asset liquidity can significantly impact the whole economy by orders of magnitude. Thus, regulation is crucial and will play a significant role in national web3 strategies. Regulating asset tokenization should be promptly accompanied by careful examination of other transactions carried out by the involved entities. It's important to note that the economy's benefits will arise from innovative actions at arms' length.

The example of securities tokenization clearly illustrates the overall importance of regulation. Once again, we focus solely on its effects within the competitive arena, particularly on influencing "chance." It's essential to understand the impact of regulations on the scope of potential strategies.

Players in the legal infrastructure

Regulations go hand in hand with the law, and we can also use the latter as a weapon in various manners. Business strategists sometimes use it daily.

The law supports the business environment with contracts and the settlement of disputes. When imperfect, the legal infrastructure can have precisely the opposite effect, tremendously increasing the market's transaction costs. Even worse, if there are political or other darker influences in the legal system, companies are exposed to arbitrary decisions, which can be devastating. So, the legal infrastructure can be a tremendous weapon.

The law as a weapon can have severe effects. It can be used for backstage attacks between companies and even between people, compromising their time and resources, thus decreasing their degree of freedom. Restraining orders, or even simple accusations, can can create a mess, especially if banks are involved, which happens more than one might imagine, sometimes with the worst of intentions. If the financial system is vital in leveraging business, an opponent can the use the law to attack with extreme effectiveness. For example, a target company might find itself unable to secure additional financial resources to sustain operations. Remember that a company's treasury is the lifeblood of its existence; without liquidity, companies fail. Using legal measures to block essential loans is just an example of the devastating indirect effect of this weapon. Companies should be prepared to withstand such attacks, among others, as unscrupulous actors will likely employ them.

Even if we are dealing with Clausewitz in the current chapter, this subdimension seems Machiavellian. In war, not everything is permissible. What counts for the analysis at stake is the use of the law to play or influence chance, that is, to influence the course of action to boost advantage. Who are the players? Where are the options? Which legal risks are we exposed to? Which difficulties can we create to our advantage? All that depends on the actors supporting the legal infrastructure—all of them.

Players in the energy infrastructure

Nothing works without energy, namely without electricity. Not even water would flow in pipes without electricity pumping it up.

Energy consumption increased tremendously during the twentieth century, and it continues to grow steadily. We are a fossil-fuel civilization where renewable energies still only account for only a tiny amount of the power we need.

On the one hand, energy tends to be a cost indexed to every specific region. In a globalized world, companies' operations abroad may stumble on different realities regarding energy costs. For example, China has been a great polluter, yet is now the most significant investor in renewable energies.[79] On the other hand, and in the same vein, rare minerals are gaining importance due to their scarcity. For instance, what would happen to Western economies, increasingly dependent on batteries, if Eastern rare mineral producers decide to leverage their bargaining power?

Regulations will continue to evolve in this arena, as well as international deals of all sorts. That will impact all facets of energy with direct and indirect effects on companies' operations for every region. Therefore, actors in the energy industry merit a Trinity subdimension to give them the importance they deserve in today's competitive landscape.

---

79   Dominic Dudley, China Is Set To Become The World's Renewable Energy Superpower, According To New Report, *Forbes*, January 11, 2019

Players in Transportation

Transportation represents tangible goods, the equivalent of the Internet for information (except for 3D printing, where it's similar). Whereas data abundance relies on communication bandwidth and ubiquity, transportation abundance still follows physical rules, meaning no zero marginal costs, meaning business as usual. Transportation evolution will never be that impressive but is happening nevertheless, with potential strategic impacts, hence the choice of including it as a specific subdimension in the second Trinity's pole.

If transports are crucial for a business, the new way to move things around can be essential to pursue. From drones to the sharing economy, things are moving fast. Uber is perhaps the most well-known example of individual transportation in the sharing economy. But this concept is spreading to other means of transportation. From bikes to skates, the sharing economy is spanning different transportation needs, like food or parcels.

Transportation companies are taking advantage of communication technologies and social networking amid regulatory unrest. The transportation sector is also related to the environment, which significantly affects the automobile industry. Therefore, we should scrutinize the transportation subdimension whenever people's movement or physical goods may affect our value proposition or our operations. The same if we can use it as a weapon against our adversaries.

The way to get our hands on this subdimension is by identifying the actors possessing core competencies in this industry and fully devising their possible strategic moves.

Players in the media and social networking

Media and social networking are subdimensions of utmost importance. Media helped shape the twentieth century's face, and it seems that social media is occupying that territory, becoming mainstream in the twenty-first. Together, media and social networking are explosive.

We consider that any type of digital communication will impact every other Trinity's subdimension. We have previously addressed media and social networking within the first pole of the Trinity, focusing on governmental and political strategy, which is accessible only to those who possess that level of power. However, our current discussion centers on impacts at the battlefield level and the role of chance, as we attempt to understand the outcomes shaped by the strategic balance established by the previous layer. This is because communications are a formidable weapon in the arsenal of armed forces.

Today, the mix of social networking and the media for information awareness is typical for businesses and our personal lives. As mentioned earlier, social networking has a powerful influence on our mindset, with both positive and negative implications. Although, we consider social networking and the media together due to the outstanding synergies involved. In this regard, the above example about WikiLeaks's role in US elections is more than enlightening.

Companies should brace themselves for this challenging communication environment, as there will inevitably be attacks. Going offensive is probably the best way to defend because learning how to attack also unveils our own fragilities, thus fueling a reinforcement approach on all identified weaknesses. Moreover, our opponents may refrain from their attacks when becoming aware of our attacking capabilities. According to Clausewitz, war is attrition, but hampering can be sublime for balancing the competitive environment. Still, we will deal with deciding where to attack and how. Sometimes a passive-aggressive approach is the best of attacks.

This subdimension is worrisome because its negative side is so much more effective than the positive. For example, going nefariously offensive means fabricating news to get leverage when anything goes. But are we prepared to go that far? What happens if we suffer the same kind of attacks?

On the other hand, social networking can help develop a positive image on the market, and we will use it in battlefield tactics, as we shall see in the next chapter.

The same happens in the media. We can pay for advertisements, but with luck, the company can appear in the news for free, and for all the right reasons. Sometimes this can also have roots in social networking.

We should assess the media and social networking playground, never leaving it to chance. We also should identify all possible actors encompassing media companies, Big Techs, and social networking to determine then, one by one, their positioning in the competitive landscape. We should leave no room for surprises.

Direct influences from the other two dimensions

This Trinity's pole is also prone to influences from the other two.

Pure reason, or strategy, is fueling high-level decisions from governments through the subdimensions depicted in the previous Trinity's pole. These decisions impact this second pole by setting the boundaries and the rules for all subdimensions. So, for the current pole's aggregated analysis, we go subdimension by subdimension, understanding the current situation and what may happen due to rational strategic decisions affecting each one. For example, China's blocking access to many websites is not so difficult to foresee after all. Russia, Turkey, and the Middle East also have different communication environments due to varying rules in place. So, we should anticipate all possible moves in the upper Trinity's pole regarding their combined potential impact on the various subdimensions here. Political decisions influence the armies, and the former should be under scrutiny here with that repercussion in mind.

Influence from the other pole, that is, people's power, is less obvious and not to be disregarded as well. People are part of companies and other organizations, affecting the armed forces through their values and behavior. That is a matter we will put in place when covering engagement using Sun Tzu's frameworks. Therefore, inside the company, we should have the means to manage that kind of influence.

But politics can be ineffective with people. Just look at all the demonstrations and strikes happening all over the world. There are several forces able to mobilize people for various reasons, and we should consider them all. That mobilization happens at a grassroots level, but its consequences influence all subdimensions of this pole. Therefore, the grassroots element, that is, the third Trinity's pole, should be considered in its impact on each of the current pole subdimensions, one by one. We should leave nothing to chance here as well.

Trinity's Second pole - The armed forces' framework in action

The time has come to create a global picture of what occurs in this second Trinity pole by considering all its subdimensions simultaneously. At this point in the strategic analysis, we also create a scenario where all subdimensions are coherently involved. Coherency is the right word here as it reflects the interrelated nature of the subdimensions under discussion.

The outcome of this Trinity's pole final analysis is a scenario pointing out the dominant armed forces at stake, their intents, and the possible use of the various weapons before defining how to go to battle, which will take place in Part II. This scenario will be crucial to explain the rules of engagement with Sun Tzu's frameworks.

ELEVEN
TRINITY'S THIRD POLE - THE PEOPLE

The third Clausewitzian Trinity pole is the fabric of armies, policies, and leadership, that is, the individuals who make everything happen. Clausewitz refers to people as "a blind natural force" with "primordial violence, hatred, and enmity."[80]

It is curious to see Clausewitz using the attribute of "blindness," for it's the opposite of pure reason, converting the third pole in the antithesis of the first. Blindness is a powerful way to describe this force because the lack of eyesight at ground level leaves no room to question orders. By referring to blindness, Clausewitz wants to keep individuals under control so that violence initiatives are visible and certain, thus dominating the battlefield. There is no time to think. Nor chance. Only actions.

Therefore, in this pole, we must identify the actors and all possible actions in the battleground. Effectiveness comes from both unleashed violence and engagement spirit. This analysis puts forward all contributions for struggle on the battlefield.

---
80 Clausewitz, On War, 1976, page 89

People's behavior

People on the battlefield are the first subdimension because they are a significant element of any organization's armed forces. Knowing what we are capable of is key, so we start the analysis by identifying the troops. Not an easy job because there are lots of grey zones in getting this type of information; know-how is tacit, thus hidden. This involves internal intelligence, where ethics must be always the foremost consideration.

Knowing the composition of adversaries' troops and their moves is even more challenging as intelligence is not synonymous with spying. Today, a vast amount of information is accessible on the Web, which is powerful but not sufficient. We need to devise an approach to acquire the necessary information about all relevant entities and their capabilities at the field level. Intangible assets, such as intrinsic know-how, are of paramount importance. For instance, how can we comprehend a painter's genius? By admiring the outcome of his know-how or performance.

In the end, we need to list the most influential persons involved in the battlefield and what to expect from them. That will help most of the tactical vision required for the needed bottom-up approach when putting a strategy in place because we build strategies with sequences of tactics.

Culture is also a vital aspect to consider because different regions have different cultures, and it may matter. Some cultures and some people are just more dependable because contracts cannot solve everything. Remember that mighty deceit is best perpetrated by the most trustworthy.

Finally, the social context also impacts people.

Social context

People live in social contexts, which influences their behavior and interactions. The social aspect has gaining importance, becoming paramount in virtually all areas. Because companies are intricate social systems, we can deploy social networks create the most significant network effects. Moreover, social systems span every boundary. Industries, education, politics, beliefs, entertainment, you name it, are all based on social interactions.

For this third Trinity's pole, we consider the social context due to the previous pole's weapons, namely social networks, media, and law/regulations. In this context social behavior is what matters and is our primary focus.

Cause-effect relationships are paramount, and there are three facets to consider.

The first facet of the social context is the communication climate, which we follow to interpret for social practices. Communication sparks may create new and unforeseen social behaviors that depend on each region and its culture. Still, culture is sometimes not easy to grasp because, to understand it deeply, we have to be open to its communication nuances, and maybe only a belonging element can attain full comprehension. The difficulty comes from its implicit nature, which takes time to absorb and master. So, because our belonging choices are limited by nature, we have to prioritize the social groups to follow. And sometimes we do not even have a chance to enter a group to fathom its social context.

Burgeoning demonstrations are an excellent example of what to expect regarding social behavior. For example, broadcasted news can be echoed by social networking with tremendous impact. Some even say that the Arab Spring has roots in media and social networking sparks.

Understanding each social environment unveils cause-effect relationships, which may be activated when needed. Only some energy in the form of an additional spark is all that is required to start profound unrest, so, knowing what works will make all the difference in battle.

The second facet of social behavior is the internal social context, or intra-company communications. Most often than not, big companies are quite tricky to grasp, mainly when resulting from mergers. Indeed, mergers are an excellent example of competing, sometimes clashing, subcultures challenging to manage by nature. In any case, shaping social contexts is an important key to play and should be mastered for leadership.

The third facet to consider is the myriad external social contexts. We should identify pertinent companies, politicians, or any other vital groups and duly note all needed information about each one. Remember that these are forces to be activated, either by our adversaries or by us. Intelligence will be vital to spot early moves. Mastering these forces is also key.

All in all, analyzing social contexts in this pole identifies social groups, their characteristics, goals, happenings, and what to expect in all cases.

Company behavior

We overviewed company behavior in the previous Trinity's pole, the armed forces of the competitive environment. Now, we focus on their practice, or what Clausewitz calls "violence, hatred, and enmity." We start with the list of companies already identified in the previous pole analysis and focus on how they act when on the battlefield.

It all depends on companies' tactical objectives because we are dealing with tactics at this level. We should identify the tools companies use to attain these objectives and the coherency between goals and methods. Of course, we can get it by looking at companies' history of tactical moves, taking into account the context of their leadership style at every moment in time because leaders tend to leave a tactical signature.

For example, have you noticed the difference between Jeff Bezos and Mark Zuckerberg? One just needs to look at what each company has been betting on over the years. When exploring innovative ideas, failures are immense because trial and error are epistemic. The difference lies in the type of ventures launched and how successes are exploited. In this regard, looking at both companies' set of achievements, we all have more to learn from Amazon.

But we can use two other hints to grasp companies' tactics by looking at them with the angles of assets and strategy.

The first hint comes from the company's assets—the intangible ones. What are its capabilities? Competencies? They result from their investments and development over the years. If the company is successful, agile, and forward-looking, the competitive landscape evolution dictates which capabilities to develop. Only by adequately adapting to an evolutive environment can we possess the needed skills for success. Forward-looking means that the information required on probable future scenarios is gathered through intelligence activities. We can use the same intelligence instruments to determine which skills are part of our adversaries' arsenal.

The second hint comes from strategy. What is the company trying to achieve? What works or has worked in the past? What would we do in their place? These questions will allow focusing companies' moves upfront because it's impossible to mobilize resources for attack without somehow unveiling it. By looking for what may be in preparation underneath, we can grasp future discontinuities in the company's behavior. By looking at tactical objectives upfront, we can foresee the right logistics to attain them.

In today's B2C environment, platforms lead the way and provide outstanding tactical capabilities. We can find useful hints on the type of violence contenders will deploy by looking at tactics for building network effects, as well as assets or skills needed to create these, which is a critical aspect of the environment of new platforms. Maybe even the most important one.

Special organizations' behavior

How powerful are Big Techs? How influential are platforms in our lives and business environments? Big Techs are examples of special organizations, with a kind of leverage only attained by governmental-level organizations. The current subdimension grasps their violence capabilities to perceive the competitive environment and establish possible tactics.

Global and ever more ubiquitous communications have created the right conditions for platforms to appear, taking over large chunks of the economy. Information and communication technologies have evolved from simple support activities to the most influential companies on earth. Their profitability and capitalization are a success measure. These platforms exploit core competencies and may even constitute natural monopolies in their regions, which, in most cases, is limited only by language and Web access. The balance of network effects determines the final balance.

We feel compelled to mention these companies because they can be overwhelming on a regional basis. No company with true global reach exists yet, as there are several distinct worldwide webs in existence today. For example, Tim Berners-Lee's dream of a flat namespace for all interconnected data resources has been under attack by the Dark Web.

The infamous Big Techs are well-positioned to take over the Western World in their industries, and no one knows how enormous their scope will be. In the West, we are daily consumers of Big Tech, which predominantly originates from the United States. Europe, in contrast, does not have its own Big Tech companies.

With Baidu and its ecosystem, China is different and effective. Super Apps like WeChat and Alipay are utterly successful, just to mention just two of the most important. Singapore has Grab. Indonesia has Gojek. Vietnam has Zalo. Europe has none. Super Apps are platforms with colossal network effects and convenience, benefiting the economy beyond what a scattered App environment can offer.

Africa is another story, building on the success of mobile payment systems started by M-PESA as early as 2008. Thus, Africa is also on the Super App path.

The adaptation of Super App ecosystems to their unique environments makes it intriguing to observe their development, especially since globalization appears to be unstoppable. For this pole, what counts is the direct influence these platforms have on the market, meaning the tactical options we face for every geography.

Platforms are evolving quickly. At this point, there are four main kinds of successful platforms, depending on the underlying technology.

The first and traditional type of platform is web-based, resulting in everybody exchanging information on the Web, creating a user network. Platform users can be both consumers or suppliers, and, when both are present, we call these platforms multisided. TaoBao in China, eBay in the West, Amazon, or even Facebook are good examples of multisided platforms. The Web induced platform development, entailing epistemic fostering among consumers, thus benefiting everybody, either for transactions or content. All Web contenders should respect Big Techs. Only companies with death wishes will attack platforms in their natural arena due to their network effect strength.

The second kind of platform evolved chronologically on top of the previous one and focused on communications, of which WhatsApp and WeChat are among the best-known examples. The network effects here are even higher due to permanent mobile convenience and ubiquity. In China, WeChat's power is enormous due to the positive network effects of both customers and suppliers, which grow with stakeholders' community. Less for the West, up to now, because OTT services[81] do not currently

---

81   Over The Top

offer anything more than just multimedia communication. Even payments are lagging. Still, in Africa, it seems that M-PESA may evolve into a Super App, starting with the utterly successful payment systems and bringing social networking on board (please refer to Bonga[82]). In summary, different regions have thus been evolving their communications platforms distinctively, depending on local culture and regulations.

Cloud computing is the cornerstone of the third kind of platform, supporting services like e-mail, mapping, or any other functionality. Google and Microsoft Western World's kings and China has their own platform service suppliers.

But a new fourth kind of platform is emerging, not based on a single supplier but on web3 distributed applications, like, for instance, Decentralized Finance (DeFi). This trend may be disruptive at the ecosystem level for various reasons. First, they are attacking the hegemony of ancient platforms. Second, by being distributed, no single entity can create their usual monopolistic rents, which is itself disruptive. And third, and this is the most critical reason, these distributed apps are trustless. By the way, the Bitcoin is a simple DeFi example. Cryptocurrency valuation, and other web3 topics, can obscure the most crucial aspect of asset tokenization. On a broader scale, a wide variety of tokens encompassing assets in the regulated economy are paving the way. Welcome to the new, wonderful, and profoundly disruptive world of web3.

Concluding the discussion on this critical subdimension, we should duly scrutinize all platforms of all four kinds. Remember that it's easier to possess network effects upfront and broaden

---

[82] Safaricom rolls out Bonga social networking platform to augment M-PESA, TechCrunch, April 30, 2018

its functionality scope than the reverse. That is why Super Apps are currently leading the way, and examples like Amazon define success itself by building on the already established community and network effects. In contrast, scattered and independent apps do not evolve as quickly when starting from scratch for the difficulties in building network effect's critical mass.

The violence felt on the battlefield has been more and more influenced by these crucial companies, and it will not stop. Quite the contrary, planforms can decide to enter virtually any industry, posing a significant risk for incumbents.

Remember that network effects are always underneath these platforms' success, and that is why platforms are so important. So, for this subdimension, we should identify all relevant platforms, as well as their intentions and actions.

Technology and communications and media available

In the current Trinity's pole, we have to evaluate the use of technology, including telecommunications and the media. Where in the previous pole, technology, telecommunications and media, are armed forces, at this level, they are deployable tactics. So, in this subdimension, we analyze its violence and consequences on the battlefield.

We first start with information technology and communications. More and more, these two technologies cannot be separated, which is why they are sometimes referred to as ICT (Information and Communication Technologies). For instance, Industry 4.0 requires the use of both technologies for production facilities, a tactic with a substantial strategic impact. Thus, we should go deep into the usage of meaningful technologies, in any form, including cloud computing, fog computing, or edge computing, and verify its strategic impacts as tactical weapons. In the current environment, AI is essential for the new flavor of analytics, including the traditional Business Intelligence for structured data and Big Data techniques for its unstructured version. Generative Learning is popping up with multiple uses.[83] Quantum Computing is also an emerging strategic tool for analytics. Yes, platforms are crucial as tactical weapons, including distributed apps in the realm of web3.

More than reviewing technologies, the trick is to devise how to use these technologies to foster business, valid for any contender. Promoting business is violence in this case. Analyze threats firsthand, upgrading all that we can into opportunities when possible. Remember that if we do nothing, opportunities naturally become threats.

Then comes communications. Things have been evolving fast and will develop even more quickly with 5G. Remember that communications multiply information's value in all its forms. With 5G, cloud computing platforms will evolve, unleashing ubiquitous computing power everywhere and in real-time. It may even happen that this decentralized set of computing devices will grow into distributed computing. That is a significant trend in the short term because it will put several interesting tactics in place, with tremendous opportunities. However, opportunities will evolve into threats if we do nothing.

Finally, consider the media. Broadcast media has limited bandwidth, but on the other hand, it has the advantage of being

---

83 Eric Mac, Generative AI Like ChatGPT Is Popping Up Everywhere. Your Questions Answered, CNET, Feb 23 2023, frhttps://www.cnet.com/science/generative-ai-like-chatgpt-is-popping-up-everywhere-your-questions-answered/

seen by many people simultaneously. Relevant news, mostly visual ones, can be compelling and so powerful they can significantly amplify all meaning and cause subsequent impact. Unfortunately, the shady side is always more substantial, and this has been exceptionally well exploited by political forces. The relationship between the media and the other communication channels, including social networking, should also be evaluated with care. The negative side is potentially hazardous, but the free ride in increased exposure is tempting.

Energy, transportation and the sharing economy

Energy supply and transportation are part of any army's arsenal. We now concentrate on their tactical effect on the battlefield, that is, Clausewitz's violence. The current subdimension is straightforward, for we just have to identify how these two types of services can be used in practice, both for offensive and defensive purposes.

Maybe this subdimension is still mild because we are talking mostly about services, which are public goods, abundant and cheaply available to everybody. Energy and transportation are both part of the underlying and almost imperceptible economic infrastructure, and if nothing were about to change, it would be uninteresting. But the fact is that energy is enduring a significant transformation because it can be produced in a decentralized manner, cheaply, which will also foster communities with potential outstanding network effects. That is an unexpected repercussion of the energy infrastructure as a weapon. There may be others due to the necessary evolution it will fast endure.

On the other hand, transportation depends on energy, so any evolution in energy supply will have consequences on transportation. Moreover, transportation is not just a question of technology but a cultural issue as well. And that is where the sharing economy enters, and not only just for transportation. The sharing economy has roots in network effects—a weapon of terrifying capabilities. That is the angle of analysis we should use for this subdimension, or how can our contenders profit from riding the wave of these network effects to their advantage? How can we build on the same network effects?

TooGoodToGo is an example working in more than a dozen countries, its business model relies on connecting traditional restaurants and other conventional businesses related to food, with consumers willing to buy their "magic boxes" containing a complete meal for a fraction of the price. Restaurants prepare these boxes with good surplus food that otherwise would be discarded. On top of additional revenue, suppliers also benefit from free publicity, allowing future customers to try their food out. That is "positive" violence, having good effects on the market.

Direct influences from the other two dimensions

As with the other two Trinity's poles, this subdimension makes the difference when going through Clausewitz's framework for strategic analysis.

More than just identifying subdimensions, we scrutinize the cause-effect relationships between strategic and tactical levels, together with the various types of actors. As with so many things in life, details matter. Counter-intuitiveness is vital here.

We must uncover the influence that reason and chance have on "violence, hatred, and enmity," keeping in mind that the former is the consequence of the inner feelings driven by the other two.

Violence is enacted by people, and the emotions associated with it also reside within individuals. Moreover, the way to perpetrate violence depends on the terrain's tactical conditions. Thus, people and terrain conditions are the other two Trinity's pole influence in this one.

Starting with the first Trinity's pole, that is, reason, we assume that governments and similar powered entities can and should influence people in the direction that suits their strategic objectives, which is valid for all armies to the extent of their capabilities. There are five main tactics of influence to consider in this third pole:

- The effectiveness of leadership, inflaming passions, and engagement.
- The effectiveness of social networking also the inflaming of passions and engagement.
- The effectiveness of laws and regulations, both for emotions and tactical engagement.
- Communication infrastructure capabilities; why some governments are fully controlling it; there is a discussion going on about how free and unregulated networking sites should be. Note: we are not considering the infrastructure, but the impact of its use, as well as regulations.
- The same with energy, transportation, and shared economy rules with tactical impact on this pole, through all its subdimensions.

Moving to chance, we should look for the outcome of the deployment of armies in this third pole. It's a bit more than chance because, at a higher level, probabilistic reasoning is what Clausewitz is expecting to accomplish when deploying his armies. But at the army level, leaders have their own strategy and influencing their soldiers in the best way possible. Clausewitz dedicates a good part of *On War* to engagement.

Once again, we should look at armies' subdimensions and interpret their impact on this pole:

- Companies: by nature, leadership has a direct effect on people; this effect is authentic and robust because people do pass a lot of their awake time at work, and the impact can be positive as well as negative; get inspiration from leadership.
- People: we can also assess the previous subdimension by looking at people and devising their leaders' impact.[84] What counts here is not the violence we already evaluated in the related subdimension above but the previous pole's influence on this one. Please note that people may feel other impacts from the army apart from the leaders, which we should also assess; in this regard, social networking also comes to mind.
- Social networking and media can significantly impact peoples' passions; it has evolved for the last two decades, first with the Web 2.0 and more recently with mobility; it will continue to grow, and we should watch it with care.

---

84 A few years ago, I supervised the commercial branch of a pharmaceutical company. We trained all employees to be attentive to their colleagues daily and report their findings. After a few months, the leadership actions from all competitor's leaders became obvious.

- Payment systems and other facets of the financial infrastructure can also impact here; are we creating a new entrepreneurial era? Or are they just cash-burners in the making? Attitude is everything for this pole.
- Other organizations, including Big Techs: the army subdimension for Big Techs and organizations with significant influence also affects people; we analyze its impact at the tactical level; what happens, for example, if the West evolves into a Super App environment? What happens if WhatsApp includes other functionalities in the platform, like payments? How will people's behavior develop?

The same with energy, transportation, and shared economy practices with tactical impact on this pole, through all its subdimensions.

Trinity's Third pole - The people's framework
This final analysis ascertains all subdimensions of this Trinity's pole to create comprehension, understanding the meaningful tactical conditions and the region at stake, thus fully depicting the terrain.

It is only natural that we understand our business environment taken from our own experience, so the combined cause-effect relationships of all other subdimensions become more comfortable to grasp. But knowledge isn't everything, and situations may happen all around us, out of our previous appraisal scope. In this regard, this analysis is particularly critical and useful when going abroad, navigating unchartered waters, exploring.

We thus reassess the various business dimensions above and pinpoint what may be necessary for our venture. For example:

- Consumers: What are the market dimension and demographics? Which communication channels are available? How effective are these?
- Social environment: is there social unrest? Are there political risks?
- Security and safety: other than cyber warfare, how safe is the region for business? Is there a risk of theft or other physical threat? What about legal threats?
- Products: how innovative is the market at stake? Are there incentives for innovation? Is it well seen? Credible? How easy is it to find venture capital?
- Is there the right supplier's availability? Are they easy to contact and negotiate? Or is there concentration or some kind of coordination between suppliers, unlawfully increasing transaction costs?
- Competitors: Who are they? How do they compete?
- Platforms: how dangerous are they? How can they be used to compete?
- Resources: How can energy, transportation, and communications be used to compete?

The list could go on, mostly inspired by all other subdimensions of this Trinity's pole. The most important thing is to pinpoint what may be essential to check upfront when designing a strategy. It also increases our real appreciation of the competitive environment testing the applicability of tactics.

For example, the terrain for innovation in Europe is different from the United States, Africa, or China. If innovation is the answer, it should be tackled differently depending on each environment. It's not just a question about culture, but which mechanisms are actionable on top of the networks and habits in place, among other possible dimensions. The more we observe and consider, the more robust and effective our strategy will be.

TWELVE
CLAUSEWITZ COMPLETE FRAMEWORK

The time has come to finish and complete Clausewitz's Trinity analysis using the results obtained in the Trinity's poles with all their subdimensions and cross-effects among them. That is the richness of Clausewitz's vision: pure, although beyond what traditional business strategy frameworks can contemplate.

The objective is a coherent scenario, which is a conclusion about what is happening in our chosen operation region. Our goal now is to grasp the combined results and develop the corresponding integrated insight.

The conclusion to be developed now should put forward a high-level strategic aim. It's not a strategy yet because we cannot draw a complete strategy from external analysis alone. By looking at external factors, we set up the overall picture defining what is real and not. Our concrete strategy will emerge by combining internal analysis, which should guide the best path through our preparedness in the context of the outer strategic space. Moreover, we do not engage in a strategy just because we can, not just any strategy. We chose the one promising more effectiveness, which we will uncover after balancing its risks and returns according to our profile. We will need a lot of internal analysis for this, which we cover in Part II.

Nevertheless, a good Trinity analysis can reveal the following aspects of a complete external strategic scenario:

- Identify the major contenders.
- Define the terrain and the primary deployable tactics around.
- Find out about unwritten rules to keep in mind.
- Unveil potential counter-intuitive contender objectives.
- Unveil unexpected political moves with an impact on our terrain.
- Unveil Big Techs' positioning, both as a contender and as a tool.
- Reveal weapons in the context of information warfare.
- Reveal tactics underneath economic warfare.
- Reveal the importance of soft powers underneath laws and regulations.
- The list goes on and on; you just have to complete it following your analysis.

Part II starts precisely at this point. We descend one level down on the strategic ladder by considering how to deploy our armed forces in the best way possible, with a meaningful internal analysis, adapting our capabilities to the ground rules and achievable objectives in the context of Clausewitz's Trinity. Thus, we will be using Sun Tzu's frameworks to define a strategy, building on a complete situational analysis, using the frameworks conceived with the reasoning stated in *The Art of War*.

PART II
SUN TZU ON ENGAGEMENT

It is not by chance that we find General Sun Tzu's book, *The Art of War*, on many shelves dealing with general strategy, business, military, or any other kind of strategy. Sun Tzu's teachings were apparently written 2400 ago but continue to inspire strategists all over the world. Enduring the test of time is the best proof of its value.

This work follows the translation General Samuel Griffith published in 1963, including all his additional Chinese insights, by citing several meaningful Chinese thinkers to interpret Sun Tzu's verses.

> *1.1 War is a matter of vital importance to the State, the province of life or death, the road to survival or ruin. It's mandatory that it be thoroughly studied.*[85]

In Part I, we used Clausewitz's Trinity analysis to encompass strategic landscapes in all its details, including all contenders,

---
85   Samuel Griffith, *Sun Tzu The Art of War*, Oxford University Press, 1976, page 63

business, politics, mutual relationships, terrain, powerful influence weapons, and even the people involved. It somehow replaces external analysis with a military flavor. Creating a high-level vision is essential for strategy development, but it is not yet a complete strategy in itself. A strategy depends on various other factors underneath battlefield engagement, both internal and external. Only then can a strategy be adequately determined.

In this Part, we discuss Sun Tzu's strategy applied to business confrontation.

To define a military approach for strategic engagement in the business landscape, we deploy Sun Tzu's teachings to develop a complete business strategy framework. We chose Sun Tzu among other military writers for this step, including Clausewitz, due to the simplicity and cleanliness of Sun Tzu's concepts. In a book of thirteen short chapters, Sun Tzu overviews all needed facets for strategic engagement, focusing on internal capabilities, including leadership and intelligence. For Sun Tzu, a strategy is a dynamic sequence of moves, that is, a sequence of tactical operations, and not just planning. When taken together, all these dimensions apply to business strategy, hence Sun Tzu's success in our era.

Sun Tzu considers all the seemingly essential ingredients to the military during wartime. Business strategists can deploy Sun Tzu's unparalleled approach for an encompassing view on strategic engagement. And knowledge is paramount here. We must not only meticulously study the enemy, the terrain, their weapons, and the possible tactical scenarios in advance, but also establish an intelligence process to collect the needed information for real-time adaptation during confrontations. Even covert operations, which is the most aggressive version of intelligence, explicitly appear in the thirteenth chapter of Sun Tzu's masterpiece[86], adding other references about information and intelligence throughout the book.

Sun Tzu considers the Command-and-Control Leadership virtues of being the base of any strategic action. He mentions ten virtues to appraise leadership capabilities for any strategy at stake. Eternal knowledge-gathering comes after leadership to build a victory, attacking enemy's strategy.[87]

We ought to know everything about the enemy, and Sun Tzu even mentions the five estimations behind the victorious leader[88]. So, for Sun Tzu, the chances of victory are assessed with knowledge [89], starting with awareness and insight, both external and internal.

The scope of the organizational aptitude is another aspect of utmost importance for Sun Tzu. We should only fight battles that we deem capable of winning, and this totally depends on our capabilities.

In remarkable sequence of four verses[90], Sun Tzu puts forward the epistemic dynamics of internal and external factors. Therefore, he bases victory on learning and adaptation about every relevant aspect of war, and that is why we engage in intelligence before anything else. The military refer to it as situational aware-

---

86 Griffith, *Sun Tzu The Art of War*, page 148, verse 13.16
87 Griffith, *Sun Tzu The Art of War*, page 77, verse 3.4
88 Griffith, *Sun Tzu The Art of War*, page 88, verse 4.16
89 Griffith, *Sun Tzu The Art of War*, page 84, verses 3.31 to 3.33
90 Griffith, *Sun Tzu The Art of War*, page 100-101

ness,[91] and Sun Tzu explicitly identifies five factors.[92] However, as we shall see below, there is a sixth one.

Including both internal and external aspects is interesting because intelligence usually considers only the external environment. For Sun Tzu, situational awareness, in all its forms, precedes strategic action.

Tactics and terrain are other fascinating aspects of Sun Tzu's work, as he sees both in terms of the impact they can cause on our adversaries. Strategy's building blocks start with the effects of each possible tactic in each specific terrain. There are eleven types of tactics identified and nine types of terrain, creating a massive set of combinations. Because we cannot analyze them all one by one, and also because there are other elements to consider, which further increases strategic planning complexity, we will use General Ferdinand Foch's Economy of Force's superior principle to assess the impact of all tactical moves without entering into the detail of all possible combinations. Sun Tzu's work sounds very much like Foch's Economy of Forces underlying principles, but their aggregation in an explicit trilogy effectively belongs to General Foch.

Sun Tzu mentions leadership, intelligence, terrain, tactics, and the impact of using tactics and weapons throughout his book. After considering all this combined advice, we can begin formulating a strategy.

A strategy differs from a plan in that the latter is static. A good strategy always depends on our tactical ability to adapt

---

91 Oswald Boelcke, a German pilot in WWI, came up with a list of air combat principles, often referred to as the "Dicta Boelcke", in his book "An Aviator's Field Book: Being the field reports of Oswald Boelcke, from August 1, 1914 to October 28, 1916". Situational Awareness is part of his findings.

92 Later on, we see that six facts are part of the lot, due to a reference Sun Tzu makes at the end of the first chapter.

because "no plan survives the first encounter with the enemy".[93] Whereas strategic planning lives in the minds of strategists, engagement happens on the battlefield. Sun Tzu emphasizes building strategy from the bottom up, focusing on tactics that aim toward a specific objective. This involves deploying a sequence of tactical moves and reacting accordingly to our adversaries' responses to our attacks. That kind of dynamic has incredible value for business strategy, much beyond classical strategic planning. Consequently, following Sun Tzu's teachings, we define a strategic engagement methodology to be put in action after Clausewitz's Trinity analysis.

Starting with the strategic objectives, as defined in Part I:

1. we first assess the five Leadership Virtues to bootstrap internal awareness;
2. assessing the terrain comes next to bootstrap external awareness; this assessment includes the nine types of combat grounds, the possible weapons and their effects on the adversary;
3. we then fully expand situational awareness deploying a complete internal and external intelligence policy with Sun Tzu's six situational awareness factors;
4. with all situational awareness factors at hand, we explore the ten possible types of tactics;
5. we assess the best sequence of tactical moves for the strategic objectives with the Foch Economy of Forces superior principle to depict the chosen strategy; we

---

93 Helmuth von Moltke, *Militarische Werke*. vol. 2, part 2., pp. 33-40; found in *Moltke on the Art of War: selected writings*, Daniel Hughes, Presidio Press, 1993, New York

should recall strategic objectives defined by Clausewitz's Trinity as discussed in Part I;
6. the chosen strategy then passes through Sun Tzu's dynamic checklist for competitive dynamic's assessment and further strengthening;
7. finally, Sun Tzu's teachings do not end here, because, before moving forward, he also proposes two tactical health checks; (i) the first one deals with applied tactics and considers six factors, that is, the Six Tactical Losing Conditions; (ii) and the second finishes the analysis by reconnecting to the very beginning of Sun Tzu's strategic reasoning, which is leadership, or the Six Command Losing Factors.

And that is Sun Tzu's exciting reasoning in a nutshell with a little help from Clausewitz for a sound upper-level strategic acumen and from Foch for tactical strength measurement. Each step is mirrored in a dedicated framework you can find summarized in Annex I.

THIRTEEN
SUN TZU'S 10 COMMAND AND CONTROL LEADERSHIP VIRTUES

Victory is tactical because it depends on the battlefield's leverage over the enemy, and we do not have to be excellent, just better than our opponents. The victory thus emerges from the clash between adversaries and how they deploy their capabilities. Decision making in command is the first necessary winning condition.

Sun Tzu highlights leadership at the start of his book referring to five qualities [94], subsequently mentioning six additional virtues [95]. We will review all these leadership traits mentioned with the detail they deserve. This discussion aims to lay down the foundations of an assessment framework to verify leadership conditions for any endeavor at stake.

Sun Tzu's hint is clear: we should assess leadership before anything else because no one can go into battle and expect to win without it.

---

94 Griffith, *Sun Tzu The Art of War*, page 65, verse 1.7
95 Griffith, *Sun Tzu The Art of War*, page 136, verse 11.42

Military strategists know about the defender's advantage. Only by maneuvering extraordinarily is it possible for an attacker to win with meager forces, which totally depends on captainship. That is the case of the already referred Napoleon's example in the battle of Austerlitz.

Alexander the Great is perhaps the best example of leadership, expanding Macedonia's influence beyond belief in just a decade. This inspiring king was considered an example to follow both by Napoleon and the German Chancellor at the end of the second 30-year war in Europe.

The relationship between political purpose, strategy, tactics, and leadership is vital. Victories are tactical in nature because they always happen on the field, whatever field we may be talking about. So, strategies do not win wars: tactics do! But tactics are meaningless without strategic context, which is itself driven by political purpose. Clausewitz's Trinity propels this purpose, which we may call strategic intent, overviewed in Part I. So, tactics create the reality of the strategic intent, Sun Tzu's primary concern, with leadership as its cornerstone. That reveals leadership's strategic importance.

In summary, leadership is key in all regards. In Samuel Griffith's translation a good commander is referred to as "The Respected One". Are you, or do you want to be that one?

We overview all ten leadership traits referred to throughout the book, which are the basis of the "Command & Control Ten Leadership Virtues" framework.

Leadership Virtue #1 - wisdom

Griffith recalls Tu Mu (803-852) to define wisdom as the ability "to recognize changing circumstances and to act expediently".[96]

There is a notable difference between wisdom and knowledge. Acquiring knowledge stems from our encounters with information, and, over time, our learning is enhanced through the recognition of patterns.

On the other hand, wisdom, according to the Chinese interpretation above, goes one step further. Wisdom enables the leader to feel, understand, and grasp new situations without prior experience! Whereas knowledge can be tacit or explicit, wisdom is unspoken, hence a feeling on top of everything else. Wisdom behaves like an intangible insight.

Nevertheless, action is necessary, as from the interpretation mentioned earlier, simply recognizing change is inadequate, and measures must be expediently taken.

For Sun Tzu, wisdom surpasses the capabilities of the ordinary man,[97] emphasizing that true wisdom requires a leader to perceive beyond the apparent. Consequently, it's this wisdom that leads to the sought-after victory without resorting to battle.[98]

Leadership Virtue #2 - strictness (rewards and punishments)

Strictness thus emerges from the leader's actions and is a cultural trait.[99] Hence, the basis for measuring it lies in experience of those being led. Their appreciation is what truly matters. So, for

---

96 Griffith, *Sun Tzu The Art of War*, page 65, verse 1.7
97 Griffith, *Sun Tzu The Art of War*, page 86-87, verses 4.8 to 4.11
98 Griffith, *Sun Tzu The Art of War*, page 87, verse 4.14
99 Griffith, *Sun Tzu The Art of War*, page 65, verse 1.7

this virtue, we consider two sides of the same coin: the leader's attitude and how it's perceived by others. Regarding the latter, Griffith appeals to Ch'ên Hao (Song dynasty) when referring to a leader's dignity at the eyes of his subjects.[100]

Sun Tzu assesses strictness through moral, discipline, and the consistency of orders, including rewards and punishments.[101] It appears that strictness goes hand in hand with trust because Sun Tzu considers a direct relationship between this trait, through rewards and punishments, and sheer victory.[102]

Therefore, this is primarily about discipline, with the focus on subject's perception. Consequently, it's worth discussing the true meaning of rewards and punishments.

Rewards and punishments represent positive and negative outcomes, aligning with each individual's expectations. Thus, it's a subjective view that we may have on everything all around us. The focus here is the leader, but we may also feel rewarded, or punished, by unexpected happenings amid complexity, just by chance. Is the bottle half empty or half full? Only each one of us can offer the answer to this question, individually.

Consequently, expectations serve as the dynamic baseline for guiding the application of rewards and punishments. More often than not, rewards are disregarded if becoming a habit, precisely because expectations have evolved. In this case, rewards can even become a punishment when not provided.

Therefore, rewards are tricky to manage due to diverse expectation of every individual. Sun Tzu's approach emphasizes maintaining consistency as it fosters a culture easy to predict.

---

100   Griffith, Sun Tzu The Art of War, page 121, verse 9.37
101   Griffith, Sun Tzu The Art of War, page 126, verse 10.14 and page 123, verse 9.49
102   Griffith, Sun Tzu The Art of War, page 66, verses 1.13 and 1.14

That is why Sun Tzu added "sincerity," which we discuss further down. Still, nowadays, life is more complicated, and extra care has to be taken regarding expectations. The double-sided nature of "strictness" thus dictates the need to handle changing expectations as well.

But what is the meaning of positives and negatives regarding these expectations? Broadly speaking, we view these as stemming from each individuals' emotions. For the current virtue—strictness—we focus on the influence a leader may have on people's emotions, as anything that elicits positive emotions is deemed a reward, while elements that induce negative emotions are viewed as punishments. That counts both for intentional and unintentional implications because a leader cannot excuse himself not to be paying attention to any relevant detail. It falls upon the leader to seek relevant information about subject's expectations and the effects of his actions.

So, what can originate positive emotions? Well, everything, really, and the tools are immense, from tangible and straightforward rewards such as salary, fringe benefits, and promotions, to subtle rewards in personal communication, social networking, and the like. A smile is powerful, only if we are not smiling all the time. Remember that only scarcity creates value, and this is also true for intangible assets, like a smile or a message from the leader saying, "I am happy with your engagement." Although, if the leader sends it to everybody, diminishing scarcity, it also reduces its value. Worse yet, if the leader sends it to undeserving subjects, it will even be considered a punishment for the deserving ones due to the already mentioned evolving expectations.

The same for punishments. But we must be careful here because the negatives are so much stronger than the positives. If rewards are not exaggerated because we want to avoid diminishing scarcity, this is even more true for punishment. The negatives are so strong that we are already living and experiencing the punishment even before it happens if we already have them embedded in our expectations. And when injustices are promoted to traumas, they will never be forgotten.

Thus, it's an excellent idea to make a list of tools that work in each culture and strategically deploy them according to the organization's needs.

And what if the leader is also the subject of another leader? This is the relationship between generals and sovereigns. The question here regarding strictness has two facets. The sovereign may override the general and give orders to his own subjects, or the sovereign may instruct the general with specific tactics, thus replacing the general's judgment. Both factors decrease the general's ability to lead effectively, and Sun Tzu is very clear about the importance of a general's strictness to remain unaffected by interference.[103]

Leadership Virtue #3 – humanity or benevolence

Griffith cites Tu Mu (803-852) for a fascinating interpretation of humanity, one that builds on the leader's actions towards those all around him.[104] Communication rules. Behavior matters. Respect and veneration go both ways.[105]

---

103   Griffith, *Sun Tzu The Art of War*, page 83, verse 4.29
104   Griffith, *Sun Tzu The Art of War*, page 66, verse 1.7
105   Griffith, *Sun Tzu The Art of War*, page 118, verse 9.20

Humanity also directly reflects the relationship between the leader and his troops, which can only be measured when assessing the leader's recipients. Thus, the manifestation of humanity is a consequence.

But there is a yet more compelling reason for this virtue, which is influence. Individuals should follow the leader, not from obligation, but for their beliefs.[106]

Moral influence is the first of the five of Sun Tzu's "fundamental factors" of war. It's that important. Humanity and benevolence are forms of influence. In today's world, that means prioritizing ethics. It's no coincidence that corporate social responsibility and ESG (Environmental, Social, and Governance) practices are gaining traction every day.

Leadership Virtue #4 – courage, engagement

Griffith's translation mentions courage several times, either by Sun Tzu or by other Chinese authors' citations for a coherent and expanded Chinese interpretation of the concept. That is the interpretation we adopt. Griffith references Tu Mu (803-852), who believed that courage is intrinsically linked with engagement.[107] This is why this virtue embodies both characteristics.

The leader builds respect through the consistency of his decisions, as well as his behavior under battle. That is what "without hesitation" effectively means. Engagement and resolve are thus essential because courage inspires and transmits certitude, and Griffith mentions Shen Pao-Hsu that sense.[108]

---

106   Griffith, *Sun Tzu The Art of War*, page 64, verse 1.4
107   Griffith, *Sun Tzu The Art of War*, page 65, verse 1.7
108   Griffith, *Sun Tzu The Art of War*, page 65, verse 1.7

Sun Tzu advises the leader to be courageous and follow his certitudes beliefs.[109] And Griffith points out an interesting interpretation of this by citing Sun Tzu's contemporary ruler in China, King FuCh'ai (495–473b.c.).[110] In a word, leadership thrives on true engagement.

Still, this virtue alone also has its risks. Citing Tu Mu (803-852) again, Griffith mentions the following curious and sharp assessment of courage:

> 8.18 ...*A general who is stupid and courageous is a calamity.*[111]

That is why this virtue alone is not enough, and we can give examples of this throughout history. However, I will refrain from doing it because of its negativity and the risk of subjective and differing appreciations. Maybe you will smile as I did with the faces of stupid and courageous leaders coming to mind.

So, to assess this virtue, the leader should verify the two sides of the same coin. On the one hand, his own decision-making process and resolve, and on the other hand, his engagement as perceived by everybody else.

Even if we did not create a separate virtue trait for engagement, due to its interconnection with courage, Sun Tzu identifies engagement as a catalyst for assured victory.[112]

Engagement is definitely key.

---

109 Griffith, Sun Tzu The Art of War, page 112, verse 8.8
110 Griffith, Sun Tzu The Art of War, page 112, verse 8.8
111 Griffith, Sun Tzu The Art of War, page 114
112 Griffith, *Sun Tzu The Art of War*, page 117, verse 98.

Humanity also directly reflects the relationship between the leader and his troops, which can only be measured when assessing the leader's recipients. Thus, the manifestation of humanity is a consequence.

But there is a yet more compelling reason for this virtue, which is influence. Individuals should follow the leader, not from obligation, but for their beliefs.[106]

Moral influence is the first of the five of Sun Tzu's "fundamental factors" of war. It's that important. Humanity and benevolence are forms of influence. In today's world, that means prioritizing ethics. It's no coincidence that corporate social responsibility and ESG (Environmental, Social, and Governance) practices are gaining traction every day.

Leadership Virtue #4 - courage, engagement

Griffith's translation mentions courage several times, either by Sun Tzu or by other Chinese authors' citations for a coherent and expanded Chinese interpretation of the concept. That is the interpretation we adopt. Griffith references Tu Mu (803-852), who believed that courage is intrinsically linked with engagement.[107] This is why this virtue embodies both characteristics.

The leader builds respect through the consistency of his decisions, as well as his behavior under battle. That is what "without hesitation" effectively means. Engagement and resolve are thus essential because courage inspires and transmits certitude, and Griffith mentions Shen Pao-Hsu that sense.[108]

---

[106] Griffith, *Sun Tzu The Art of War*, page 64, verse 1.4
[107] Griffith, *Sun Tzu The Art of War*, page 65, verse 1.7
[108] Griffith, *Sun Tzu The Art of War*, page 65, verse 1.7

Sun Tzu advises the leader to be courageous and follow his certitudes beliefs.[109] And Griffith points out an interesting interpretation of this by citing Sun Tzu's contemporary ruler in China, King FuCh'ai (495–473b.c.).[110] In a word, leadership thrives on true engagement.

Still, this virtue alone also has its risks. Citing Tu Mu (803-852) again, Griffith mentions the following curious and sharp assessment of courage:

> *8.18 ...A general who is stupid and courageous is a calamity.*[111]

That is why this virtue alone is not enough, and we can give examples of this throughout history. However, I will refrain from doing it because of its negativity and the risk of subjective and differing appreciations. Maybe you will smile as I did with the faces of stupid and courageous leaders coming to mind.

So, to assess this virtue, the leader should verify the two sides of the same coin. On the one hand, his own decision-making process and resolve, and on the other hand, his engagement as perceived by everybody else.

Even if we did not create a separate virtue trait for engagement, due to its interconnection with courage, Sun Tzu identifies engagement as a catalyst for assured victory.[112]

Engagement is definitely key.

---

109 Griffith, Sun Tzu The Art of War, page 112, verse 8.8
110 Griffith, Sun Tzu The Art of War, page 112, verse 8.8
111 Griffith, Sun Tzu The Art of War, page 114
112 Griffith, *Sun Tzu The Art of War*, page 117, verse 98.

Leadership Virtue #5 - Sincerity

Griffith appeals to Tu Mu (803-852) for an interpretation of sincerity that is demonstrated through one's actions over time.[113] Sincerity is conquered with consistency, where the appropriate use of rewards and punishments is paramount. It's just not about being fair when rewarding or punishing, but also about revealing one's truthfulness.

Just keep in mind that a single mistake can potentially jeopardize everything. A leader's actions must consistently be just and seem just[114], which means that sincerity has a profound impact on the relationship between the leader and his troops.

Nevertheless, the classical understanding regarding sincerity relies on communication and should not be disregarded. The leader should also look sincere to reinforce trust.

Leadership Virtue #6 - is serene and self-controlled.

For Sun Tzu, a leader must be serene[115], or "not vexed".[116]

The leader should never be agitated, a capability particularly challenging to endure, especially in warfare situations. Serenity is an implicit trait, part of the leader's nature as an individual.

It is only natural to see war's violence-inducing vexing individuals along the way, including its leaders. Thus, self-control is part of this leadership trait, which Griffith interprets, citing Wang Hsi (317-420): "if self-controlled, not confused."

Enduring the violence of war with serenity is not for everybody, and, in many situations, it relies solely on self-control.

---

113   Griffith, *Sun Tzu The Art of War*, page 65, verse 1.7
114   Griffith, *Sun Tzu The Art of War*, page 123, verse 9.49
115   Griffith, *Sun Tzu The Art of War*, page 136, verse 11.42
116   Griffith, *Sun Tzu The Art of War*, page 136, verse 11.42

Therefore, serenity is more than a leader's intrinsic capability but the result of his enlightened will, or, in other words, the outcome of self-control.

Moreover, the importance of serenity and self-control leads Sun Tzu to use against the adversaries[117]. Griffith references Li Ch'uan (618-907) and Mei Yaochen (1002-1060), also known as Chang Yu, to further explore the connection between anger and confusion in leadership, suggesting its strategic utilization[118].

Irritation and confusion are precisely what the French endured with already referred Bismarck's Ems dispatch in 1871.

Creating conditions for the adversary's leader to lose his serenity and self-control will compromise his ability to lead[119], meaning a victory of ours over a confused adversary. Thus, in an ideal scenario, a composed leader faces an adversary who is in a state of confusion. Serenity and self-control together form a strength and a virtue in leadership, as well as a target for provocation. Thus, attacking an adversary's emotions can be effective. Being immune to provocations is its corresponding crucial strength.

Leadership Virtue #7 – inscrutable

According to Sun Tzu, inscrutability means that no one should guess your thoughts, adversaries, and officers included. Where lies its strategic importance? In victory itself because "all warfare is based on deception",[120] and deception is the base of decisive action[121]. Therefore, inscrutability must be forged bottom-up in the minds of the adversaries. This principle applies equally to

---

117 Griffith, *Sun Tzu The Art of War*, page 67, verse 1.22
118 Griffith, *Sun Tzu The Art of War*, page 67, verse 1.22
119 Griffith, *Sun Tzu The Art of War*, page 82, verse 3.23
120 Griffith, *Sun Tzu The Art of War*, page 66, verse 1.17
121 Griffith, *Sun Tzu The Art of War*, page 69, verse 1.26

the strategic actions of our armed forces and the intentions of the leader.

Let's start with the former—adversaries. In Sun Tzu's course, deception plays a key role,[122] inducing the enemy to perceive weakness where there is actually strength. That is how we compel adversaries to attack where victory is inevitable for us, hence the necessary inscrutability of our intentions.

In time, a leader's strategy may become evident because repetition is only natural. Therefore, to maintain our intentions entirely out of adversaries' reach, tactics should be varied and misleading, "making it impossible for others to anticipate".[123] Griffith appeals to Wang Hsi (317-420) to advocate the immense power of inscrutability[124], ensuring that adversaries cannot get to us either way—a cornerstone for victory.

But there is a final, vital, and challenging aspect to this critical leadership virtue: the leader's loneliness. According to Sun Tzu, leaders should hide their intentions to even their closest allies and trustful subordinates.[125]

And this is difficult because trust is always built on some perceived vulnerability when sharing seemingly strategic information. And trust grows with time. There is thus a subtle balance between inscrutability and trust.

As a result, the leader will build trust when sharing strategic information with subjects only to increase the risk of exposure. This is because adversaries can use various kinds of intelligence operations to exploit these new potential sources of information.

---

122 Griffith, *Sun Tzu The Art of War*, page 140, verse 11.01
123 Griffith, *Sun Tzu The Art of War*, page 122, verse 9.46
124 Griffith, *Sun Tzu The Art of War*, page 136, verse 11.42
125 Griffith, *Sun Tzu The Art of War*, page 122, verse 9.43

Sun Tzu discusses the challenging task of disclosing tactics to subordinates while maintaining the secrecy of the overall strategy.[126] This can only be achieved if the leader's actions remain unpredictable to both adversaries and his own team, by constantly altering tactics and methods[127] to prevent any pattern or repetition[128].

Unpredictability is thus key for inscrutability.

Leadership Virtue #8 - impartial

Sun Tzu highlights impartiality is as a key virtue.[129] Griffith refers to Wang Hsi (317-420) to illustrate that a principled leader upholds truthfulness in all matters,[130] thereby fostering a culture of fairness and impartiality over time.

Sun Tzu elaborates that an upright leader cultivates humanity and justice,[131] he refers to as the Tao. Griffith draws on Tu Mu (803-852) to explains its significance.[132] Impartiality also has a moral influence with an impact on benevolence.

Sun Tzu also relates impartiality with strictness, adding strong morality as a necessary success factor.[133]

The last two leadership traits are referenced throughout Sun Tzu's book. Even though they are not directly mentioned by the master, they remain important as they form the foundation of his strategic reasoning.

---

126   Griffith, *Sun Tzu The Art of War*, page 100, verse 6.25
127   Griffith, *Sun Tzu The Art of War*, page 122, verse 6.45
128   Griffith, *Sun Tzu The Art of War*, page 100, verse 626
129   Griffith, *Sun Tzu The Art of War*, page 136, verse 11.42
130   Griffith, *Sun Tzu The Art of War*, page 136, verse 11.42
131   Griffith, *Sun Tzu The Art of War*, page 88, verse 4.15
132   Griffith, *Sun Tzu The Art of War*, page 88, verse 4.15
133   Griffith, *Sun Tzu The Art of War*, page 126, verse 10.14

Leadership Virtue #9 – open to learn and adapt

As mentioned earlier, we have emphasized the significance of knowledge and learning, and well as its dynamics. Sun Tzu emphasizes the need for adaptability.[134] The leader learns from the various situations and interactions, playing with his adversaries to gather valuable insights.[135]

Victory hinges on the defeat of the adversary,[136] learning from each situation to capitalize on their weaknesses,[137] rather than imposing this task on subordinates.[138]

Sun Tzu goes as far as saying that without learning, defeat is mandatory.[139]

In conclusion, for Sun Tzu, learning and adaptation underpin every kind of victory.

Leadership Virtue #10 – humble

Not seeking personal fame reveals the leader's humble attitude in command.[140] Additionally, Sun Tzu's strategy relies on willingness to learn,[141] which requires recognizing one's own lack of knowledge and being humbleness about it.

Learning is a solitary journey because it relies on each individual's willingness to engage. The learning effort can involve different forms, such as actively memorizing information (explicit learning), or acquiring practical know-how through experience (tacit or implicit). Regardless the method, learning is always a

---

134 Griffith, *Sun Tzu The Art of War*, page 139, verse 11.56
135 Griffith, *Sun Tzu The Art of War*, page 100, verse 6.21
136 Griffith, *Sun Tzu The Art of War*, page 85, verse 4.2
137 Griffith, *Sun Tzu The Art of War*, page 140, verse 11.60
138 Griffith, *Sun Tzu The Art of War*, page 93, verse 5.21
139 Griffith, *Sun Tzu The Art of War*, page 122, verse 9.46
140 Griffith, *Sun Tzu The Art of War*, page 128, verse 10.19
141 Griffith, *Sun Tzu The Art of War*, page 65, verse 1.9 and 1.10

deeply personal endeavor, and cannot be forced to achieve excellence. The most we can do is to inspire and motivate others to learn.

Humbleness precedes learning because acknowledging unknowns is mandatory, with either a tacit or explicit nature. Without this recognition, learning cannot occur.

On the one hand, being humble with explicit knowledge means being honest about ourselves. When we acknowledge what we don't know, it's easy because we can take deliberate action to acquire that precise knowledge. But how can we become aware that there is something new to learn when we are unaware of what we should already know? That is why learning is a constant search for the unknown, with humbleness as its cornerstone. Each individual should recognize their lack of tacit or explicit knowledge and start learning from there.

On the other hand, humbleness towards tacit knowledge happens with the right attitude towards others. Most probably, tacit learning implies other people's involvement when training and learning from someone. Furthermore, acquiring know-how involves experiencing frequent failures as striver to master what we need to learn. So, how can we endure this laborious learning process, with failure at stake, together with the shame it may originate? The solution lies in being humble and having personal commitment. Here, commitment means finding satisfaction in simply attempting things, even if we fail. It's not just about tolerating failure but actually finding it rewarding. It all comes down to being humble.

Additionally, with tacit learning involved, we also must consider the relationship with others. Humbleness also underpins sincerity, as already discussed above. Only this time, it specifically relates to the way we communicate. How do others perceive us? Take notice that only the humble leader deserves to be helped in any way possible. The overconfident leader may foster jealousy and other negative feelings, all not helping their leadership by any means.

Therefore, we consider "not seeking personal fame" in all its forms, always with humbleness in the background. Although not explicitly mentioned by Sun Tzu, humility is a crucial element underneath his cherished attitude towards learning, which forms the foundation of his strategic action.

The virtues framework

After discussing all the traits of the "Command & Control Ten Leadership Virtues" framework, the time has come to put it into action. It's extremely simple and a good auto-evaluation and introspection exercise. The framework presents four columns for each trait: the first lists questions identifying its details, followed by strengths, weaknesses, and then next steps.

After grasping each subdimension's essence, by answering the questions in the first column, we summarize why we believe we have strengths and identify weaknesses, the latter being an act of humbleness. With this information available, we proceed with determining the steps that should be taken to reinforce that same subdimension.

FOURTEEN
THE NINE COMBAT GROUNDS

Sun Tzu mentions the battleground with a mysterious, almost metaphysical, allure. For Sun Tzu, there are nine heavens and nine different earth types,[142] the former related to the attack and the latter to defense. Why the difference between heaven and earth when both offense and defense may happen on the same ground anyway? Sun Tzu advises that invincibility should be established through defense, while offense should be used to exploit vulnerability.[143]

Thus, the earth is defense, and heaven is offense. Some commentators describe the "nine-fold" as a metaphor. Still, the fact is that Sun Tzu identifies nine different types of terrain, each one directly influencing tactical maneuvering.

Moreover, studying all possible confrontation grounds enlightens the choice of the most appropriate tactics for each one, thus effectively deploying resources and increasing the chances of victory. In business, victory equates to return on investment,

---
142 Griffith, *Sun Tzu The Art of War*, page 85, verse 4.7
143 Griffith, *Sun Tzu The Art of War*, page 85, verses 4.2 and 4.5

meaning achieving maximum revenues with the minimal use of resources. Sun Tzu advocates for meticulous consideration of tactics in relation to the chosen terrain for battle, the available personnel, and the specific situation at hand.[144]

Combat ground #1 - dispersive (feudal)

Sun Tzu defines feudal ground as dispersive.[145] We are naturally strong in our geographical surroundings, meaning our market and our clients. In our ground, we are aware of all surroundings so that an attacker will have difficulties in succeeding. There are both switching costs for customers and learning costs for invaders.

When attacking, the defender's territory, known as *dispersive grounds*, may be unsurmountable. This depends on the strength of the feudal lord, often linked to entry barriers in business. Will anyone dream of attacking Amazon on their playground? Will Amazon dream of attacking Alibaba, its Chinese counterpart, in their own Eastern playground? Certainly not! Even eBay lost in China just three years down the road after entering the market, despite its initial victory, swiftly annihilated by TaoBao.

Griffith appeals to Ts'ao Ts'ao (155-220) to characterize dispersiver grounds *as uncomfortable*.[146]

Ts'ao's assessment includes both strengths and weaknesses. On the one hand, the officers defending their own territory will fight bravely, but, on the other hand, they are not in desperate positions, by nature. Sun Tzu advocates[147] that a hopeless situation can build significant strength. This lesson also serves the eight

---

144 Griffith, *Sun Tzu The Art of War*, page 133, verse 11.24
145 Griffith, *Sun Tzu The Art of War*, page 124, verse 11.2
146 Griffith, *Sun Tzu The Art of War*, page 130, verse 11.2
147 Griffith, *Sun Tzu The Art of War*, page 134, verse 11.33

grounds covered below. In the case of *dispersive ground*, not being in a desperate position can be a weakness to be exploited by our adversaries.

Finally, dispersive grounds are dangerous to attack due to the feudal defender's increased knowledge and awareness. Sun Tzu advice is thus to avoid attacking on dispersive grounds[148] and instead seize the opportunity to concentrate forces.[149]

In conclusion our strategy when attacking should avoid combating in dispersive grounds. Instead, we should lure the adversary to other and more favorable types of terrain.

Combat ground #2 - frontier ground (shallow penetration)

Sun Tzu characterizes frontier ground as a limited incursion into enemy territory.[150] We will be just scratching the surface in this terrain, as there is nothing significant to gain than knowledge about the adversary[151] or to pass to more compelling grounds.[152]

Sun Tzu advises to be careful because surprises may happen on frontier grounds.[153] Even if the adversaries do not feel violence yet, they may take the opportunity to attack our base when our forces are more dispersed. In this regard, Griffith appeals to Mei Yao-Ch'en (1002-1060) for confirmation.[154]

In conclusion, on frontier grounds, we are on the move, and we should take care not to be attacked. However, we can benefit from seizing resources and challenging the opponent or partner to learn from the situation. That is, for example, what *series A*

---

148   Griffith, *Sun Tzu The Art of War*, page 131, verse 11.11
149   Griffith, *Sun Tzu The Art of War*, page 132, verse 11.15
150   Griffith, *Sun Tzu The Art of War*, page 130, verse 11.3
151   Griffith, *Sun Tzu The Art of War*, page 100, verse 6.23
152   Griffith, *Sun Tzu The Art of War*, page 131, verse 11.11
153   Griffith, *Sun Tzu The Art of War*, page 132, verse 11.16
154   Griffith, *Sun Tzu The Art of War*, page 132, verse 11.16

funding means for venture capital. In this regard, Sun Tzu advises exploration with prudence.[155]

When probing a market, we are on shallow ground. After probing, real offense can take place, although on a different type of ground.

Combat ground #3 - key ground (equally advantageous)

Key ground has vital importance for Sun Tzu[156] and he defines it as equally advantageous[157] for opponents.

Every business should diligently seek for *key ground* because it will become a source of competitive advantage when occupied. It's important to acquire it quickly because the contender who controls it will gain significant leverage.

Confrontation does not depend solely on defending forces but also on the ground's characteristics, so, we'd better take *key ground* to ourselves and use it as another tool for victory. Still, victory is costly and laborious, always preceding exploitation with profit in mind. Should confrontation continue to occur, costs will be too high to produce good returns. This strategic facet is so crucial that we will dedicate the next chapter to discuss it, only this time using Machiavelli's extraordinary vision on this very issue.

To effectively seize *key ground*, Sun Tzu recommends swiftly concentrating all forces,[158] including the "rear elements." Griffith, interpreting this concept, refers to Ch'én Hao from the Song Dynasty and Chang Yi from the Han Dynasty,[159] suggesting this

---

155   Griffith, *Sun Tzu The Art of War*, page 100, verse 6.23
156   Griffith, *Sun Tzu The Art of War*, page 131, verse 11.12
157   Griffith, *Sun Tzu The Art of War*, page 130, verse 11.4
158   Griffith, *Sun Tzu The Art of War*, page 132, verse 11.17
159   Griffith, *Sun Tzu The Art of War*, page 132, verse 11.17

approach as a means to outmaneuver and outpace the adversary in order to secure a tactically advantageous position.

Thus, this interpretation has two facets. On the one hand, we should occupy *key ground* as concentrated as possible, and that is why we should be quick, not leaving the rear behind. Dispersion is a weakness, and, if for some reason, the adversary lags his force behind, that spot is attackable, with the expectation of occupying the *key ground* before him. The only situation where offense should be used in relation to *key ground*, is when the enemy has not arrived yet, presenting a weakness to exploit. So, as soon as the *key ground* is fully occupied, we should halt and direct our strategy elsewhere.

In conclusion, we first must identify all *key ground* and always look for all the leverage we can get. We should do everything necessary to conquer but be cautious to attack only if there are weaknesses to exploit. We should aim and occupy *key ground* swiftly and without fighting whenever possible.

Therefore, the single most important element of strategies involving *key ground* is identifying it promptly. Spotting it out before others gives us the advantage to occupy it ourselves while conserving resources.

An excellent example of *key ground* are markets with economies of scale or network effects acting as entry barriers. Big Techs conquered their *key ground*, and most startups dream about creating the next one.

Combat ground #4 – communicating ground (open, not key)

Sun Tzu defines *communicating ground* as equally accessible by all contenders.[160] We may also call it open ground. It's the opposite *key ground* in the sense that it will never generate, by itself, any competitive advantage whatsoever. Most confrontation grounds today are equally accessible and can thus be considered *communicating ground*s.

Therefore, *communicating ground* refers to a battleground that no contender has yet established as *key ground*, similar to unexplored or emergent markets.

Because communicating ground is open, our forces will be vulnerable. Therefore, unlike *key ground, open ground* can never be a source of strength. This means we need to take extra care with our troops,[161] monitoring both ours and carefully following our adversaries.

Sun Tzu goes even further, providing instructions on what to do, maintaining cohesion to ensure strength so that attrition will not weaken our forces in case of attack.[162] Griffith also refers to Tu Mu (803-852) to confirm the interpretation[163] because open ground does not provide shelter, and defense is paramount.

The offensive is yet the other facet of confrontation on open ground. Sun Tzu only refers to the uniting with allies,[164] a move good to both offense and defense.

But everybody's fate is confrontation, and struggles are most likely to happen on an open ground, as most grounds are

---

160 Griffith, *Sun Tzu The Art of War*, page 130, verse 11.5
161 Griffith, *Sun Tzu The Art of War*, page 132, verse 11.18
162 Griffith, *Sun Tzu The Art of War*, page 131, verse 11.12
163 Griffith, *Sun Tzu The Art of War*, page 130, verse 11.5
164 Griffith, *Sun Tzu The Art of War*, page 111, verse 8.3

communicating by nature. Therefore, our offensive strategy should count on attrition working to our advantage and get leverage by weakening our adversaries.

Just remember that overall strategy is more encompassing than any single tactical operation and that we can deploy simultaneously other tactics on different grounds with victory in sight. In this sense, we will consider thorough tactical maneuvers further down when devising the strategic path.

Combat ground #5 - focal ground (enclosed and critical)

Sun Tzu defines *focal ground* as enclosed by three other contenders.[165] It's hazardous and politically surrounded, which is different from the *encircled ground* discussed later. Here, there is no single adversary; instead, multiple adversaries could potentially ally, quickly creating the more dangerous *encircled ground*.

Sun Tzu proposes political level actions to deal with focal ground's dangerous situation.[166] Griffith appeals to Mei Yaochen (1002-1060) to confirm the interpretation.[167]

So, armed forces' tactics cannot deal with a *focal ground* situation; only political actions can. Sun Tzu goes as far as admitting that an isolated political entity can only survive with significant political support,[168] mentioning All-under-Heaven.[169]

---

165 Griffith, *Sun Tzu The Art of War*, page 130, verse 11.5
166 Griffith, *Sun Tzu The Art of War*, page 132, verse 11.19 and page 131 verse 11.13
167 Griffith, *Sun Tzu The Art of War*, page 132, verse 11.19
168 Griffith, *Sun Tzu The Art of War*, page 130, verse 11.15
169 All-under-Heaven is the Chinese Empire.

Combat ground #6 - Serious or deep ground

Sun Tzu defines *deep ground* as a far hostile territory.[170] So, *deep ground* is a serious matter and Griffith cites Ts'ao Ts'ao (155-220) to highlight its difficulty.[171] So, we need to be conscious of the risks when moving into *deep ground*, and it's simply a question of taking the right precautions.[172]

Better still, we can save efforts and resources by utilizing the terrain we are already passing through.[173] Still, this is easier said than done. A known example where plundering failed and turned against the invader is Napoleon's victory in Moscow. Its invasion became meaningless when the Russian engaged in scorched-earth retreat, a method previously used by the Portuguese with complete success against Napoleonic invasions two years before.[174] Being so far from home and unable to ensure a supply chain, Napoleon could no longer rely on local resources, which meant immediate defeat.

Nevertheless, being difficult or risky ground does not mean we are weaker, but it does mean we should be cautious. Napoleon was victorious in the battle of Austerlitz, as well as in the invasion of German states, both against superior forces, which proves it all depends on strategy.

In the business world, profiting from other companies' investments, like market creation markets or simple ideas, comes to mind. It's not unusual to see a startup developing a good idea only to see it exploited successfully by others. For example, who is

---

170 Griffith, *Sun Tzu The Art of War*, page 131, verse 11.7
171 Griffith, *Sun Tzu The Art of War*, page 131, verse 11.7
172 Griffith, *Sun Tzu The Art of War*, page 132, verse 11.20
173 Griffith, *Sun Tzu The Art of War*, page 74, verse 2.1, page 131, verse 11.13 and page 134, verse 11.31
174 The Lines of Torres Vedras: The Cornerstone of Wellington's Strategy in the Peninsular War 1809 - 12, Grehan, John, Frontline, 2015

making profits on spreadsheets? Who invented the concept? No, it's not Multiplan or Lotus. Visicalc invented it.

And what to say about Netscape, Mosaic, and Erwise, the first Web browsers? All gone.

In conclusion, our success on *serious ground* depends on overcoming entry barriers, whichever they are, and protecting ourselves from others by erecting our own. After all, serious ground is not so different from *key ground*, except that it's not an objective per se, but only a means to get to *key ground*. *Serious ground* can be used tactically both for attrition and for acquiring valuable resources.

Combat ground #7 - difficult ground

In business we always expect challenges ahead, and for a good reason. Only difficulties are exploitable, being a source of competitive advantages. Everything simple or abundant has no value at all for business. Consequently, we not only expect but wish for steep paths ahead. Welcome to the world of *difficult ground*, which Sun Tzu defines as harsh in any regard.[175] It's hazardous for everybody, adversaries included.

Sun Tzu mentions twice how to deal with *difficult ground*, by maintaining momentum,[176] and offers no other explanation or interpretation about *it*.

It seems that *difficult ground* is like a storm, which won't last forever. We just have to endure it with determination. There is also no reason to believe we will be attacked, nor will it be advisable to go on the offensive in *difficult ground*. Doing so would require

---

[175] Griffith, *Sun Tzu The Art of War*, page 131, verse 11.8
[176] Griffith, *Sun Tzu The Art of War*, page 131, verse 11.14 and page 132, verse 11.21

unreasonable amounts of resources, and these should always be conserved. Nevertheless, we should be vigilant as the enemy is likely to will precisely where we least expect him. For example, Alexander the Great got some victories exactly on this premise, by traversing *difficult ground* before striking, in ways no one even dreamed of being possible, thus taking the element of surprise. Not that attaining *difficult ground* is the objective, or even the battleground, but employing it may catch adversary by surprise.

Combat grounds #8 and #9 - encircled/death ground

Sun Tzu extensively defines *encircled ground* as having constricted access, a tortuous way out and being exposed to even small forces.[177] Griffith's reference by Tu Mu (803-852) further explains its danger.[178]

Encircled ground is suitable for offensive operations but terribly difficult to defend. One should probably avoid moving forces to such terrain unless a desperate attack is necessary. However, should the adversary commit the mistake of entering *encircled ground*, we can use it for attrition with a small number of our forces, much like guerrilla warfare. Guerilla, by the way, could never be carried out on the open ground.

In any case, *encircled ground* is challenging[179] and intriguing.[180]

Encircled ground should not be regarded as completely inaccessible, as this would equate to being on *death ground*. Therefore, Sun Tzu recommends blocking access to such areas,[181] effectively transforming them into death ground. Griffith, cites Tu Mu (803-

---

[177] Griffith, *Sun Tzu The Art of War*, page 131, verse 11.9
[178] Griffith, *Sun Tzu The Art of War*, page 131, verse 11.9
[179] Griffith, *Sun Tzu The Art of War*, page 111, verse 8.5
[180] Griffith, *Sun Tzu The Art of War*, page 131, verse 11.4
[181] Griffith, *Sun Tzu The Art of War*, page 119, verse 9.22

852) to explain that an exit must be available in encircled ground; otherwise, the adversary will fight to the death,[182] a notion that is affirmed by Sun Tzu himself.[183]

Sun Tzu points out that blocking access to encircled ground can prevent the adversary from receiving reinforcements, which is straightforward. However, regarding egress, Tu Mu (803-852) interprets that this applies to our own forces if they are encircled. This is because encircled ground results in the highest attrition, allowing us to use it to our advantage against adversaries. We should do everything possible to avoid being encircled ourselves, but if we do find ourselves in such a situation, it's better to avoid attrition and adopt an all-or-nothing stance, turning the *encircled ground* into *death ground*. This transformation depends solely on us, by blocking the point of egress.

Managing the fine balance of encirclement to achieve victory is indeed unique. On the one hand, it allows for the possibility of victory without actual battle.[184] But on the other hand, it carries the risk of turning the situation into a *death ground*. Griffith references Li Ch'uan (618-907) to corroborate this latter point.[185]

The right balance is thus to encircle for victory while avoiding the risks of encirclement becoming *death ground*. Thus, encirclement is a measure of adversaries' desperation, and, if the enemy is prepared to die, we should be prepared to endure such attrition. Otherwise, we'd better leave an escape route and devise another strategy, probably through *key ground* and not encirclement.

---

182   Griffith, *Sun Tzu The Art of War*, page 119, verse 9.22
183   Griffith, *Sun Tzu The Art of War*, page 109, verse 7.31
184   Griffith, *Sun Tzu The Art of War*, page 79, verse 3.10
185   Griffith, *Sun Tzu The Art of War*, page 79, verse 3.10

The Nine-combat grounds framework

At this phase, we are only classifying opportunities and situations. It's not strategy yet, although strategy will unfold in one or more of the nine grounds.

Focal ground is different from all others, and we should consider it only if political alliances are at stake.

Most struggles will probably happen on open grounds, with *key grounds* always under our eye, wishing to conquer their contribution to competitive advantage.

When the enemy already occupies *key ground*, maybe there are unsurmountable entry barriers, as is the case of platforms holding natural monopolies. But if not, the unbalance of having an adversary on *key ground* must be circumvented with strategy by luring him on other types of grounds. Open grounds will be most probable for confrontation, but, with some chance, we may encircle our adversaries and increase attrition.

We may also look for strategies on several grounds simultaneously, not to be enclosed by the unbalance of one.

We should avoid dispersive and death grounds, even if the latter can motivate our forces when in desperation. On the other hand, we should use frontier grounds to probe the adversary with few resources and enter *deep ground*s only if required.

We will further discuss all these dynamics when considering already occupied grounds and their adequacy for the strategy at stake.

FIFTEEN
THE 6 FACTORS OF SITUATIONAL AWARENESS

Before going to war, we must evaluate everything needed to devise a winning strategy carefully. In this regard, Sun Tzu acknowledges the importance of knowledge[186] and detailed measurement,[187] emphasizing the importance of prior knowledge and constant learning about all events in the combat arena.[188] So, awareness during confrontation depends on intelligence, which needs to be actively maintained.

Intelligence plays a key role in Sun Tzu's teachings, with the final chapter dedicated to convert operations and spies. Therefore, procedures for intelligence gathering strategic the strategic foundation of Sun Tzu's philosophy. In military terms this is known as situational awareness, which is the focus hence of the framework under discussion. Its importance is probably the reason why Sun Tzu begins his book with the previously fundamental factors of war. In the first three verses he outlines the five key factors to con-

---
186 Griffith, *Sun Tzu The Art of War*, page 130, verse 11.51
187 Griffith, *Sun Tzu The Art of War*, page 88, verses 4.16 and 4.17
188 Griffith, *Sun Tzu The Art of War*, page 82, verse 3.25

sider: "moral influence, weather, terrain, command, doctrine,"[189] emphasizing the importance of measurement and appraisal.[190]

Sun Tzu's war factors are thus a very encompassing vision on war's strategy. Tactics and strategy dynamics should follow the initial appraisal. Advancing in war requires total awareness about our own capabilities and limitations, as well as our adversaries' strengths and weaknesses, on top of combat conditions, including terrain.

We spontaneously added adversaries' capabilities because we also consider a supplementary sixth war factor. We need to include it because Sun Tzu extensively mentions it in the last verse of the first chapter.[191] One should remember that the first chapter's title is Estimates, which, according to Griffith, is just another word for appraisal. It refers to the "estimation of our strength when compared to the enemy". So, how could this factor not be part of his situational awareness approach? We believe it's hidden in the mysterious seven elements mentioned in the second verse of the same chapter.[192] However, these elements are impossible to pinpoint throughout the rest of the book. Still, later chapters emphasize the importance of thoroughly evaluating the opponent from all perspectives,[193] including the enemy,[194] the terrain,[195] and various other factors.[196]

---

189 Griffith, *Sun Tzu The Art of War*, page 63
190 Griffith, *Sun Tzu The Art of War*, page 65-66, verses 1.10 to 1.14
191 Griffith, *Sun Tzu The Art of War*, page 71, verse 1.28
192 Griffith, *Sun Tzu The Art of War*, page 63, verse 1.2
193 Griffith, *Sun Tzu The Art of War*, page 84, verse 3.31, page 127, verse 10.15, page 144. Verse 13.2 and page 100 verses 6.20 and 6.22
194 Griffith, *Sun Tzu The Art of War*, page 100, verses 6.20 and 6.22
195 Griffith, *Sun Tzu The Art of War*, , page 127, verse 10.17 page 138, verse 11.51
196 Griffith, *Sun Tzu The Art of War*, page 113, verses 8.12 and 8.13

Consequently, there is no doubt that the adversaries are a sixth war factor and we will consider it in the "Six situational awareness factors" framework.

Situational awareness factor #1 - terrain

Having discusses Sun Tzu's nine types of grounds earlier, we understand the significance of terrain for combat.[197] Griffith appeals to Mei Yao-Ch'en (1002-1060) for a deeper interpretation on the advantages of terrain intelligence.[198]

Distances describes the difficulty and cost when deploying the armed forces, which also depends on the competing ground. For example, no company will ever compete with a current monopolist in its competitive environment. The "degree of difficulty of traversing the ground"[199] confirms this interpretation.

Interestingly, determining the size of required forces and deciding where and when to engage in battle offers a fresh perspective on how terrain influences strategic dynamics. Clearly, we can only devise the needed forces when facing the adversary, which is the next dimension to consider. Still, the terrain also greatly affects the strength, deployment, possible tactics, and strategic planning.

Additionally, the idea of "chances of life and death"[200] encompasses both the risks involved and the potential rewards. It prompts us to consider the likelihood of success in our actions and how changes in the environment might impact our tactics. For Sun Tzu, this level of awareness is essential.[201]

---

197 Griffith, *Sun Tzu The Art of War*, page 64, verse 1.6
198 Griffith, *Sun Tzu The Art of War*, page 64, verse 1.6
199 Griffith, *Sun Tzu The Art of War*, page 64, verse 1.6
200 Griffith, *Sun Tzu The Art of War*, page 64, verse 1.6
201 Griffith, *Sun Tzu The Art of War*, page 104, verse 7.10

Assessing terrain is performed in two steps. The subdimensions of Clauzewitz's Trinity are part of this terrain reflection; they encompass all aspects of the current confrontation. The competitive landscape currently extends beyond just business-level actors, as we also experience significant political influences, economic warfare, regulations, and other forces mentioned earlier. Therefore, summarizing all the influences identified through Clausewitz's approach is the first step in the situational analysis of the terrain. The second step involves interpreting this summary through the lens of combat grounds covered earlier, using the "Nine Combat Grounds" framework. This framework categorizes various aspects of the confrontation at high political and strategic level based on their suitability for our tactics and capabilities. At this stage, we are not yet selecting a strategy, but this information will aid in outlining our range of possibilities and also in identifying significant threats. For example, all *key ground* assets possessed by our adversaries are substantial threats. All unoccupied *key grounds* are opportunities and good strategic objectives to set. All open grounds will define the main confrontation tendencies, that is, where fighting may take place. All frontier grounds set the scope of our exploration. And so forth.

But how can we define the characteristics of terrain?

Let's start with the geographical boundaries, remembering that, in today's world, customers can be just one click away. We are concerned with current or intended regions where customers are located.

All decisions and perceptions occur in the minds of stakeholders, which means that understanding these perspectives is crucial for defining combat grounds. How easy, or how hard, is it to get in touch with customers? Is it a leveled-up ground, easily accessible to everybody, and thus open? Or is it difficult due to language, regulations, or sheer technical difficulties? What to say about the imperfections caused by attractors on social networks, thus influencing every Internet consumer's access to information? The never-ending list of influences just goes on, and we should duly consider all these factors.

In a highly interconnected technological world, defining the market, sector, or industry becomes increasingly challenging. For example, platforms are known to target multiple industries at once, with Amazon being a prime example of this trend. Nevertheless, we should also identify the sectors we wish to compete in, classifying them according to the "Nine Combat Grounds" framework.

Essential aspects of terrain are their political milieu, including laws and regulations, which can be very subtle, mostly due to unwritten rules and influences coming from less obvious forces or contenders.

Finally, we should evaluate our intelligence sources concerning all aspects just covered as this relates to maintaining awareness. Remember that weak intelligence may lead to unpredictable outcomes, most undoubtedly adverse.

Situational awareness factor #2 - Adversaries

As already discussed earlier, the adversary dimension is an integral part of *The Art of War*'s first chapter, culminating in a final and apotheotic verse about calculations against enemy forces. Additionally, awareness about adversaries is also thoroughly mentioned at least in six out of the thirteen chapters. We shall thus consider adversaries a significant factor in warfare in their own right.

Adversaries are bound to their geographical area of operation, their terrain. Still, the best way to define the reach of our adversaries is through the boundaries of our customers. That is where the real battleground lies, especially in a world that is becoming increasingly digitally interconnected. All contenders intending to fight for our customers, are also our adversaries. In a broader sense, adversaries include all companies capable of reaching our customers, even if currently they do not show intentions to compete.

Identifying adversaries is part of a challenging and risky balance. Focusing on a few adversaries increases analysis' effectiveness but risks not considering some critical emergent enemies. Always remember that the most dangerous contenders are those we are not still aware of. Still, expanding the set adversaries' for analysis may increase the noise to a level that risks disregarding vital sparks. Identifying adversaries can be challenging.

Besides traditional ones, there are two types of potential enemies tough to identify. On the one hand, we have all entities with enough assets to compete, even if they are not operating in the concerned market yet. For example, all companies with exceptional social networking, like Big Techs, are prone to extend their tentacles to other industries, just because they already own the customer base to a large extent. That is already happening in China with Super Apps, and it may occur in the West as well. Are we all going to wait for Big Techs' next step in the financial sector? Amazon has been very active, experimenting with different value propositions throughout the years. Google has been increasing its reach with Google Pay,[202] and even Facebook dreamed of becoming a global central bank with its Libra/Diem cryptocurrency. Maybe all this is just smoke, but risk in the financial sector is genuine due to Big Tech's tremendous and relevant intangible assets.

On the other hand, we have the startups which can be even more challenging to sopt. They remain off the radar until secure enough funding to start growing, but by that time that may already be too late. Only entities like venture capitalists and business angels have some access to a startup's value proposition before it becomes a threat. However, this information is not available to most other meaning the majority of us are unaware of these emerging competitors. After launch, each startup largely depends on its available resources and market reception in its early life, as only a promising newcomer attracts funding. The best we can do is to set up intelligence sources areas we believe are key and develop excellent capabilities for generating insight.

The Big Techs give us a glimpse of a not-so-recent trend in the world of platforms and ecosystems. The reality of ecosystems is not new, and the last decade was immense in the development of platforms, largely drive by the explosion of mobility and social networking. Still, their influence has barely just begun.

In the world of platforms, the usual linear value chain of buyers and suppliers does not exist anymore. Some call it the unbundling of the value chain, and China seems to be leading the pack with successful and astonishing examples like Haier and Xiaomi. Welcome to the new ecosystem-based environment, where a mesh of new complex relationships is developing amid

---
202 Google signs up six more partners for its digital banking platform coming to Google Pay, Sarah Perez, TechCrunch, August 3, 2020

new unbundled value chains. The cause-effect relationships typically encountered in traditional value chains do not have a place here, replaced by the new system's balances to be found among all ecosystem participants. That is why intelligence is also paramount here.

The list of adversaries is just the first step of this war factor. Sun Tzu refers to the following:

- By enemy forces, we consider adversaries' capabilities and competencies, including operational and intangible ones.
- Situation and dispositions are enemies' tactics, both visible at the moment or already used in the past.
- Plans and strategies are more difficult to foresee, although much can be done with a reasonable intelligence approach.

The key takeaway from this discussion is critical importance of sublime intelligence for situational awareness regarding adversaries. Please consider it with seriousness.

Situational awareness factor #3 - Weather

Weather, as Sun Tzu's thirds factor situational awareness, detailed in chapter 10,[203] is defined as the interaction of natural forces.[204] In the case of business, the weather means the result of the market's both written and unwritten rules.

For Sun Tzu's concept of weather, the primary considerations are the existing laws and regulations, as well as any foreseeable changes in them. How are these affecting the competitive

---
203   Griffith, *Sun Tzu The Art of War*, page 129, verse 10.26
204   Griffith, *Sun Tzu The Art of War*, page 64, verse 1.5

landscape? Do they represent opportunities or threats? Currently, everything related to the environment is prone to generate many changes. From taxes to new rules, anything goes. We should spot every new possible regulation with change factors in mind. In this context, the change factors to consider are trends with a high probability of occurrence and a significant impact on the competitive business environment, as anything less impactful is of little interest. Change factors are also essential for both written and unwritten rules.

Because laws and regulations have a life of their own, it's important to track and understand these changes as well. Regulations are continually updated, with new versions always on the horizon, due to the thousands of lawyers working globally on upcoming legislation. Additionally, regulatory bodies are influenced by politicians, who in turn are affected by factors such as the electorate, media, and both overt and covert lobbying from various entities, including companies. Therefore, depending on the terrain defined in the first war factor above, the regulatory ecosystem should be an essential subdimension to scrutinize.

Unwritten rules are more challenging to navigate because understanding them typically requires being an integral part of the ecosystem to fully grasp the ongoing dynamics. It's a question of culture. For example, some cultures attribute much value to nationally produced goods, whereas others believe precisely the opposite, preferring imported goods from specific countries. Consumer habits have also been changing with concerns for the environment, and who knows what will eventually happen? Only early warning can timely spot new trends.

Another relevant subdimension is the balance induced in the market by companies that wield this kind of influence. That is why we referred the companies with political level impact in the previous chapter when discussing the upper-level Clausewitz's Trinity's pole. In his regard, Big Techs have already been mentioned and are a threat in every sense. Their influence has been reinforced during the last decade, building on the synergy between mobility and social networking. Even more dangerous are perhaps Eastern Super Apps, already looking for international expansion. However, these are just examples. We should always be on the lookout for any company that has significant marketing capabilities and influence over consumers, customers, clients, buyers, and politicians. Needless to say, companies also possess unwritten rules.

In conclusion, all the elements we've discussed under this third factor boil down to situational awareness, which is fundamentally based on intelligence gathering. We should ask ourselves: How useful and complete are your intelligence sources for what in understanding the market dynamics? How effective are we in identifying early warnings, threats, and opportunities?

Following the market should not be so difficult from the intelligence point of view because much of the needed information is public and abundant. Too abundant, as a matter of fact. Our capabilities should include proper market research, filtering, and subsequent insight generation. It's an iterative process because research depends on what we already know when formulating the next set of meaningful questions to learn what matters. Insight results from proactive research, and feedback loops tremendously increase the subsequent research wave's effectiveness. That is intelligence at its best: a knowledge puzzle built proactively and iteratively.

For information not publicly available, that's another story. With covert operations, we have to create relationships with entities with privileged access to relevant sources such as regulatory bodies.

Situational awareness factor #4 - Doctrine and resources

Following discussions on adversaries, weather, and terrain, Sun Tzu focuses on internal aspects of the organization. We need to assess what is within our reach and what is not, conserving our resources by engaging only in battles we are capable of winning.[205]

Thus, knowing oneself is a crucial war factor, and we consider it part of situational awareness. Although Sun Tzu specifically mentions doctrine, we find it necessary to include resources in the name of this factor. This is because resources are inherently a part of Sun Tzu's concept, and it would be misleading not to acknowledge their significance. For Sun Tzu, doctrine encompasses organization, control, structure, and logistics.[206] He particularly highlights the strength that comes from good organization.[207] Sun Tzu also discusses the use of hierarchical ranks as a conventional method for assigning and delegating responsibilities within an organization, which is essential for maintaining control.[208]

Sun Tzu also refers to "supply routes" and "principal items," representing the tangible and intangible resources at our disposal.

---

205   Griffith, *Sun Tzu The Art of War*, page 84, verse 3.31
206   Griffith, *Sun Tzu The Art of War*, page 65, verse 1.8
207   Griffith, *Sun Tzu The Art of War*, page 91, verse 5.1
208   Griffith, *Sun Tzu The Art of War*, page 93, verse 5.19

We account for the typical tangible resources, as commonly recorded in accounting, which include human, financial, and technological resources, all acquired and utilized for operations. Intangible resources are more difficult to define by nature. However, they are the most important for success in the long run. Patents, know-how, and brand come to mind. The Calculated Intangible Value is an excellent example of research on how to measure intangible assets' value.

Lastly, the management of resources is crucial. The organization should be effectively managed and controlled, ensuring that engagement happens through the deployment of appropriate resources with efficiency in the relevant competitive environment—this embodies the organization's competitive capabilities. For example, is the company prepared to take risks? Are the officers capable of managing and tolerating uncertainty? Are co-workers willing to explore and learn?

Situational awareness factor #5 - Command

We previously addresses command in the context of the "Ten Leadership Virtues" framework. We can begin by summarizing its findings for this war factor, which include wisdom, strictness, humanity, courage, engagement, sincerity, serenity, self-control, inscrutability, impartiality, the ability to learn and adapt, and humbleness.

We may further enhance the analysis by evaluation aspects of civility and encouragement for this war factor.[209]

---

209   Griffith, *Sun Tzu The Art of War*, page, page 123, verse 9.48

Situational awareness factor #6 - Moral influence (the harmony with leadership)

Moral influence[210] is the final war factor mentioned by Sun Tzu, as noted earlier. It's an intriguing factor to consider, as it's not commonly included in traditional strategic planning exercises. However, for Sun Tzu, it holds the same level of importance as all others.

Measuring this war factor in the mindset of individuals is intriguing. Engagement relies on the involvement of everyone, so it's crucial to consider each person in the field. Moral influence is challenging to gauge because there's often a disparity between what people say and what they actually think. Simply asking individuals about their beliefs is insufficient for leaders, as it doesn't fully capture the depth of their true sentiments or commitment.

In a world where intangible assets are of utmost importance, trust emerges as the currency capable of handling subjects indoors.

Sun Tzu postulates that moral influence is centered on trust and belief. Shared objectives inspire individuals to work towards the same goals, while trust motivates them to take risks. Thus, significant achievements are attainable only on a foundation that combines both trust and shared belief.

However, trust and belief are intangible traits, revealed more through actions than words. Yet, for individuals with highly strategic capabilities, even actions may only show intended impressions rather than their true nature. Therefore, deeds are the most reliable indicators for measuring this war factor. It should be assessed with careful consideration.

---

210   Griffith, *Sun Tzu The Art of War*, page 64

Until this point, our focus has been on estimations. The next step involves exploring possibilities and making choices that will solidify a strategy. These possibilities present themselves as various potential tactics. Sun Tzu outlines ten such tactics, which we will delve into in the next chapter.

SIXTEEN
SUN TZU'S TEN TACTICS

With situational awareness in place, the time has come to think about action—to start devising a strategy! However, we're not quite there yet. With Sun Tzu's bottom-up approach, tactics take precedence and must be addressed first.

The more we know about the competitive environment in all its facets, the better we will be prepared to engage in successful tactics.

A strategy is like a film composed of multiple frames, where each tactical maneuver represents a single frame in its narrative. Before making any move, we analyze its market impact and anticipate the likely reactions of others, like a chess game. However, unlike chess, there may be multiple adversaries in this scenario. Alternatively, we may wait and observe the adversaries' moves if we believe it's better.

Strategy happens both at battleground level as well as in the political heights. There is a relationship between both; following Clausewitz's thinking, war is just a facet of politics by other means. Still, Sun Tzu's ten tactics include political moves as well, which is impressive.

Sun Zu dedicates a whole chapter to maneuvering and refers to how difficult it is. Strategy unfolds itself through a series of tactical moves, and the enemy will respond with his own actions. This back-and-forth sequence continues someone achieves victory or face defeat (like bankruptcy or acquisitions). Thus, we consider tactics to be a set of battleground level possibilities upon which we can develop and deploy our strategy.

Consequently, tactical capabilities are paramount. They are a necessary condition for victory, and the more options we possess, the better. Thus, our first job is to fully understand all tactical possibilities, the current chapter's objective. Note that possibilities differ from capabilities. Possibilities are dependent on external conditions while capabilities are solely reliant on our own internal resources and strengths. Still, successful tactics consider both our aptitudes and market' circumstances in all battlefield dimensions.

More than the resources we can gather, victory also depends on adversaries, competing grounds, as well as the weather at every moment in time. All the elements resulting from situational awareness thus ought to be duly considered when conceiving every tactical move. We should assess the various tactical possibilities before each play, using the current insight of players or stakeholders.

Tactics are also influenced by the freedom of movement within the market, a factor that applies to everyone involved. Each tactical snapshot of any strategy will compromise the related resources, which can be a strength if resources are abundant, or a weakness if they are scarce. The same for our adversaries. Each tactical move aims to enhance strategic positioning, either by creating a surplus of resources or by weakening our adversaries. So, tactics are the answer to situational awareness, and strategy is the outcome of these tactics.

Thus, tactics are a crucial warfare's intermediary element, aggregating our knowledge and capabilities to play the strategic melody. The most robust melody will win.

Sun Tzu puts forward ten different types of tactics to create strategies, divided into three sets.

The first set of two tactics operates at the political-level and aligns well with the previous analysis inspires by Clausewitz's Trinity. The next group of five tactics addresses strategy dynamics at the battleground level. The final set of three tactics functions at the support-level, enhancing the power of all previous ones.

Sun Tzu's writings are nuanced among tactics, strategy, strategic dynamics, and intelligence. They are not necessarily easy to grasp, although crucial to understand the power of his acumen.

Political-level tactics

Sun Tzu's first set of high-level tactics is fascinating and unusual in traditional business environments. Instead of looking at the market to compete, we attack adversaries' strategy by any means, including their political-level ties. That has been a most neglected field of action by traditional business strategists, although it has become common in the battlefield of economic and information warfare between nations.

Tactic #1 - subdue the enemy without fighting by attacking his strategy

In his discussion about the ultimate goal of achieving victory by capturing the state, enemy armies, and assets intact without engaging in battle, Sun Tzu demonstrates profound strategic insight. This can be termed as the tactic of avoiding battle, focusing instead on undermining the enemy's strategy.[211] The start of the third chapter is rich with such statements.[212] Griffith also references Li Ch'uan (618-907), particularly regarding the concept of attacking the enemy's plans.[213]

Attacking an enemy's strategy is not a strategy in itself, but rather a tactic. At this point, everything depends on the previous situational awareness exercise. By profoundly knowing the enemy while interpreting and anticipating his moves, there is always the possibility to block out adversaries without any confrontation. In military operations, this may mean blowing up a bridge, for example. For business, we may think about blocking access to funding or influencing regulations to thwart adversaries' moves. Well-positioned companies, playing at the regulation level, do have that kind of power. What if a Volkswagen adversary released the information that ultimately originated its hefty fines, but most of all, obliging the company to lose its strategic focus?

So, why is this not strategy in the first place? Because the operations at stake are just tactics and should be defined as such. After identifying all possible tactical moves, one of them will be chosen, depending on its strategic strength.

---

211   Griffith, *Sun Tzu The Art of War*, page 76, verse 3.4
212   Griffith, *Sun Tzu The Art of War*, page 76, verse 3.1, and page 79, verse 2.10
213   Griffith, *Sun Tzu The Art of War*, page 76, verse 3.4

To attack the adversary's strategy, we may draw inspiration from the previous analysis of the Clausewitz Trinity. By using the subdimensions of Trinity as a guide, we can anticipate probable strategic moves of the adversary, thereby revealing the underlying tactics they might employ. This approach allows us to preemptively counteract their strategies by understanding and targeting their tactical foundations, which is the same as attacking enemy's plans, as referred by Li Ch'uan (618-907).

Examining threats in the plans of enemies is another crucial aspect, and Sun Tzu addresses these threats directly and pragmatically. He emphasizes the importance of understanding and anticipating potential challenges posed by adversaries and formulates strategies to effectively counter them. Thus, we will develop a menu of tactical counter-threat options, which may not depend on dealing with the market, but on subtler, even sublime, attacks to adversary's dispositions.

Sun Tzu also recalls the importance of winning without fighting[214]. Following his discussion on tactics in chapter 3 of *The Art of War*, Sun Tzu offers a reminder in chapter 4, titled Dispositions, dedicated to the application of tactics in strategy. We adopt a similar approach here. After considering all ten of Sun Tzu's tactics in this chapter, we will delve into their strategic deployment in the next.

Tactic #2 - disrupt alliances and the armies only after
Sun Tzu mentions a second tactic that operates at the high political level. Instead of directly targeting the adversaries' strategy, this tactic involves concentrating on their allies.[215] Griffith elaborates

---
214   Griffith, *Sun Tzu The Art of War*, page 87, verse 4.14
215   Griffith, *Sun Tzu The Art of War*, page 78

on this by citing Tu Yu (733-812), Wang Hsi (317-420) and Chang Yi (Han Dynasty) [216] explaining how targeting the political alliances and supports of an adversary can indirectly weaken their position.

For this tactic we do not necessarily need to be aware of enemy plans. Instead, we focus on their current or possible allies to weaken our their tactical positioning. Remember that our adversaries need to deploy tactics in some form, as inaction is not a viable option. In the current interconnected world, where competition often transforms into coopetition (cooperative competition), success is increasingly measured at ecosystem level. Therefore, we must identify which segments on the value chain strengthen our enemy's positioning and explore tactical options for luring these entities away from our adversaries. Maybe it's not easy, but strategy never is. If we can devise quickly and decisively.

Since it's impractical to deploy all possible tactical options on the field, this initial exercise results in a menu of opportunities. We then select the most appropriate tactics to include in our strategy, as a series of tactical moves, according to the available resources and situational awareness at each moment. This ensures that our strategic decisions are both relevant and feasible.

Take startups as an example; they can be fascinating cases to monitor. These new and small companies with innovative ideas have the potential to become strategic powerhouses, capturing significant portions of the competitive landscape.

Consider the substantial investments made by banks, venture capitalists, or others, in fintech startups. By gaining control over startups' knowledge, assets, and market access, these enti-

---

[216]   Griffith, *Sun Tzu The Art of War*, page78, verses 3.5 and 3.6

ties can influence the ecosystem in a way that diminishes their competitors' tactical capabilities, including at political or regulatory levels.

Clausewitz's Trinity analysis can be very useful in contextualizing these maneuvers. Griffith, citing Ts'ao Ts'ao (155-220) highlights the potency of such tactics,[217] like breaking alliances to weaken feudal lords, thereby asserting a position of authority with "prestige and virtue". Achieving victory without engaging in direct combat aligns with Sun Tzu's principle of the highest form of victory.

Ground-level tactics

The second set of Sun Tzu's tactics is battle-level, the most discussed type of tactics, and central for strategy dynamics. Sun Tzu's writings are again insightful because his thinking emerges from experience, thus effectively deriving the true war's success factors, instead of just theoretical ideas.

The five following tactics are interdependent so that no single one should be deployed without thinking and assessing the other four.

Tactic #3 - Bring the enemy to the field of battle

Now we start engaging the enemy on the battlefield, and the issue is where it will take place. A good part of fighting will take place in consumers/clients/costumer minds for business. Only this time, much unlike the traditional military battlefield, the enemy follows our moves in the market and responds accordingly, which includes all business and marketing dimensions.

---

217   Griffith, *Sun Tzu The Art of War*, page 138, verse 11.53

Still, markets have greatly transformed in the digital age. This is because digital connections among all participants can be private and one-to-one unlike the traditional way of broadcasting market information. That is possible due to the post-internet zero marginal costs of handling personalized multimedia communication. So, digital markets tend to be less transparent due to these one-to-one connections, and everybody may have limited awareness of their adversaries' tactical moves. In contrast, in pre-Internet markets, we could easily access all market information, including services and pricing. However, with e-business, that same information may tailored to each consumer becoming opaque for everybody else. Nonetheless, we can still access it through specialized intelligence measures, which aligns with Sun Tzu's advice in the last chapter of his book dedicated to covert operations. In any case, luring the enemy can always be achieved using the most visible market communication channels, following ethical and legal practices.

The current tactic brings to mind the early days of online supermarkets in the late 1990s. E-commerce is a harsh competitive environment, prone to discounts, dynamic pricing, and sheer price reductions, sometimes even giving products or services away for free. So, why would supermarkets want to go online and face increased competition? High margins require low competition, and the more competitive an environment is, the less profitable it will be.

In the 1990s, only the big supermarkets, capable of enduring devastating pricing wars, could sensibly provoke their adversaries to go online. Their bargaining capability regarding suppliers could prevent newcomers from price-cutting because challenger's supply chains and procurement capabilities would never be as effective. In the meantime, everybody learned from Amazon, and differentiation became king with valuable one-to-one communication, that is, personalization. Anyone can replicate Amazon's website but no one can truly match the vast knowledge and insights that Amazon has accumulated from serving countless customers over time.

Going online or going mobile fosters different competitive landscapes where the traditional business models will probably not work anymore. Sun Tzu advises to take the lead when attacking.[218]

As per Sun Tzu's teachings, bringing the enemy to the field of battle can be challenging. If unsuccessful, it will mean jeopardizing crucial resources, thus compromising other possible strategies on possibly different terrains. For example, what if Libra/Diem's Facebook announcement was just a significant hoax, preventing others from moving forward, by merely luring competitors in the wrong direction?

Sun Tzu recurrently refers to tactic #3 in four different chapters.

Initially, he suggests using deception as a tactic to guide adversaries to our desired location[219], a strong move with combat in mind.[220] So, this Sun Tzu's tactics can entail a confrontation to reduce adversaries' tactical capabilities by forcing them to waste their own resources.

Remember that we should occupy new unexplored battlegrounds with entry barriers, that is, thus establishing an advan-

---

218   Griffith, *Sun Tzu The Art of War*, page 96, verses 6.1 and 6.2
219   Griffith, *Sun Tzu The Art of War*, page 66, verse 1.20 and page 120, verse 9.28
220   Griffith, *Sun Tzu The Art of War*, page 93, verse 5.20

tageous position. With the current tactic, fighting is mandatory because we invite the enemy onto the battlefield, resulting in resource depletion on both sides. Therefore, we'd better be sure to win. Otherwise, only companies with death wishes should deploy such tactics, either due to an ongoing takeover is going on an impending all-or-nothing situation.

It is always better to think about *key ground* upfront, thus igniting a dispute, while hoping for peace, counting on possible entry barriers that might well happen in adversaries' minds.

Typically, the fittest will win. We may win without fighting by luring competitors to move towards a new battlefield,[221] provided that we master the needed competencies with new environment requiring the first mover's advantage. Building network effects is an example of such tactics.

Information warfare can indeed produce powerful battlegrounds. Weakening enemies this way can be as reliable as burning their tangible resources out. Unfortunately, the most prominent examples are shameful and related to politics, with populism at its cornerstone. For instance, after Bolsonaro's election in Brazil, Facebook found more than seventy rogue accounts used but his followers, impersonating public figures to spread fabricated news.[222]

The crux of the next tactic is occupying a battlefield without fighting.

---

[221] Griffith, *Sun Tzu The Art of War*, page 96
[222] Facebook suspends disinformation network tied to staff of Brazil's Bolsonaro, Jack Stubbs, Joseph Menn, Reuters, July 8, 2020

Tactic #4 - Create a position not to be defeated and grab every opportunity

After the political maneuvering with the initial tactics, we now enter the decisive set of confrontation tactics.

The counterpart of bringing the enemy to disadvantageous grounds is to free better-positioned grounds for us, thus creating leverage. Sun Tzu recalls the impactful use of resources when in advantageous terrain.[223] Griffith appeals to Mei Yaochen (1002-1060) for a portrayed example:

> *5.25 Chang Yu: When one man defends a narrow mountain defile, which is like sheep's intestines or the door of a doghouse, he can withstand one thousand.*[224]

The current tactic is likely the most common approach, often at the forefront of and managers' minds when struggling for competitive advantage.[225] The opportunity lies in utilizing our strengths within that particular terrain, although opportunities can also arise around the terrain's characteristics, and we should be quick to adapt accordingly.

The opportunity presented to us lies in leveraging our forces within that specific terrain. However, we should also be prepared to quickly adapt to opportunities that may arise from the unique characteristics of the terrain.[226]

Besides, because the *key ground* is at stake for the current tactic, we should be vigilant about potential threats. Sun Tzu warns

---
[223] Griffith, *Sun Tzu The Art of War*, page 95, verse 5.25
[224] Griffith, *Sun Tzu The Art of War*, page 95
[225] Griffith, *Sun Tzu The Art of War*, page 55, verse 1.13
[226] Griffith, *Sun Tzu The Art of War*, page 140, verse 11.59

about the risks that adversaries may pose when occupying the *key ground*, and we should every precaution avoided such risks.[227]

But occupying *key ground* can be tricky. We should carefully consider the appealing first mover's advantage because dealing with markets can be expensive, and it all depends on how costly market creation is. Moreover, because *key ground* is irresistible, we should carefully plan how to defend it because we will surely be under constant attack.

Therefore, *key ground* depends on entry barriers because, without them, it would not be *key ground* in the first place. In this case, that ground would be plain competitive, therefore not contributing to create any leverage. For example, entry barriers can exist in form of switching costs for consumers, which is a compelling strategic ingredient. Strategic because maintaining *key ground* is the source of competitiveness and hence profits, a discussion we will continue in Part III on Machiavelli.

So, let's talk about entry barriers.

The first inherent entry barrier is the expense of establishing a market, followed by the cost of playing in it. While we may not like the former because it may be out of our reach, it's essential to create entry barriers, thus seizing the advantage of being the first mover and aspire to achieve a natural monopoly in that market or niche. Natural monopolies are ideal for this tactic. For instance, Big Techs found this especially true in their own environment, and now no one is willing to fight them in their conquered territory. Even if we can mimic Big Tech's value proposition, the consumer will always experience switching costs when moving to an alternative provider. And the latter does not possess the implicit

---

227 Griffith, *Sun Tzu The Art of War*, page 131, verse 11.12

information gained from previous experiences, which is crucial for the value proposition. This switching costs may be minimal, although enough to exploit that *key ground*, thus grabbing every opportunity. That us currently the situation of the most valuable companies on earth, GAFAM[228] and BATX.[229]

If we cannot afford market creation, the option is to let someone else do it, get into the bandwagon, evaluate its probable final balance and verify if there is space for more than one. Being a follower may be ok. If so, we just must find a way to erect entry barriers in our newly conquered *key ground*. Customer intimacy has been a traditional approach here. But remember that, if the final balance tends toward a natural monopoly, we'd better possess the resources to try to play that game.

The other types of entry barriers come from playing in the market and have the effect of naturally reducing the number of contenders while erecting fences in the form of hurdles. One of the barriers is the cost of playing the game. Venture capitalists with big pockets naturally mitigate the power of this barrier since they can provide funding for startups, enabling them to compete with the largest sharks in their respective markets. Fintechs come to mind. The other barriers happen in consumers' minds and can be measured with switching costs. Consider all needed assets to overcome these switching costs as the hurdles representing entry barriers.

In essence, this tactic addresses the traditional opportunities and threats, centered on *key ground*. It involves always keeping

---

228   Alphabet (i.e., Google), Amazon, Facebook, Apple, and Microsoft – only leaving Saudi Aramco out.
229   Baidu, Alibaba, Tencent and Xiaomi, in China.

potential advantages in mind for future exploitation, and this approach can make all the difference.

Tactic #5 - Create momentum

We now enter the crux of military tradition. Sun Tzu illustrates[230] momentum creation, which is equivalent to General Foch's Concentration of Forces[231] explained later. Even water, an elastic element, can move mountains.

Time is money: when time is essential, energy should surge. Time is critical in most common business situations, so we should always be prepared to mobilize resources as Sun Tzu commands. The issue is where and when. Precision is Sun Tzu's advice.[232]

Thus, the trick is to create an overwhelming momentum, concentrating our effort where needed,[233] always to acquire market advantages. For Sun Tzu, with the above referred Concentration of Forces, victory is certain.[234]

Moreover, we can use the Concentration of Forces also when luring the adversary, to provoke him. Additionally, we can employ the Concentration of Forces tactic to entice and provoke the adversary.[235] Deception must also be involved because the enemy will never attack a stronghold. And if the enemy is deemed to attack, he'd better move against anything that does not bring us harm while compromising his own resources.

---

230 Griffith, *Sun Tzu The Art of War*, page 92, verse 5.13
231 Marshal Ferdinand Foch *The Principles of War*, (Chapman & Hall Ltd, London, 1903)
232 Griffith, *Sun Tzu The Art of War*, page 92, verse 5.15
233 Griffith, *Sun Tzu The Art of War*, page 122, verse 9.46
234 Griffith, *Sun Tzu The Art of War*, page 91, verse 5.4
235 Griffith, *Sun Tzu The Art of War*, page 67

All in all, momentum is crucial for both attack and defense, hence this tactic. Using it in *key ground* will probably be the typical case of our strategic chess's timeline.

Tactic #6 - Conserve your strength and maintain your freedom

As put forward with the previous tactic, momentum is the base for any victory, but surely not the single one because Sun Tzu also elegantly believes in victories without fighting.[236]

Not fighting at all is the utmost strength's conservation strategy, but surely seldomly possible because investments are implicitly part of the game when conquering new markets. Still, it's also true that already installed monopolists will have less trouble conserving their resources than everybody else because natural monopiles are not easy to attack. Big Techs come to mind again.

The more we spare resources, the better, because of its direct impact on investment return and for maintaining competitive capabilities on the high side.[237]

From the previous tactics, we already have a good idea about opportunities or where attacks are possible. But are we able to attack everywhere? Probably not. The most important lesson from this tactic is that we should only engage the most relevant battles and not in all possible conflicts. Consequently, we should use resources and energy just to fit, although with enough strength to win.[238] Therefore, knowing that resources are always limited, we must decide where to set them up. On the one hand, if we bet everything on one single project, should it fail, we are out

---
236   Griffith, *Sun Tzu The Art of War*, page 77, verse 3.3
237   Griffith, *Sun Tzu The Art of War*, page 134, verse 11.32
238   Griffith, *Sun Tzu The Art of War*, page 139, verse 11.57

for good. That is why we sometimes hear not to put all our eggs in a single basket. On the other hand, if we disperse resources in multiple projects, we risk that no plan will ever be sufficiently strong to win.

Besides, there is another reason to spare our resources. Winning a battle does not mean winning the war. First, we must study the strategic battleground, decide which campaigns are critical, and conscientiously deploy the needed resources. Should we fail to spot any decisive battle, lacking the resources required to win it, this will weaken our tactical positioning, and the result may be sheer defeat. As we will see later, Foch calls this the Freedom of Action. By sparing resources and correctly deciding our battles to fit energy levels, we increase our winning chances and profitability.

We should also not forget to maintain defenses high, which requires husbanding the related resources. The previous tactic of creating momentum is deemed to be dynamically deployed in either offensive or defensive operations. Sun Tzu clearly articulates the vital importance of building momentum and concludes that envisioning victories should align with maintaining freedom of action.[239]

We have to be skilled in both attack and defense, and that is why we need to conserve our strength, thus maintaining enough reserves to be deployed when needed. Moreover, in the same way, we cannot attack everywhere, and we will never have the resources to defend everywhere. Before entering the multiple tactical battleground dynamics, we should identify weak spots upfront by carefully analyzing the enemy and acting accordingly.

---

239   Griffith, *Sun Tzu The Art of War*, page 96, verse 6.8

Strengths and weaknesses are relative concepts and always relate to the relationship between contenders. We only have a weakness if a corresponding vigorous enemy's capability can attack it, and Sun Tzu is also clear about this.[240]

Sun Tzu's insightful approach to strategy matches adversary strengths with weaknesses in the considered battlefield. We then derive the set of defensive actions at stake and mobilize the corresponding resources, and only those. That will conserve strength and spare reserves for tactical offense or defensive deployment where needed.

The related property of strengths versus weaknesses also puts forward another way to deal with defense, focusing on curtailing an enemy's strengths instead of just defending weak spots.

Tactic #7 - Prevent the enemy from concentrating

Sun Tzu recommends disrupting the enemy's ability to concentrate their forces,[241] a strategy that counters the two previously mentioned tactics.[242] First, in blocking an enemy's momentum, we may not even need to protect corresponding weaknesses. And second, because without momentum, enemies will see their defensive capabilities hampered.

Griffith recalls Mei Yaochen (1002-1060) to exemplify partition of enemy's will.[243]

Therefore, according to Griffith, this tactic may even be deployed at the political level.

---

240 Griffith, *Sun Tzu The Art of War*, page 67, verse 1.21
241 Griffith, *Sun Tzu The Art of War*, page 69, verse 1.25
242 Griffith, *Sun Tzu The Art of War*, page 67, verse 1.21
243 Griffith, *Sun Tzu The Art of War*, page 69, verse 1.25

Combining both concentration of forces, or momentum, with an enemy's dispersion, creates the best balance to create advantage. Sun Tzu is utterly clear about it.[244] Additionally, Sun Tzu reminds the importance of dividing the enemy, both at battleground and political levels.[245] And Griffith recalls Mei Yao-ch'en (1002-1060) to justify it.[246]

To disperse the enemy, we must be convincing. We can achieve it, either by moving our forces on the ground, or, better yet, with information warfare, or deception, because "all warfare is based on deception."[247] Deception flows through Sun Tzu's veins.[248]

Preventing the enemy from concentrating is thus part of strategy dynamics but can only be achieved with focused tactical moves—which is what this tactic is all about. Each movement on the battlefield should always tackle an adversary's disposition. This unbalance it creates can indeed be used to our own advantage by deploying the previous tactic and concentrating our forces to conquer *key ground*. In other words, we prevent the enemy from concentrating first and then create momentum to win against week adversaries spots so that we can then add another tactic to build entry barriers and explore our conquest.

---

244 Griffith, *Sun Tzu The Art of War*, page 98, verses 6.13 to 6.15
245 Griffith, *Sun Tzu The Art of War*, page 132, verse 11.52
246 Griffith, *Sun Tzu The Art of War*, page 132, verse 11.52
247 Griffith, *Sun Tzu The Art of War*, page 55, verse 1.19
248 Griffith, Sun Tzu The Art of War, page 92, verse 5.18

Support-level tactics

The final set of three Sun Tzu's tactics should be deployed in conjunction with the two previous groups, for they cannot produce any result per se. However, they are critical in increasing our tactical strength.

Tactic #8 - Use extraordinary (special) forces ("infinite as the heavens on earth")

Sun Tzu unveils the existence of special forces.[249] They are a particular case of momentum, and the difference lies in the type of resources to unfold.

Whereas we can achieve momentum by concentrating regular forces, we can also deliver a high penetration potential with special forces, even if in small quantities.

For Sun Tzu, the power of special forces can be overwhelming.[250] These forces assume prior high investments, usually endure high training, and handle advanced tools, just like SWAT teams. The cost of preparing special forces is thus extremely high, thus justifying its usual scarcity. The return on investment of special forces comes precisely from the reinforcement of regular forces' effectiveness. Therefore, deploying both regular and special forces are at the core of the current tactic.[251]

We consider special forces all assets requiring high investments while offering outstanding benefits. Deciding which capabilities to endow is the first challenge to contemplate. Due to the necessary expenditure on special forces, we need some prior understanding of what may become essential in the competitive

---

249   Griffith, *Sun Tzu The Art of War*, page 91, verse 5.6
250   Griffith, *Sun Tzu The Art of War*, page 91, verse 5.6
251   Griffith, *Sun Tzu The Art of War*, page 91, verse 5.3

environment, which will be the single most crucial challenge of this tactic. We shall now consider their nature.

Special forces can be both tangible and intangible. The former relies on the use of tangible assets and depends on sheer financial investment. The more we have, the better. The tactical importance of extraordinary tangible resources may be limited because they may be somehow easily attainable by any contender.

On the other hand, intangible assets are the very definition of knowledge itself, including know-how and time dependency. Time dependency cherishes increased strategic importance. While both types of assets require investment, only knowledge acquisition requires effort in time, which means that advantages may exist just by being first mover. The strategic significance of this tactic can thus be superlative.

Knowledge is also more interesting because its usage does not decrease its availability. Quite the opposite, because the more we use knowledge, the more we reap, in a never-ending learning cycle. That is why so many companies invest in learning abilities, hence the incredible success of AI nowadays.

In summary, the special forces tactic consists of two strategic facets. The first involves deploying assets during the confrontation to bolster momentum, primarily intangible assets. However, perhaps the most important one is the timely creation of intangible assets. Since strategy is heavily time-dependent, whenever these unique assets can be the deciding factor, only those already in the contender's possession will emerge victorious. This means that, beyond simply reinforcing momentum, the tactic also has a vital impact on preserving Foch's Freedom of Action, or in other words, conserving strength.

In summary, extraordinary forces entail two challenges. The first one is its timely development and acquisition. And the second is the decision to deploy them wisely due to their implied scarcity.

Tactic #9 - Capture enemy resources

Possessing resources is a much-debated aspect in Sun Tzu's book and appears in four chapters. Taking possession of resources is a corollary of winning without fighting.[252] Sparring resources on both sides is good because if the enemy only capitulates after fully deploying its own resources, nothing will be left.

Still, there are more reasons than meet the eye. Using the adversaries' resources decreases the need to supply our own.[253] Sun Tzu is thus quite bold about plundering.[254]

This tactic fits well with the current business environment when considering both the earlier-referred facets we now discuss.

On the one hand, profiting from the investment of a first mover is a usual second movers' advantage; yes, there can also be advantages for second movers. Creating new markets is utterly expensive and makes sense for those wanting to benefit from being first movers while creating entry barriers in *key ground*. But what if these barriers are not strong enough? Or, what if there is a natural space for more than one contender in the concerned market? These two possibilities open opportunities for riding the wave created by others, which is just great. The second mover can profit from the investments of the competitor and sharing that market's returns. Occasionally, this can extend to different

---

252 Griffith, *Sun Tzu The Art of War*, page 79, verses 3.1, 3.2 and 3.11
253 Griffith, *Sun Tzu The Art of War*, page 74, verses 2.9 and 2.10
254 Griffith, *Sun Tzu The Art of War*, page 80, verses 3.15 and 3.18 and page 81, verse 3.20, pager 120, verse 9.31 and page 106, verse 7.14

industries because the market becomes ripe thanks to a spillover effect. Alternatively, we may be the first movers in another market without initial competition. Fintech companies like Revolut or N26 are actively establishing new habits, but the question is, who will ultimately profit from all that cash burn? Will fintechs grow and rip the rewards, or will traditional banks, or even Big Techs, take the created market space to their own advantage?

On the other hand, in a second approach to this strategy, adversaries can be maneuvered into losing control of their resources. In today's world, intangible resources hold great significance, but they are often the most challenging, if not impossible, to directly seize. However, it's important not to be overly naive. Covert operations do exist in this world and should be considered, even if only for defensive purposes.

Nonetheless, there are alternative methods to acquire the knowledge and expertise of adversaries, such as through takeovers or reverse engineering. While a substantial portion of intangible assets is available on the market, we can also explore ways to obtain them. Mindshare comes to mind.

Tactic #10 - Throw your troops to prepare to die (throw the army into a desperate position)

The last support tactic mentioned by Sun Tzu is a bit creepy, but it's emphasized repeatedly and we simply cannot simply not ignore it. This tactic is more directed to our own forces than to the adversary. It may even be ethically questionable, but it's what it's. Sun Tzu highly believes in it, and the engagement attitude he intends to foster can make all the difference, mostly in military environments.

The Art of War's chapter 11 thoroughly elaborates on the significance of this last tactic while discussing possible battlefield grounds. It becomes especially relevant when addressing the concept of death ground[255] and the desperation of fighting to the death.[256] Additionally, Sun Tzu believes that desperation can also be advantageous in other situations and on other grounds.[257]

Furthermore, it appears that a situation of desperation is inherently motivating, obviating the need for a leader to take any additional steps to drive or enforce actions among their troops.[258] Sun Tzu illustrates this by detailing how to place troops in a desperate position through four consecutive verses at the conclusion of the same chapter[259], explaining how to "snatch victory from defeat".[260]

Sun Tzu is quite clear about the minds of subjects when mentioning that everything happens according to their beliefs. In fact, they do not need to be in that desperate situation in reality. They only have to believe it.

This tactic's counterpart is the escape route mentioned by Sun Tzu, which we mandatorily deploy when the enemy finds himself in *encircled ground*. Instead of finding themselves in a totally desperate situation and fight to the death, adversaries will tend to flee through the opening offered intentionally, and we can take advantage to increase attrition with much leverage. We can maneuver with momentum, whereas the enemy is deemed to cope with his forced dispersion. Only an enlightened opponent will

---

255 Griffith, *Sun Tzu The Art of War*, page 133, verse 11.23
256 Griffith, *Sun Tzu The Art of War*, page 133, verse 11.23
257 Griffith, *Sun Tzu The Art of War*, page 134, verse 11.43
258 Griffith, *Sun Tzu The Art of War*, page 134, verse 11.44
259 Griffith, *Sun Tzu The Art of War*, page 137, verses 11.47 to 11.50.
260 Griffith, *Sun Tzu The Art of War*, page 139, verse 11.55

push encirclement into death ground and go for an all or nothing situation instead of just trying to survive. In that case, attrition will be too high, and we should disengage.

In our current world, encirclement relates to engagement and a sense of urgency by considering all entities' rules of engagement at stake. Customers, employees, coworkers, and partners are part of the lot. We may acknowledge that coworker's engagement, in all its facets, can be dealt with through leadership and communication techniques, but that is not the crux of the current tactic. We are concerned here in maneuvering for naturally fostering that same engagement as well as a sense of urgency, without saying a word or communicating anything.

Strategy

We now have everything we need for defining a business strategy, totally inspired by military concepts. Unlike tactics, strategy is just an idea that lives within the minds of leaders and is a largely untapped intangible concept.

After carefully studying the terrain, the competitive environment's rules, the adversaries, as well as all tactical prospects between them all, the time has come to decide how to proceed. That is strategy, which translates into practice when executed by a sequence of tactical moves. The strategist's crux lies in determining each concerned tactic's details when to deploy each one and their coherent succession. For Sun Tzu, battles are akin to music,[261] with interacting forces[262] forming the melodies and available tactics acting as the notes that compose these melodies. Together, these sets of melodies create the symphony of warfare.

---

261   Griffith, *Sun Tzu The Art of War*, page 65, verse 1.8
262   Griffith, *Sun Tzu The Art of War*, page 92, verses 5.11 and 5.12

But a plan is just a plan. The experienced military knows that any plan is immediately outdated at the moment of the first engagement. In this regard, Helmut von Moltke (the elder), the commander-in-chief of the Prussian army during the unification wars in the nineteenth century, is usually cited, among others, as follows: "no plan survives contact with the enemy." Thus, the strategic plan should continuously be revised with feedback from the battlefield, either by confirming our initial assessment or updating it with new information. The impact of this feedback loop may be as substantial as imposing a new strategy. Once again, it's like chess. We believe we are grasping adversaries' moves. Still, we may well be surprised along the way, either because the enemy proves to be unpredictable or by the unforeseen evolution of the market itself. In this regard, we should recall that political-level moves will also impact the battlefield at the Clausewitz Trinity level. The same for unpredictable external influences that can be as large as the global response to the Covid 19 pandemic.

Fortunately, Sun Tzu's first set of tactics already contemplate dealing with this type of risk. Even if tactics are all that we can see, we are compelled to "attack enemies' strategy" with the first Sun Tzu's tactic, developing the corresponding strategic insight just by looking at enemy's moves. Devising the enemy's strategy is indeed the most effective way to attack it. When choosing tactical moves, we are always obliged to engage in simultaneous tactical and strategic thinking, following Sun Tzu's teachings.

Because strategy is just an idea, we can never see our adversaries' strategies, but only their visible tactics. And the same also happens the other way around. So, adversaries can and should be misled. In Sun Tzu's words, war is an art, and warfare is a matter of deception. We should look weak where strong and vice-versa. With such an unbalance, adversaries will never attack where they should, and this approach can also protect us with little effort. Sparring forces will leave enough free resources to create momentum against the enemy's weak spots and conquer *key ground*. And deception goes both ways. Through deception, the enemy will be weak where we need it, and victory will quickly happen because trickery also conceals the crucial strengths underneath decisive momentum. In Sun Tzu's words: "a solid acting upon a void."[263]

Moves are tactical; vision is strategic. Even in chess, where all steps are open for everybody to see, we also only see tactics to address an opponent's strategy. The real intentions behind their actions will only be unveiled later when natural and visible strengths emerge. When any contender deploys real momentum, thus compromising resources, they reveal the existence of some of their strengths, and these say much more about their strategy than any set of intangible words ever will. For that matter, even intelligence is not the reality, only depicts it.

In contrast, actual tactical actions compromise real resources and witness the very world we live in, because some happenings never lie. The enlightened commander should deceive and never be deceived. It just came to mind that, in the Blockchain's world, proof-of-work emerged precisely for this purpose, where its counter-deception reliability is justified by the resources compromised during the process. In summary, there are times when we can defeat deception. These moments of truth are critical for intelligence insight and interpretation of strategy, which is the definition of enlightenment itself.

---

263 Griffith, *Sun Tzu The Art of War*, page 91

All tactical movement is thus subject to interpretation, so we can also mislead adversaries by playing with their perception. Even if tactical moves are openly accessible, their understanding is what counts. It's on us to devise how to create the most fruitful scenario in the minds of our adversaries. That is probably the significant difference between military strategy and traditional business strategy: the former always looks upfront to the terrain with detail and adversaries with utter care. The latter is primarily focused on the market and internal competencies. Where businesspeople talk about strategy, the army sees tactics. Sun Tzu's proposal is to look at the market through the eyes of competitors with everything happening at tactical level. Therefore, our strategy will be the result of detailed tactical scrutiny of all previously covered dimensions.

Our job now is to lay down the logical steps for strategy execution as devised by Sun Tzu.

Sun Tzu's approach to strategy is crystal clear, and the first two verses of his book immediately point it out.[264] Such an introduction motivates the reader to learn about relevant concepts for handling warfare, Sun Tzu calls factors. In a nutshell, all previously covered frameworks are an organized summary of these teachings.

While theory alone is insufficient, mastery of all the factors outlined by Sun Tzu, encapsulated in the previously mentioned frameworks, paves the way for execution. This execution is fundamentally built on knowledge and awareness.[265]

The ground and the weather are the external factors already covered in the "Nine Combat Grounds" and the "Six Factor Situ-

---
264 Griffith, *Sun Tzu The Art of War*, page 63
265 Griffith, *Sun Tzu The Art of War*, page 84, verse 3.31 and page 129, verse 10.26

ational Awareness" frameworks. The latter also covers the needed insights about adversaries before battle. And the "Leadership Virtues" framework provides some additional information about us.

But then, we must know everything about everybody under fire, and this does not only relate to resources and the information we got from the three mentioned frameworks above. A good part of crucial information will only be revealed during battle such as when to apply the previous chapter's tactics. Only considering the dynamics of engagement in the context of the market such as the terrain and the weather will we grasp the real meaning of the competencies and capabilities of all contenders. That is why tactical analysis is crucial for insight, which really makes the difference for strategy effectiveness. Thus, we interpret Sun Tzu's words with this amount of depth and wisdom.

With the previous reasoning in mind, we now propose a methodology for strategic deployment of the various tactics, as a sequence of plays that most authors call strategy. But how can we get a sense of strategic effectiveness for every move? How can we assess if each action is successful and attains some advantage? Businesspeople have a name for this: competitive advantage and several authors have searched for its source, just like for a holy grail. Michael Porter's (*Competitive Strategy*) five forces in the 1980s come to mind. Bruce Henderson (*And the Sea Will Tell*) and others researched advantages from internal capabilities or competencies, calling it the Resource-Based View of the Firm. Yet, others have been preoccupied with adapting competencies to an ever more unpredictable world and calling it Dynamic Capabilities, which we consider the firm's knowledge-based view. The fact is that a competitive advantage can have many sources, both internal, originating from non-replicable competencies, and external, stemming from unique opportunities, as long as these are not available to anybody else. In any case, one thing is certain: a competitive advantage always depends on the conditions of each particular competitive environment, so that the immutable and nontemporal source of advantage is probably not a real possibility. Therefore, we are going to assume that some tactic positioning always originates an advantage. Maybe some examples will be nontemporal and replicated throughout time, perhaps not. After all, it should not matter because the quest for the holy grail in strategy is probably misleading. We will settle just for what we can have at each moment in time, which should always work. Besides, searching for long term sustainability is not incompatible with this approach. Quite the opposite, as we will see.

Still, the issue remains: without any traditional high-level rule on building some strategic capability, or positioning, or both, how can we assess the intended strategic impact of our tactical moves? That is our enthusiastic quest because, as already mentioned, strategy always derives from tactics.

The traditional business approach to strategy derives from classical strategic planning. The ends justify the means, some say. It's true that planning surely is an evolution of any ad hoc approach, unfortunately not so unfamiliar, still nowadays. But planning is not enough for two reasons. First, because without good tactical knowledge, no strategy will ever be sound because the planner will always be missing unseen options for both sides of the barricade. A typical classic example of this dysfunctional decision-making happens every day in the laws, rules, and regulations imposed by those that never leave the office in any environment. And second, because no plan ever won any confrontation like action does, i.e., tactics. So, we'd better start thinking about tactics upfront and then proceed to planning. Opportunities may come from any quadrant, and tactics has been a most important and disregarded one. Although not for the military.

The military typically have a tactical assessment solution in the form of an honorable trio of concepts, a superior principle for strategic assessment, discussed next. The idea is to use this trio as a tool, or a rule of thumb, to assess the tactical strength of every move—and that is the best we can when predicting strategic success.

SEVENTEEN
GENERAL FOCH'S ECONOMY OF FORCES

Strategy in action is much like playing a game of chess, where victory is an aftermath of a sequence of tactical moves. Nonetheless, the business environment is considerably more complicated than chess because there is more than just one adversary at stake. Moreover, the surrounding environment may unexpectedly shift, which is why the chapter on Clausewitz and his Trinity for strategic evaluation holds. So, it's complicated. Still, we require some sense of direction for each tactical move, much like a chess player. While chess operates with unchanging rules and complete transparency regarding current tactics, the business world differs in significant ways. In business, not everything is readily visible, and the rules of the game can shift, either due to legal alterations or unforeseeable circumstances.

Moreover, the most fearful opponents sometimes are the ones we did not see coming in the first place. That is why intelligence operations essential for companies, much like they are for armies. However, while military strategy relies heavily on intelligence, practical business strategy has not always embraced this approach. Military war rooms are common practice, but in business, situational rooms typically established only in particular situations. For instance, during the pandemic there was a surge in scenario planning conducted in situational rooms to address with the unexpected and unpredictable health crisis that had a profound impact on economies around the world. Still, perfectly or imperfectly, business strategists use the information they have at hand and take their decisions, which are the genesis of all tactical moves. Strategy then emerges from these field struggles.

After discussing Sun Tzu's tactics, the next challenge is determining the best sequence for their application. We chose a specific tactic at each moment while considering a potential but recognizing that this sequence may need adjustment given the outcome of each move in the market and our adversaries' response. With our strategic objectives in mind, which tactical move should we choose among an apparently equally valid set of actions? How to play each tactic for the most effective strategy?

Before delving in Sun Tzu's deployment of tactics for crafting strategy, we can draw insights from General Foch's Economy of Forces. In his book *Principles of War*, Foch presents a superior principle, another admirable trio of concepts. His system can act as a lens to assess the strategic power of each tactical move. We will naturally choose the most potent tactic, and this tool provides a tangible means for an enlightened decision.

Indeed, to the best of our knowledge, military geniuses have implicitly applied Foch's superior principle. This apparent in the tactical dispositions of past battles, from Alexander the Great to Napoleon, to any other modern military leader. Once more, it's clear that tactics ultimately dictate the outcome of a conflict, rather than strategy, which primarily influences tactical choices. We can also discern Foch's principles in the writings of military leaders whose ideas have been documented and published.

Foch's principles aligns well with Sun Tzu's mindset. Indeed, Foch's system could be supported solely by Sun Tzu's writings. Still, Sun Tzu's direct mention of Foch's principles is not explicit in The Art of War, so I chose to follow Foch framework in depth to honor the intellect behind the comprehensive and coherent concept. Moreover, General Gil Fiévet also contributed to clarifying the Economy of Forces system in his book[266] about military business strategy, detailing several military examples that illustrate the interpretation of conflict's balance using each of the three underlying principles, which we will discuss further below.

We intend to incorporate Foch's perspective when working with Sun Tzu's tactics while building the emerging strategy. This way we ensure that the contribution of each tactic for the strategic balance becomes an immediate assumption. Moreover, since strategic action involves the sequential deployment of several tactics, appealing to Foch's superior principle serves as a means to assess the potential success of proposed sequence's at each point in time. Just like a simple rule of thumb.

Foch was a preeminent French military commander and strategist during WWI. He was the commander-in-chief of the allied armies that put an end to the German Empire offensive by 1918. More than a theorist, Foch needed to test his ideas and his convictions in the most intense, complex, and risky of all playfields. But more than his accomplishments as a commander

---

266   Gil Fiévet, *De la Stratégie Militaire à la Stratégie d'Entreprise*, InterEditions, Paris, 1992

during WWI, Foch's vision was prophetic when, after the signature of the Versailles Treaty at the end of WWI, he stated: "This is not peace. It's an armistice for twenty years."[267] it's quite remarkable that World War II began precisely twenty years later. So, what is underneath Foch's extraordinary vision about the outcome of tactics on strategic balance?

He published two books before WWI, *The Principles of War* and *On the Conduct of War*, respectively in 1903 and 1904. Like other authors, including Clausewitz and Napoleon, Foch's doctrine is still a reason for controversy, and its discussion finds no place in this work. Nevertheless, his Economy of Force's superior principle, proposed in his first book, is useful in getting the rule of thumb we are looking for.

Foch unmistakably recognizes the power of tactics[268]. Like Clausewitz, Foch draws lessons from Napoleon, who did not publish any book, although Emmanuel-Auguste-Dieudonné de Las Cases kept Napoleon's memories in writing. Foch opens the pivotal third chapter by citing Napoleon,[269] to define the tactical drive that generates a shock effect by assembling and engaging all necessary forces. And yet, he chose Economy of Forces for the title of this third chapter, and that may seem almost deceptive at first sight because, to win, we have to deploy as many forces possible at the point of engagement, as mentioned by Napoleon. But the Economy of Forces superior principle has much more than meets the eye. For Foch, economy entails more than just "sparing one's forces", it's "the art of knowing how to spend."[270]

---

267 Williamson Murray and Jim Lacey, The Making of Peace: Rulers, States, and the Aftermath of War. Cambridge University Press, 2009
268 Marshal Ferdinand Foch, Foch, The Principles of War (Henry Holt and Company, 1920), page 49
269 Foch, *The Principles of War*, 1920, page 48
270 Foch, *The Principles of War*, 1920, page 51

The apparent paradox between sparing forces vs. fully deploying the same resources is solved when Foch discusses the relation between both, which is the crux of his superior principle. This relation is found in the art of maneuvering, well between concentration and dispersion of forces. And the recipe is simple: to win, we concentrate our forces while preventing our adversaries from doing the same, that is, concentration vs. dispersion. What is particularly intriguing is that Foch deems concentration to be nearly impossible to attain due to the dispersed nature of the forces in the field, and he is right. We also must remember that front lines are, by definition, an immense field space for operations. So, how to achieve concentration through dispersion? To successfully apply the forces "together on a given spot; on the basis of unity of time and unity of space.[271] In a word, the Economy of Forces. That is why there is more than meets the eye to this outstanding concept. Additionally, according to Foch's own words, the reference about "time and space" is probably directly borrowed from Clausewitz's "union of forces in time and space."

Consequently, the Economy of Forces principle emerges from the dynamic and evolving nature of gathering the appropriate forces in the right place at the right time. We are, therefore, not just talking about (i) economizing forces and (ii) concentrating effort, but also about a third one representing time and space, or (iii) the freedom of action. And Foch illustrates this third principle in practice by explaining that "you cannot hunt two hares at the same time."[272]

The comprehensive definition of Foch's Economy of Forces superior principle is as follows:

271 Foch, *The Principles of War*, 1920, page 50
272 Foch, *The Principles of War*, 1920, page 50

> *The Economy of Forces is the art of making the weight of all one's forces successively bear on the resistance one may meet and organizing these forces using a system.*

By looking deeper into his explanation about his Superior Principle, we can draw the three underlying principles, as follows:

1. **The Economy of Effort:**
   sparing one's own forces, being careful not to disperse one's own efforts,[273]
   which Foch refers to as being only "part of the truth," because we still need to "know how to spend, in a useful and profitable way, to make the best possible use of available resources[274]" (which is tackled in the following two principles),

2. **The Concentration of Forces:**
   the art of pouring out all one's resources at a given moment on one spot,[275] [or]
   to engage battle with all possible forces by employing the mass,[276]

---

[273] Foch, *The Principles of War*, 1920
[274] Foch, *The Principles of War*, 1920
[275] Foch, *The Principles of War*, 1920, page 51
[276] Foch, *The Principles of War*, 1920, page 55

3. The Freedom of Action:
   deploying forces in both ways – of the mass and of detachment –...on the basis of unity of time and space,[277] [or the] *union of forces in time and space*[278] when and where it matters.

Therefore, the Economy of Forces encompasses all three of these principles simultaneously. When consistently applied together, they unveil the mechanics of Foch's system. The previously mentioned work by General Gil Fiévet illustrates these principles.[279] Each principle is intriguing on its own, but it's the combination of all three, when brought together, that truly deserves merits to be considered exceptional.

This chapter thus reviews each of the three concepts and the reasoning behind their combination, only to be used as a rule of thumb for tactical assessment when deploying Sun Tzu's tactics for strategy outgrowth.

Economy of Forces factor #1 - Concentration of forces
The Concentration of Forces shapes victory, and, in this regard, Foch cites Napoleon:

to be stronger at one given point, at one given moment.[280]

---

277 Foch, *The Principles of War*, 1920, page 50
278 Foch, *The Principles of War*, 1920, page 97
279 Gil Fiévet, *De la Stratégie Militaire à la Stratégie d'Entreprise*, InterEditions, Paris, 1992
280 Foch, *The Principles of War*, page 294

Considering the baseline set by Foch's Superior Principle, we just need to deploy sufficient strength to win at every single confrontation event. Even if the adversary has more forces overall, only the effective tactical impulsion counts when the battle takes place, and that is why Napoleon's eighteenth-century doctrine advised "all-in." On the other hand, Foch's Superior Principle provides clues against deploying all available forces, hence its name Economy of Forces. That is why we need to deconstruct this superior principle in its fundamental components, Concentration of Forces being the first one.

So, how do we use this first principle? We evaluate each tactical move for its contribution to a strategic unbalance of forces to our own advantage. Even if we cannot always be entirely sure about the importance of the confrontation locus, this fortunate unbalancing should dictate the advantage of this principle regarding the tactical play at hand. Most importantly, merely concentrating our forces is insufficient because we need to calculate the positive leverage against our adversary's forces, hence the need to continually assess all forces on the battlefield. Besides, the importance of factoring in our opponents underscores that this principle on the battle as a whole, as it considers all the significant elements to assess the referred unbalance. Once again, we observe the need to incorporate real-time intelligence into strategy dynamics, affirming Sun Tzu's unique approach to strategy based on situational awareness.

In the business environment, "forces" is the same as organizations' resources, like people, technology, market space, and every other asset at our disposal. Time does not play a role in this first principle, although it becomes a prominent factor in the subsequent principle, as we shall see.

How will we use our forces at each moment? Will we engage in a single major project, or several minor ones? Some say that we should not put all our eggs into one basket, but what if we disperse the same set of eggs in many baskets so that each project does not really have the required resources or strength we need to succeed? Dispersion weakens. Where is the balance between these two opposite approaches? How much dispersion should we tolerate? In the business world, the need for various activities and projects arises frequently, and this poses a significant challenge as resources are inherently limited.

Organizations typically have two categories of activities: one for operations and another one for projects. This distinction can vary in terms of resource flexibility over time. Even when projects and operations are entirely separate, there are instances where the same resources are allocated to both types of activities. This can be challenging because projects are inherently strategic, and operational urgencies may take precedence, potentially leading to detrimental impacts on project timelines.

Still, there is another major difference in project genres with consequences on resource prioritization. On the one hand, we have projects intending to increase and fortify organization's current activities, which we normally refer to as exploitation. And on the other hand, we have completely different projects for exploring new ideas, where we should be prepared to fail and learn from these setbacks, which we call exploration. In the realm of exploitation, victory is often concrete and results in increased business performance. Exploration involves intangible assets and may manifest as knowledge when experimenting with new ideas. Despite the less direct nature of exploration, the ultimate goal is to harness these intangible assets for long-term exploitation, generating the expected returns over time.

Consequently, in the context of the Economy of Forces system, and with the Concentration of Forces principle in mind, we should evaluate, what is necessary to achieve success for each project. No project should move forward without a reasonable perception that all the required conditions are met in terms of resources and a realistic probability of success. Although, that does not mean guaranteed victory because, as Clausewitz puts it, the future is always foggy, and success is contingent on all market forces. And victory may come in the form of profitability or learning.

Is the *Concentration of Forces* principle clear in Sun Tzu's writings? By all means! it's critical for fighting, even if just through dispositions on the battlefield, thus avoiding engagement. Like the sport Sumo, a lot happens before actual clashes may occur, and it may happen that victory now emerges even without fighting. For Sun Tzu, the moment of truth totally depends on dispositions, avoiding strengths and striking weakness[281] and estimating the enemy situation correctly to concentrate strength and capture him.[282]

So, Sun Tzu postulates the concentration of forces,[283] while avoiding enemy's strengths,[284] skillfully circumventing the

---

[281] Griffith, *Sun Tzu The Art of War*, page 101, verse 6.30
[282] Griffith, *Sun Tzu The Art of War*, page 122, verse 9.46
[283] Griffith, *Sun Tzu The Art of War*, page 139, verse 11.57
[284] Griffith, *Sun Tzu The Art of War*, page 67, verse 1.21

adversary's strongholds, coupled with a comprehensive situational analysis, to dynamically engender and capitalize on imbalance.[285]

Concentration relates to timing only in the realm of the following principle, as elucidated by Sun Tzu.[286]

Amazon is probably the best and most successful example of a company using all its available resources to simultaneously strengthen its course of action (exploitation) and experiment with new ideas (exploration). Even if Amazon's innovation failure rate is exceptionally high, which is a natural outcome for all real experiments, its success is unquestionable. Amazon's diversification of businesses and business models is admirable. Who remembers its venturing into real-estate (Amazon Local), payments (Amazon Wallet, WebPay, and Local Register), travel (Amazon Destinations), smartphones (Amazon Fire Phone), among other failures? From selling books to the most powerful cloud computing platform on earth, Amazon is now advancing into physical retail, financial services, healthcare, and AI-led computing. Amazon's successes are impressive. The same cannot be said of Facebook, for instance, where successes do not compensate the extensive list of failed projects.

So, how to balance the concentration of forces among so many challenges? The answer to this challenge doesn't come in isolation within the current principle. Every move and every play are integral components of Foch's superior principle, both influenced and influencing all three underlying principles in unison. Therefore, the only way to evaluate the Concentration of Forces is to strike a balance in terms of strength based on the specific

---

285   Griffith, *Sun Tzu The Art of War*, page 98, verse 6.15
286   Griffith, *Sun Tzu The Art of War*, page 116, verse 9.5

requirements of battlefield needs, regardless of their nature the decision The decision about which battles to fight from a tactical perspective is left to the next principle.

Finally, as per the previously mentioned Fiévet's reasoning, all three basic principles have underlying pillars. The pillar supporting the Concentration of Forces is sheer willpower. We must actively desire to concentrate our forces because this will not occur spontaneously. In the midst of hostilities, the recurring questions are: what should we do? What do we want to accomplish? Hence, the foundational pillar that should be firmly rooted in our minds, in a first-person perspective, is "I want," with the underlying overarching Principle of Volition.

Economy of Forces factor #2 - Freedom of action

Foch characterizes to the *Freedom of Action* principle as "a corollary of the theorem of the Economy of Forces." It primarily revolves around dimensions of time and space, specially focusing on the when and where of battles. Foch cites Xenophon (431-354 BC) to highlighting that "war is … the art of keeping one's freedom of action."[287]

Xenophon's statement may initially appear contradictory because it suggests the importance of maintaining freedom of action in war, even though war inherently involves some form of conflict, whether tangible or intangible, such as in information warfare. However, the essence of his statement lies in the idea that while conflict may be inevitable, the strategic goal is to ensure that you have the flexibility and capability to choose when, where, and how to engage in battle, rather than being forced into unfavorable

---
287 Foch, *The Principles of War*, 1920, page 101

circumstances or reacting solely to your adversary's actions. In other words, it emphasizes the importance of maintaining strategic initiative and control over the situation.

Therefore, it's imperative to combine the Concentration of Forces with the Freedom of Action because success can only be achieved when we have the ability to concentrate our forces where needed, and this is possible when we are free to do so. The synergy of both principles is key to achieving strategic goals effectively.

Engaging forces in any battle is a compromise that decreases the capability of deploying these same resources elsewhere in another struggle because, as already cited, "you cannot hunt two hares at the same time." The very nature of the Freedom of Action principle naturally emerges from the sequence of plays establishing strategy. In the very beginning, before engaging in any fight, we are free to deploy our forces wherever we like, but this freedom is somehow lost in the course of battle due to mandatory engagement. And the burden is on us not to lose this freedom, or, at least, to lose as few as possible.

Besides, Clausewitz explains that war is a process of attrition, consuming resources, and losing corresponding degrees of freedom due to resources unavailability. On the other hand, acquiring resources strengthens this principle. Therefore, a holy balance connects the two principles, the Concentration of Forces and Freedom of Action. As we shall see below, this balance is the restricted principle of the Economy of Forces we will call the Economy of Effort.

Foch requires intelligence capabilities in place to successfully implement the second principle. Without intelligence, an army would be struggling in the blind. Without eyesight, forces will be easily misled and concentrated in the wrong places, therefore easily dispersed. In summary, the Freedom of Action requires a clear understanding of where one can be and where one should be. Victory then emerges from the careful balance between our opponents' moves and our capability to engage with the right amount of forces in the right place at the right time, or, in other words, maintaining Freedom of Action to engage when and where it matters. Additionally, given that engaging forces necessities preparation and maneuvering, placing available resources in advance where they make a significant impact is crucial. In summary, intelligence plays a pivotal role in supporting this second principle, which should always be a consideration for every tactical move.

Thus, tactical movements preparing for battle are part of the game. In this regard, military strategists have learned to foresee where conflicts may occur just by following the logistical preparations, although these movements can also be misleading, well understood. Like the previous principle, the Freedom of Action is also embedded in Sun Tzu's strategic approach, and it's all about dynamics, movement, and timing.[288] So, we will never deploy the Freedom of Action principle without intelligence because, in alignment with of Sun Tzu's doctrine, every strategic endeavor begins with a complete situational awareness assessment on an intelligence bedrock.

So, what is Sun Tzu's advice? We have to play the adversary, luring him to lose his freedom,[289] and let the *Concentration of Forces* do the rest.[290] Sun Tzu dictates exploiting enemy's unpre-

---

[288] Griffith, *Sun Tzu The Art of War*, page 92, verses 5.14 and 5.15, and page 134 verse 11.29
[289] Griffith, *Sun Tzu The Art of War*, page 93, verse 5.20
[290] Griffith, *Sun Tzu The Art of War*, page 122, verse 9.46

paredness,[291] and deception[292] also with apparent confusion, cowardice, and weakness.[293] The consequences for the adversary are dispersion and confusion.[294] And Sun Tzu even puts forward possible recipes, like offering a bait,[295] to divide and strike,[296] and keeping enemy's allies away.[297]

The Freedom of Action principle is better illustrated with examples of failure rather than successes. Unlike the previous principle, the victor does not win by strengthening its freedom. In this case, it's the underdog that loses because freedom suddenly ceases to be an option. Ultimately, companies come to a halt when running out of liquidity, much like how human life ceases when the heart stops beating. Still, t's essential to consider the reasons behind running out of money in the first place. This principle holds true for any resource a company relies on, providing an effective strategy to entice our adversaries into a situation where they disperse their resources, attention, or both, weakening their position. This approach allows us to shape the terms of the battle to our advantage. Consequently, our adversaries may capitulate both at project level, akin to a battle, or they may be forced out of business entirely by losing their freedom of action due to resource constraints. In summary, if our adversaries are not able to engage the right resources at the right time when a fight comes along, their defeat is inevitable.

An exciting example of winning through Freedom of Action is the constraint of resources in project logistics. Projects

---

291 Griffith, *Sun Tzu The Art of War*, page 134, verse 11.26
292 Griffith, *Sun Tzu The Art of War*, page 106, verse 7.12 and page 92 verse 5.18
293 Griffith, *Sun Tzu The Art of War*, page 92, verse 5.18
294 Griffith, *Sun Tzu The Art of War*, page 133, verse 11.26
295 Griffith, *Sun Tzu The Art of War*, page 66, verse 1.20 and page 134, verse 11.27
296 Griffith, *Sun Tzu The Art of War*, page 69, verse 1.25 and page 116, verse 9.5
297 Griffith, *Sun Tzu The Art of War*, page 138, verse 11.52

take time, sometimes years, to develop, and this constraint may be enough to entail defeat by lack of preparation. Much like a faraway army unable to engage in battle, should an enterprise be capable of developing a complex project in secret, followers will have difficulties catching up. The barrier will be proportional to the time and the resources needed for project completion. Worse yet, if the first movers' advantages are part of the game, defeat is inevitable for whoever fell behind.

Big Techs have flourished the current natural monopoly environments where the advantage of being first mover serves as a formidable entry barrier. The next playfield will probably come from ecosystems, as already discussed in Part I. So, strategic moves based on the Freedom of Action principle and astute project logistics are likely to become increasingly prevalent. Moreover, because Artificial Intelligence is becoming commoditized, and, in the cases where accumulated knowledge makes the difference for enhancing the value proposition, this knowledge will create significant entry barriers. That is another excellent example where victory emerges, and contenders lose, based on Freedom of Action. In this case, even if followers try to copy, there is no time to create a comparable value proposition anymore because the AI infrastructure lacks the stream of tacit touch points with consumers. Besides, these touchpoints are hardly possible to put in place by followers because each new customer will always prefer the incumbent's superior value proposition, which explains the current entry barrier to Big Tech's success. Big Techs offer value, either with high personalization levels through advanced collaborative filtering algorithms or unsurmountable social networking.

Google is the classical case for the former, and Facebook for the latter, just to give two prominent examples.

Why did Nokia lose its leading position in the smartphone business, when they were the unquestionable ahead for so many years? The same with BlackBerry. In the mid-2000s, the opportunity was there, but only Apple was able to grab it. Apple took its time to develop a new interaction model and changed the rules. Then, all players rushed to adapt because the market did not appear to be a natural monopoly at the time and it still seems that way today. What is remarkable in the subsequent story is that Google was able to copycat Apple's IOS with Android, and everybody else fell behind. Nokia was not even a real contender in that race, but Microsoft's case is worth mentioning. Microsoft had already succeeded in copying Apple's interface in the computer's operating system environment many years before, so why not do it again? The answer is that they did attempt it, although too late. In this regard, we must consider that, even if the competitive environment with multiple contenders, network effects are still essential. So, what happened? Microsoft did an excellent job with a marvelous system, not inferior to Android, although too late. Being one of the world's leading companies in terms of market capitalization, and thus with virtually unlimited access to financial resources, Microsoft tried its chance. Having the Concentration of Forces on its side was a certitude. Still, being too late ultimately led to an inevitable defeat, primarily due to a lack of Freedom of Action. Victory never does not depend solely on technology, but in winning people's minds, a lesson Microsoft had learned decades before - Success in communication markets relies on network effects. And Microsoft was well aware of this because market penetration is the primary reason behind many of its successes, including its Windows operating system's enduring standard. The same kind of defeat happened to IBM when proposing OS/2, a better system than Microsoft's DOS operating system at the time. It was also too late due to the necessary critical mass attributes to ensure market penetration. The examples are abundant, all of them eventually in the loss of Freedom of Action at some point in time, either because resources are exhausted or just because the market dictates it.

With all its resources, Google has created tremendous leverage in many markets and has been building its strength mainly with non-replicable knowledge, because victory requires more than just tangible resources. Still, Google has also been a victim of the Freedom of Action over the years, and there are two outstanding examples worth mentioning.

In YouTube's early days, Google tried its luck with Google TV, but they were not successful enough because YouTube's network effects had already reached the critical mass. Result: Google had to buy YouTube.

The second example of Google+ is even easier to understand, and one without hope. The project was good, and the resources were there, although Facebook's network effects provided an unsurmountable first mover advantage. In the same market, not even a better technology and infinite resources would be able to win. It was already too late. Facebook's threat would happen only if social networking was capable of evolving in a different direction, like mobility, for example. Facebook recognized the challenge of mobility when acquiring WhatsApp, perhaps believing then Facebook Messenger might not succeed everywhere. Surprisingly, even more than a decade later, Facebook is still exploring ways to profit from this $20bn investment.

All these examples relate to Freedom of Action for sustainable victory. However, to establish themselves as the dominant player in their respective, Concentration of Forces had to be in place. This example also intends to demonstrate that tactical moves may be deployed in succession, each with a possible different strategic objective in mind.

In the meantime, the Freedom of Action principle also has a pillar. Freedom means having the capability to take action, such as deciding which resources to use in a battle. Dispersion diminishes the freedom of our competitors, and their capacity to engage in battle when it matters. So, when dispersion happens, defeat will surely occur.

Consequently, when considering this crucial principle, we should always have its pillar in mind. As we will see, this factor is of the utmost importance when applying Foch's system to evaluate the strategic effectiveness of our chosen tactics. The pillar in our mind, and in the first person, can be verbalized as "I can," with the overreaching general Principle of Freedom as its foundation.

Economy of Forces factor #3 - Economy of effort

The Economy of Forces superior principle introduced by General Foch encompasses both of the previously mentioned principles, and the interaction between these two principles forms a the third principle in its own right, completing Foch's system. We believe Foch named his system Economy of Forces by considering the Concentration of Forces as a given while conserving forces as much as possible to achieve superior tactical positioning through

Freedom of Action. That is why we refer to this third principle as the Economy of Effort. As Foch so well remembers: "...sparing one's resources... is only one part of the truth."

The rationale behind this third principle is straightforward: conserving forces maintains reserves, a well-established concept in the military. This enhances the readiness to engage when and where needed. Hence, the decision to engage the minimum number of forces in battle is of supreme importance. Moreover, preventing dispersion, which means maintaining reserves intact and deploy them only when truly necessary, also considers the degree of freedom both in terms of both time and space. That is why Foch's Superior Principle is a system.

In summary, the Economy of Effort surfaces from the need to balance the Concentration of Forces while preserving the Freedom of Action. The essence of the Economy of Forces superior principle results in the combined action of these three underlying principles altogether, in all situations. Where victory requires that all three be present simultaneously, the loss of a single one can originate defeat. This is key.

In this regard, one surrenders (i) when the Concentration of Forces flunks, and the battle is lost. One also surrenders when (ii) forces are not immediately available for some dispute. Finally, (iii) one surrenders if resources are squandered and not available when and/or where needed.

Sun Tzu also adheres to the principle of Economy of Effort.[298]

The best examples of this third principle in action come from failures. Just like the previous principle, conserving effort

---

298 Griffith, *Sun Tzu The Art of War*, page 111, verse 8.7 and page 134, verse 11.32

alone does not entail victory. Still, it does enable the preservation of Freedom of Action, which, over time, can lead to timely engagement in the battles that may lead to success. So, what is the meaning of failure here? Well, it's cheer defeat, directly or indirectly originated exclusively from resources usage.

Cash burn is a good example of failure because cash can acquire almost all other resources except time and everything depending on time. Running out of cash is a sure path to failure because lack of a single crucial resource is sufficient to bring operations to a halt.

What is a startup really betting on? What happens when the business goes live? There are reasons for the financing of a start up to go through several rounds. Each round allows investors to continue betting on their ideas as long as the current results show potential for ongoing success, typically reflected in growth. After each round, startups may have additional resources to continue their projects, eventually becoming unicorns and continuing to grow, or they may not. Meaning that even if the ideas are great and the strategic situation is favorable, when cash runs out, it's all over. Without resources, there is no more freedom to concentrate forces and win.

Big Techs are not a suitable example here because their resources are quite abundant when compared to most other companies. This abundance of resources makes it unlikely for them to capitulate upon this principle. So, for Big Techs, we should look other types of failures.

Finally, this third principle also has its own pillar. Economizing effort relies on knowledge, although assessing the right amount of resources for each battle is easier said than done.

Therefore, the pillar that should be present in our minds for this principle, and in the first person, is "I know," with the underlying general Principle of Effectiveness supporting it.

We now consider Foch's Economy of Forces superior principle in action—how the three principles work together cohesively, using the three pillars we discussed—will, ability and knowledge—to explain it.

Foch's superior principle in action

According to Foch, the Economy of Forces solves the apparent contradiction between theory and practice. Where theory advises concentration and, possibly, inaction as well, conserving Freedom of Action is precisely the opposite because moving and unfolding forces create dispersion. While we aim for concentration, we also are doomed with dispersion because, in Foch's own words, "…battle cannot be merely defensive"[299]; "the offensive form alone…can lead to results."[300] With the Economy of Force superior principle, we learn how to "portion forces out in time and space and to employ them in both ways—of the mass and of detachment,"[301] thus solving the contradiction at stake.

Much like Sun Tzu, Foch supports every decision with extensive intelligence because tactical superiority depends as much on our capabilities as on our adversaries' moves,[302] and in real-time.[303] Indeed, Foch advises assessing Freedom of Action for both offense and defense with full knowledge of the surround-

---

[299] Foch, *The Principles of War*, 1920, page 283
[300] Foch, *The Principles of War*, 1920, page 283
[301] Foch, *The Principles of War*, 1920, page 50
[302] Foch, *The Principles of War*, 1920, page 250
[303] Foch, *The Principles of War*, 1920, page 329

ings and before committing to battle.[304] After assessing all tactical options, the next step is to attack[305] with "moral and physical superiority."[306] So, both offense and defense are necessary and deployed in a sequential manner.

Just like Sun Tzu, Foch also highlights the importance of moral superiority and emphasizes the crucial role of intangible resources during battle. The Concentration of Forces will dictate victory if coupled with Freedom of Action to guarantee a strategic safeguard. And Freedom is maintained by deploying just enough resources to win, conserving effort, which is the crux of Foch's third principle.

Verbalizing the three principles in the same sentence guarantees they are considered unitedly at each tactical decision. Neglecting one leads to a decrease our tactical reasoning and potential advantage. After all, any tactical move should entail some influence on any component of Foch's system:

- to nurture our adversary in jeopardizing his own resources (third principle),
- to lure our adversary into engaging in the wrong places to lose freedom (second principle),
- thus, preventing him from concentrating his forces where it matters (first principle).

We will gain advantage by weakening the adversary, and this is the moment to launch the decisive attack. Our adversary

---
[304] Foch, *The Principles of War*, 1920, page 250
[305] Foch, *The Principles of War*, 1920, page 298
[306] Foch, *The Principles of War*, 1920, page 349

will lose either because they have no forces left to concentrate, or because they are dispersed in the wrong place. This reduces the necessity for us to concentrate our own forces, saving our efforts and increasing our chances of victory.

The three principles are essential conditions for victory, and mastering just one is insufficient. Even mastering only two is not enough to win. Therefore, ignoring just one principle ultimately jeopardizes strategic security, and our adversary may exploit it to build our defeat. Once again, victory hinges on mastering all three principles together, while for defeat, just one is enough.

Leverage is inherently differential. Accepting a negative outcome from battle is fine as long as we do not end up worse than our adversary, Pyrrhic victories being an excellent example of this phenomenon. Therefore, coherently deploying all three principles becomes the crux of Foch's superior principle and the heart of the Economy of Forces.

General Fiévet proposes an interesting view of this system, based on the pillars already mentioned above.

- the Concentrations of Forces has to be wanted, so we **want**; this is the Principle of Volition;
- the Freedom of Action prescribes what we can do, so we **can**; this is the generic Principle of Freedom;
- the Economy of Effort requires knowledge, so we **know**; this is the Principle of Effectiveness.

Now, we combine the three principles two by in the following manner:

- the Economy of Effort (I know), combined with the Concentration of Forces (I want), has the following meaning: <u>I know what I want</u>;
- the Economy of Effort (I know), combined with the Freedom of Action (I can), has the following meaning: <u>I know what I can</u>;
- the Concentration of Forces (I want), combined with the Freedom of Action (I can), has the following meaning: <u>I (only) want what I can</u>,

Now let's see how it sounds when combining the three:

If "I know what I want," "I know what I can," and "I want what I can," I win!

The above recipe requires a lot of intelligence, exactly as Foch, Sun Tzu and Clausewitz demand, among probably all enlightened military strategists. However, it also requires a good perception of our own capabilities at every moment in time. Victory is the outcome of this system, with all three principles working together for us, whereas defeat only requires one on the negative side, preferably for our adversaries.

And that is how we use Foch's Economy of Forces superior principle with its three underlying principles to assess every tactical move's strategic power. Let's now proceed to practice.

Foch's Economy of Forces framework – assessing tactics' strategic power

The Economy of Forces superior principle is an outstanding tool to assess each possible tactic's strategic contribution and the simple rule of thumb we were looking for. Each tactic should go under the scrutiny of the three principles, both from our perspective as attackers and from adversaries' perspective as targets, for we should always have in mind that our victory is based on someone else's defeat.

Foch's system focuses on the dynamic interactions between all contenders. Therefore, when evaluating each tactic, we consider its potential to gain leverage over our adversaries. This assessment is based on three key principles, which we will examine as follows:

- The concentration of Forces — are adversaries' forces sufficiently weak to ensure our victory?
- The Freedom of Action — are we luring our adversary out of strategic focus?
- The Economy of Effort — are our adversaries jeopardizing resources?

The goal is to find one or more principles where our tactic proves effective. This method allows us to assess the substantial contribution of each tactic to the overall strategy and aids in refining it with details that could potentially undermine our adversaries' tactics. Remember that victories unfold from tactics, and that strategy is only a tool to determine the most appropriate tactic at each point in time. By meticulously evaluating each tactic against these principles, we can ensure that our strategic decisions are not only sound but also impactful, potentially leading to decisive advantages over our adversaries.

Simultaneously, we need to self-assess the Economy of Forces as a whole. Each tactic should be sound regarding each of the three principles concerning our own strategic positioning:

- Concentration of Forces — are we strong enough to engage and win?
- Freedom of Action — are we maintaining our capabilities regarding other strategic considerations?
- Economy of Effort — are using our resources just to fit?

In the latter analysis, it's not necessary to meticulously detail the assessment of each principle individually. An integrated holistic evaluation is sufficient, as the objective is not to excel in each principle individually, but rather to ensure that leverage is not lost in any of them. Several questions come to mind helping this second assessment:

- Which battle to choose next, that is, which project should we bet on?
- Can we cope with the dispersion generated by the next project? Or does it create a weakness exploitable by our adversaries?

- Are we deploying the right amount of forces, not more, nor less, than we should?

With the Economy of Forces system, we conduct both an internal and external analysis for each tactical move. This approach allows us to anticipate the impact of each action on our adversaries, as well as on our own resources and capabilities. analysis should be applied to the chosen Sun Tzu's tactics, thus assessing each one with this rule of thumb.

A strategy emerges from a set of coherent tactical maneuvers, much like a chess game where we predict the outcome of each move. When planning for strategy, we can use Foch's tactical assessment to determine the most effective sequence of tactics, which in turn help to craft a possible effective strategy. In this respect, please remember that to win, we just have to find an adversary's weakness in only one of the three principles and then fully exploit it until victory.

The next chapter revisits Sun Tzu's tactics and interprets their strategic strength using Foch's Economy of Forces superior principle.

EIGHTEEN
EXAMPLES OF SUN TZU'S TEN TACTICS USING FOCH'S ECONOMY OF FORCES

Sun Tzu's tactics are more than 2400 years old, and they indeed inspire, although it's on us to ignite them in today's reality. In this chapter, we go through each of Sun Tzu's Ten Tactics, with examples illustrating their usefulness, along with its strategic appraisal employing Foch's Economy of Forces superior principle.

Tactics depend on the tools at hand to attack the market and disrupt its stakeholders' competitive balance, from regulation to adversaries. In this sense, the use of technology has been a preferred subject by many authors in the last two decades, hence its influence on all business disciplines' content, from marketing to strategy, which is truly immense.

Indeed, storytelling is likely the most effective method to illustrate and fully grasp the mechanics of each tactic; we'll look at applying Foch's Economy of Forces superior principle to exemplify each tactic's real strategic power. The chosen examples are all about well-known companies and circumstances.

Political-level tactics

The first set of two tactics gets inspiration from strategy and politics, whereas all others focus on adversaries' tactics in one way or another.

Subdue the enemy without fighting by attacking his strategy

We already know that "to subdue the enemy without fighting is the acme of skill," which we accomplish either directly or indirectly. Battling at ground-level is the direct approach, and we will deal with these types of tactics below. Achieving indirect attacks on the adversary is accomplished by targeting the compulsory conditions underneath their tactics, thus undermining the opponents' strategy. It's indirect because the opponent is not aware of the attacks.

For example, lobbying in the United States to shape legislation and regulations is sometimes obvious, with both sides aware of the other's actions and desired outcome. On the other hand, backdoor deals are also a lobbying scenario, with legislative and regulatory proposals blindsiding the opponent.

Environmental regulations have been pushed to evolve by such advocacy efforts and the pace of change will probably accelerate from now on. Many regulatory changes worldwide have been disruptive, entailing a remarkable impact on economies.

Evolutionary regulations are incredibly effective tools to undermine adversaries' tactics. In Economy of Forces terms, regulations force contenders to spend resources in preparations, with potential negative strategic impact. On the one hand, if there is no time left to build the needed capability, companies lose Freedom of Action, independently of possessing unlimited resources. On the other hand, even if there is time to comply, for companies with limited resources, which is the case for most, spending resources is similar to dispersion. Consequently, because scattering resources has a noticeable impact on Freedom of Action, the company at stake may not dispose of enough reserves for future victories, directly influencing the third principle, the Economy of Effort. Ultimately, the current tactic may impact all three principles of the Economy of Forces.

A most interesting example comes from the automotive sector, namely, Volkswagen fines and settlements in 2017, originated by fraud in their engine software. Europe has been evolving around regulations to benefit the companies capable of embracing this kind of compliance. It's only natural to assume that the most politically powerful companies aim to exert influence for their own benefit.

Besides, governments are also interested in fostering regulations with advantages for their industrial tissue. International agreements have been difficult to achieve and take many years to concert because they represent negotiations where every nation is concentrated in creating conditions for its own economic development, with potential impacts on the three Economy of Forces principles. What is surprising in this automotive example is the irony of one of the largest automakers becoming a victim of the very environment they helped to create. Volkswagen tried to take the easiest way out, and it backfired. It's an exciting story. Conclusion: anyone wanting to seriously compete in the automotive industry must possess capabilities to influence regulators. The question now is: what if a Volkswagen contender has access to crucial information and chose to indirectly attack Volkswagen's strategy using the media followed by legal actions?

The current tactic is also accessible to small organizations. Let's imagine the following scenario. A company in Europe is prepared to move forward with some investment, with banking support. Maybe an opponent can attack its strategy by creating conditions to delay cash access long enough to hinder getting ahead? And what if there was a straightforward way to do it using the banking clearance system and the courts? In some countries in Europe, companies see their credit rating blocked if, for any reason, there is a process in court going on. Simulating a situation requiring a court process is quite simple to prepare and more than enough to attain the objective. Unfortunately, no example is readily available because it's too horrific for anyone to confess its use. However, banks have seen it quite often and sometimes also help to play this hideous move.

All in all, for attacking our adversaries' strategy, we only need to find a way to block access to some required resource, whatever it may be. And anything goes, here. Market level moves are also allowed, and information warfare has been handy and effective. Sometimes, we just have to read the news to spot such examples. But what has been even more powerful and gaining terrain by the day is cyberwarfare. More than disrupting the operations of adversaries or even blackmailing through ransomware, cyberwarfare can have the highest intelligence objectives with the lowest risk ever. Better yet, intelligence can expose adversaries in the worse possible manner. "Panama Papers" comes to mind. In 2016, millions of compromising documents of wealthy individuals were leaked following a cyberattack on someone who breached

Mossack Fonseca's computer infrastructure, a law firm and leading corporate service provider for offshore properties.

Besides, the inspiration for attacking the strategy of adversaries may come from a detailed analysis of Clausewitz's Trinity in all its subdimensions. All in all, this tactic is essential and should always be at the back of our heads.

First, disrupt alliances

At one time, several VISA credit cards started using cryptocurrency accounts, Bitcoin, and others, so that even a newspaper could be bought in Satoshis.[307] Using the VISA infrastructure to start promoting cryptocurrencies was seen as a threat to the system itself at the time. If paying with cryptocurrencies became the norm, its current payment system's fabric would become obsolete, destroying VISA's business model. If everybody starts transferring cash to software wallets and between software wallets, all this would happen outside the banking sphere. Therefore, it made no sense for VISA to continue to nurture a culture that could mark the end of the company and all the outstanding fees generated around the world for managing electronic payments.

We counted more than two dozen VISA cards handling cryptocurrency wallets, with more to come at the time. So, what did VISA do? For those companies to access the VISA network, some issuer had to provide the debit card service. It turns out that WaveCrest, with offices in Gibraltar, was issuing most of these cards. So, on January 5, 2018,[308] VISA considered that WaveCrest breached conformity and canceled its license on the

---

307 A Satoshi corresponds to 1/100.000 of a BitCoin. It was created with the intent of having a similar value of one cent of a dollar in the long run.
308 https://www.telegraph.co.uk/technology/2018/01/05/visa-locks-bitcoin-payment-cards-crackdown-card-issuer/

spot, and VISA has not even mentioned any cryptocurrency issue in that move. Still, the fact is that all these companies lost business overnight, and for good, because WaveCrest was a crucial and necessary ally.

One may argue that Revolut, an App with Mastercard and VISA cards associated, also allows cryptocurrency trading among a well spread-out community of consumers and growing by the day. In this case, the consumer is obliged to trade back and forth within Revolut's account, unable to send directly any amount of cryptocurrency to any other wallet. With Revolut, cryptocurrencies have been investments and not a payment system, therefore not posing any threat to VISA. Clever Revolut.

PayPal also started trading cryptocurrencies with the benefit of having some tens of millions of merchants in its ecosystem. Like Revolut, PayPal also switches cryptocurrencies back and forth with fiduciary money.

Ground-level tactics

Ground-level tactics include businesses attacking the market, the adversaries, or both. It's not by chance that marketing actions are put in place under the name "marketing campaign." We can search for marvelous examples of success, keeping in mind that victory always entails someone else's defeat. Victory emerges when a single of the three Economy of Forces principles dwindles at the adversaries' side, while all our three are maintained intact. The Anna Karenina principle comes to mind, which is the first sentence of the novel with the same name, written by Leo Tolstoi in 1877:

All happy families are alike; each unhappy family is unhappy in its own way.[309]

So, all successful ventures are alike, and each unsuccessful venture fails in its own way. It's thus not enough to declare why winners win. Real insight emerges from understanding why losers lose.

Victory emerges from a final struggle between winners and losers, where the Concentration of Forces does the trick for winners, although not everything can be reduced to that instant. For real insight, we have to search for maneuvering, that is, how Freedom of Action contributed to that specific instant, and the same with the Economy of Effort. If war means attrition, the first contender running out of resources will be doomed.

Consequently, throughout the examples below, we will look for both—the result of the Concentration of Forces' moment of truth through the contribution of Freedom of Action and Economy of Effort. The corollary is the following: our strategy, that is, our set of tactical choices, should get inspiration from our adversaries' weaknesses by scrutinizing the Economy of Forces' superior principle.

Bring the enemy to the field of battle

The third tactic is somehow straightforward and should represent the Blue Ocean strategy.[310] All startups have been following it, and it's also the preferred tactic for disruption.[311] A disruption

---

[309] Anna Karenina, Lyof N. Tolstoi, trans. Nathen Haskell Dole, (New York, Thomas Y Crowell & Company Publishers, 1899), page 1
[310] Blue Ocean Strategy: How to Create Uncontested Market Space and Make Competition Irrelevant, W. Chan Kim and Renee Mauborgne, Harvard Business School Press, 2004
[311] C.M. Christensen, The innovator's dilemma, Harvard Business School Press, 1997

creates a new battlefield by definition, forged with sheer innovation. For example, some authors consider Uber not disruptive because its value proposition is just an evolution of the basic car transportation service, only improving the value proposition in additional, although significant, aspects. Still, even if Uber is not considered disruptive, the company evolved tremendously the competition pattern, and all contenders had to follow the challenge. Uber's capability to win will depend on how strong their position is when attacked, which actually belongs to the fifth tactic, that is, preventing the enemy from concentrating. Uber had to sell its operations to Didi in China, although still hoping to succeed in the West.

Innovation is the best example of bringing the enemy to the battlefield, provided that consumers see a new value proposition, which is precisely what Amazon did when selling books over the Internet back in 1995. With Amazon, the bookstore business was never the same again. Other products followed, and the world changed for good with the advent of e-commerce.

Maybe the same is happening again with Blockchain-based businesses in all industries, starting with the financial sector. But that's another story.

In summary, innovation creates new battlefields, which, if successful, are Sun Tzu's *key ground*. Building *key ground* depends on the Concentration of Forces' needs of the modern marketplace. Sometimes a Blue Ocean success requires meager investments, although we have witnessed innovation and disruption entailing substantial resources, like Uber's favorite example. In any case, enduring victory in a new battlefield depends on erecting entry barriers, and these come in the form of Freedom of action and

Economy of Forces. The new incumbent ought to protect his newly acquired leverage by any means possible.

Create a position not to be defeated and grab every opportunity

The fourth tactic is pure Freedom of Action, followed by Concentration of Forces.

Once again, we will not win just by maintaining Freedom of Action, although it's necessary for striking effectively when and where needed. True victory hinges on maintaining constant attack leverage while simultaneously never losing Freedom of Action.

The world evolves and foundational knowledge with it. Companies must adapt their resources, competencies, and capabilities according to new environmental characteristics. One thing is to adjust, and another completely different one is learning how to adapt successfully to disruptions. It's double-loop learning, which means learning to learn. To circumvent this need, some companies with large pockets intensively buy any new contenders while the latter are small and cheap, fostering their competencies and getting rid of the latest threats. But is it enough?

Let me briefly narrate the fate of an important information technology company, Digital Equipment Corporation (DEC), a significant contributor to computer development. Whereas IBM developed mainframes for data processing, DEC advanced in scientific computation with minicomputers since its birth in the 1960s. DEC's unique PDP systems in the 1960s gave birth to Unix. DEC VAX/VMS systems in the 1970s had an operating system so advanced that it's still admired. Their Alpha RISC architecture was powerful, but that did not stop the company from heading downhill and ultimately being acquired in 1998 by Compaq—a move that signaled the end for both of them. DEC was a minicomputer' specialist but did not believe in microcomputers.

Microcomputers started to be developed in the 1970s and conquered the world in the 1980s. Apple II in 1977 is an excellent first example, but the IBM PC and its clones became the front runner, which still has the lion's market share today. Nonetheless, IBM made the mistake of commissioning the IBM PC Operating System to Microsoft. When IBM finally acknowledged the business importance of microcomputers and developed the more advanced OS/2 operating system, it was already too late. On the other hand, unlike IBM, DEC possessed all the world knowledge to dive into microcomputer business with complete success, but they decided not to do so. Microcomputers invaded decentralized computing networks proposing cost-effective solutions that outstanding minicomputers like the VAX were unable to match in the long run. DEC lost its Freedom of Action when choosing not to enter the microcomputer business, and it was already too late to start from scratch. So, DEC chose a threatful position, unable to grab opportunities. Their Concentration of Forces was outdated and unable to sustain their business.

Still, the same happened to Compaq in the 2000s, in an extraordinary Freedom of Action example of defeat. After acquiring DEC, Compaq could also not grasp the business models' evolution induced by e-commerce and its impact on their market. Companies like Dell, which were already accepting telephone orders, took advantage of e-commerce to nurture direct sales. Compaq was unable to perceive this trend on time, and when they tried to evolve their supply chain and marketing operations accordingly, it was already too late. Technical knowledge was not so necessary anymore, but supply chain knowledge was, namely in build-to-order operations. Compaq also lost its crucial Freedom of Action by refusing to accept the challenge of potentially cannibalizing their traditional indirect distribution channels.

In a nutshell, all DEC's foundational knowledge could not save the company when the world evolved towards decentralized computing. Similarly, the outstanding Compaq marketing capabilities were also unable to save the company just a few years after DEC's acquisition because the world had changed again with the Web. Corollary: keep your Freedom of Action at all costs regarding the meaningful competencies, or you will head to an inevitable defeat. Market evolution mandates it, so maintaining Freedom of Action always depends on the competitive landscape.

Create momentum

The fifth tactic is pure Concentration of Forces. Recall that we do not have to apply all forces we have when in battle, but just enough to win. All victories in war are the consequence of this moment of truth.

Big Techs have been unbeatable from the height of their unlimited resources, although their complete success comes mostly from their unfathomable positioning in the market. Network effects have been paramount for these companies. To build platform value with various possible business models, each Big Tech has attempted to find its own winning recipe. Yes, we can learn from them, although the probability of replicating the recipe is extremely slim, at least in their own playfield. After learning about Big Tech's winning formula, we can always try to replicate it in a new geography or another industry, but that is the focus of the third tactic, being the first mover in a new and fresh battlespace. In this tactic, we want to understand how momentum works, and, like the previous tactic, maybe defeat can be more enlightening. How much we can learn from defeat can be staggering. We propose to study two classic defeats from apparently successful giants, although rarely discussed, mostly because, like everybody else, both companies prefer to forget. We are talking about Uber's and eBay's defeats in China again.

Western company investments in China are interesting to study because they are attacking a completely different battleground. Both Uber and eBay applied with success the third tactic to enter the market, that is, bringing the enemy to the field of battle, because none of these markets existed in China. Whoever wanted to compete would have to stand against a worldwide successful first mover with lots of resources. Still, both lost and were obliged to stop operations.

Entering a new market or new geography with a unique value proposition is somehow easy because adversaries do not exist. And we are talking about already successful companies expanding their geographical scope. So, it all comes to the capability to defend the newly conquered position with entry barriers at the reach of any prosperous Big Tech with deep pockets. But apparently not in either case because momentum was not strong enough, that is, the Concentration of Forces.

Start with eBay, the worldwide conqueror of e-commerce, in the form of auctions. They entered the Chinese environment in 2002 by acquiring Eachnet. In response, Taobao, a local adversary funded by Alibaba, appeared in 2003 and started growing. In just three years, Taobao overtook eBay, and in 2007 it was over for Eachnet. eBay, the worldwide e-commerce champion, was thrown out at light speed.

In e-commerce, audiences are paramount, so there was no reason for eBay/Eachnet to lose its first mover's advantage, already with 75 percent of the global market in 2003. Everybody imagined a continued growth in absolute numbers in a promising country with a vast population. However, the adversary Taobao started growing at light speed. There were two main differences between Taobao and Eachnet's business models. First, it was relatively easy for Taobao customers to communicate between themselves before any purchase, which eBay/Eachnet did not allow. Second, Taobao did not charge any fee for transactions, so everybody was free to communicate. eBay/Eachnet hindered consumer communication before any transaction because, if consumers could speak firsthand, the transaction could take place outside the portal, and they would lose the corresponding fee. Still, there was a third difference. eBay/Eachnet used PayPal for payments, and TaoBao had Alipay with escrow services available, something that was completely out of eBay's plans at the time. No one knows why eBay/Eachnet did not react and change its business model to follow TaoBao, and the result was defeat in a nanosecond. Thus, eBay/Eachnet could not sustain the initial victory because network effects were not strong enough to maintain its leverage, and, to gain momentum, TaoBao found a solution with the right value proposition. Taobao promoted better network effects, which is particularly effective in a growing market. Even if TaoBao's value proposition was not difficult to copy, eBay/Eachtnet did not react, and the rest is history. Maybe eBay/Eachnet believed their first movers' audience of 75 percent market share would be an entry barrier strong enough to sustain its competitive positioning due to network effects, like in the rest of its markets. Or maybe eBay/Eachnet disregarded the different Chinese culture where Tao-Bao's new value proposition made all the difference. So, Taobao built a new stronger audience fast enough with stronger network effects. That was the momentum, or the Concentration of Forces, that made the difference.

Uber is an entirely different story because it happened in the mobile world. Uber has been considered a winner when looking to its value proposition. What is less clear is why Uber sold its operations to Didi in China and to Grab in Singapore. They say these were mergers and that Uber maintains shares around 15 percent in both. But why did Uber prefer owning a small part of a local player, thus leaving the market with its brand in the first place? The answer comes solely from network effects again.

The transportation business with mobile apps is a double-sided platform requiring availably and value creation to both supply and demand. Drivers join the platform if there are enough consumers worth the effort. Consumers will search for a provider if there are enough drivers around and do not need to wait more than a few minutes, preferably five and surely not more than ten. Uber entered the western market, and then the immense Chinese market, and started to win. Although there are always copycats, and it's relatively easy for both sides of the platform to play simultaneously on other platforms when the culture is already in place. Drivers just need an extra mobile phone for each new platform, which means that entry barriers are slim for the supply side. Even worse, if the number of drivers goes up, they have to share the demand, which means that network effects are adverse whenever a new driver joins the platform. And with consumers, the problems are similar for network effects on the demand side. Whenever there are too many consumers for the available drivers, prices go up, and the waiting times also increase, thus entailing adverse network effects.

Consequently, there is no way to maintain momentum during growth and to sustain the Concentration of Forces. And for Uber, what happened in China may also occur elsewhere. Uber's loss was fast due to the extremely convenient mobile communication environment with Super Apps in China, which is much more effective than in the West. Uber also did not know how to deal with Super App audiences, whereas Didi was born in its midst.

The conclusion of these two defeats is fierce: we may apply the third tactic to enter, that is, innovating, disrupting, and bringing the adversaries to a new battlefield. However, if we cannot build momentum with the first mover's advantage and erect entry barriers, copycat exposure will be a given. Both Uber and eBay did not know how to deal with the local e-commerce environment and did not adapt fast enough, which accelerated defeat. Note that Super Apps will probably happen all over the world one day, thus completely changing the competitive landscape. Companies should be knowledgeable about the new competitive arenas fast enough, or the same disasters can happen, which should be true even for today's most successful companies on earth. Incumbents do not tend to disrupt, right?

Conserve your strength and maintain your freedom

The sixth tactic is the pure Economy of Effort, so we now illustrate how to conserve strength.

No one wins just by preserving strength, but everybody will lose if there are not enough forces available to sustain the combat. The previous examples about DEC, Compaq, and eBay also could apply in the final stage of their battle, originating their defeat. The major difference between Freedom of Action and Economy of Effort is that failure depends on time in the former and on the lack of recourses in the latter. In this sense, the examples of DEC and eBay illustrate a clear case of Freedom of Action impacting the Economy of Effort.

Consider Skype versus Zoom. Skype created the OTT industry for international video communications in 2003, with a good value proposition building a comfortable first mover's advantage. The company achieved around 600 million users in just six to seven years. So, why did it fall to 100 million in a nanosecond? Moreover, by being now part of the Microsoft ecosystem, thus supported by as many resources as required, why did Skype lag behind Zoom and others grabbing hundreds of millions during the pandemic? With the current tactic in mind, where are the weaknesses? Where are the opportunities lost?

The worldwide confinement was an incredible opportunity for technology to support remote workplaces. Zoom had a few million users at the beginning of 2020, and the opportunity was there for any company to grab, namely for well established businesses like Cisco Webex and AdobeConnect. How could Skype let this opportunity slip through their fingers?

Conserving one's strength does not just mean internal resources. In the world of platforms, users are the greatest strength, and that is something we learned from the best, many years ago, just by looking at their critical success factors. It's called platform value, and network effects are the tool to build it. In the case of platforms for remote conferencing, the value proposition increases with the number of users, so the more users, the better. In this regard, Skype was not successful in maintaining the lead, which is visible through the decreasing number of users throughout the 2010s. Bottom line: They added "functionality" without adding value to the user—especially ease of use.

Skype4Busines, Cisco Webex, AdobeConnect, and others targeting the business sector, completely forgot the power of platform value and ignored the fantastic opportunity to build on everyday user competencies and influence. When everybody went home for confinement in 2020, the more convenient solution—Zoom—flourished. The previous Skype culture, the one that everybody remembers, is that Skype was free for communication between two people only. Cisco WebEx and AdobeConnect were also less than convenient in their payment plans and subscriptions when involving many users. Therefore, everybody jumped on board a 45-minute freemium solution, where limiting the number of participants was not a problem for most situations.

The value proposition is a good part of the explanation of Zoom's fantastic success in this period. Most people did not even hear about Zoom before, and a lot of them had previous experiences on other platforms. It seems that Skype's market positioning worked against growth because previous expectations of consumers did not match the change in behaviors and needs. Even if Google rushed to open their Meet video conferring this service for free, but it was probably too late because Zoom led the viral effect upfront. Google and others lost Freedom of Action here, and not because of any limitation on resources.

Skype was unable to conserve its strength and unable to grab the opportunity. And Zoom was able to build momentum with the right value proposition, which other contenders also disregarded. Still, it would be difficult for incumbents to change their pricing overnight, along with a more convenient enrolling process and communicate it in real-time with the market. What would happen to the extant customer base already paying for their licenses? That is called disruption, and the result is not pretty. Incumbents struggle to innovate but experience have difficulties in disrupting their businesses. Usually, the best they can do is to expand the value proposition and try to block disruptors. Although, that is real hard for disruptions coming out of the blue, because incumbents have no time to follow the new momentum and simply become obsolete.

Conserving strength in an evolving environment is a challenge, although mandatory. Without it, when the time comes, Freedom of Action is lost and so is battle due to a lack of momentum.

Prevent the enemy to concentrate

Preventing the enemy from concentrating is the opposite of building momentum and addresses adversaries' Concentration of Forces. Utilizing this tactic effectively weakens opponents, thereby amplifying our own momentum. As a result, we need to commit fewer resources to launch an attack and achieve victory. One idea is to create some distraction moving away our adversaries from whatever *key ground* we are aiming for. Politicians use this tactic extensively, sometimes fabricating news just to draw the public's attention somewhere else, thus avoiding discussion of something they are trying to hide.

We can use this tactic both in a tangible and intangible manner. In the former, we drive our adversaries to focus on some project well away from our real intentions, thus leaving the route free. The latter involves some counterinformation, or even disinformation, because in war, anything goes.

The first rule for preventing the enemy from concentrating is to keep our intentions in absolute secrecy because the last thing we want is to warn the enemy to ignite concentration when we want to attack. Drawing attention away is an example of this tactic and is discussed next.

The world has never seen so much innovation. It has been happening everywhere, from the unmistakable Silicon Valley to startup initiatives a bit all over. The traditional research and development (R&D) projects looking for the next big idea have been disrupted with open innovation, social innovation, and considerable investment with venture capital. Crowdsourcing and Initial Coin Offerings (ICOs) have raised the bar with investments in technology, attaining billions of USD every year. All this reduces focus and creates more difficulties for companies, dispersing attention, thus preventing the concentrating of forces.

When companies continue to exploit their business, by including more functionalities in their value proposition, they become more predictable than when exploring new ventures in any innovation ecosystems. Incumbents hardly originate disruptions due to difficulties in going out of their comfort zones, increasing predictability. And external predictability is good, not to be surprised by our adversaries concentrating precisely where we do not want them to. So, we want to achieve the exact opposite of predictability for adversaries with dispersion, and Xiaomi is an outstanding example.

Xiaomi has excelled in unpredictability, making its moves virtually impossible to anticipate and attack. Founded in 2010, Xiaomi invests in technology, including smartphones. Even if its products are similar to those of other competitors, like Apple, Samsung, or Nest Labs, their approach is different. Do you remember when Apple learned how to make money by harnessing platform value? It all began with the iPod, or, better said, with iTunes. Apple would never have achieved this level of profitability without its community. Xiaomi innovated even more in this sense because, on top of consumer communities, the company created a complete ecosystem for product development, and its benefits happen in the form of knowledge underpinning the development process. Xiaomi connects consumers with entrepreneurs, merchants, developers, advertisers, and everybody else you may think of. And it's not in the standard streamline waterfall version we are accustomed but in a real multi-connected ecosystem. At Xiaomi, even venture capital plays the game this way. Xiaomi is thus pure platform value throughout the complete value chain and not only at the final consumer and mobile app marketplace.

Any adversary trying to attack Xiaomi will see its resources dispersed and will never be able to concentrate against a single potential weakness. The attacker would have to target the platform itself. Still, in this case, we are talking about a complete and resilient ecosystem with many allies, some of them consumers themselves. Xiaomi is an outstanding example of a moving target.

Support-level tactics

The following tactics complement all the previous ones and can be used for strategic enhancement.

Use extraordinary (special) forces ("infinite as the heavens on earth")

The use of special force may seem strange in modern times, but it's not. When attacking, we create momentum with all we have. So, how are special forces different?

What explains victory beyond fair amounts of tangible resources available? The proposal is to look for notable victories. For example, is there any company winning in Big Tech arenas? The first mover's advantage cannot be the explanation, nor availability of resources. So, let's see some examples.

Facebook gained traction in 2006 and pulverized competitors such as Hi5, Friendster, MySpace, and SixDegress, the original social networking site, among others. Even if Facebook was lagging behind Friendster, its growth rates excelled fast. Where Friendster was attracting everybody and treating them like a simple audience, Facebook exercised controlled growth with some exclusivity for its users. The new value proposition increased traction, and its consumers did the rest by becoming their special forces. Never underestimate the power of crowdsourcing. The community became the force in Facebook's case.

Why did Google win when Altavista, Lycos, Yahoo, and MSN, among others, were already in place? The answer is PageRank, an intangible asset, the AI algorithm that finetunes Web page search results. That was Google's special force.

Dollar Shave Club is also an inspiring example. With a single successful viral video, they were able to acquire around 12,000 clients overnight, and this success ensured subsequent funding and a growth rate out of the ordinary. The special forces came in two forms, people and money, both necessary conditions to win. The first one was spontaneous social networking, and with enough audience and funding secured. The company never stopped growing while receiving appropriate financing, and the rest is history.

Special forces boost momentum and positively contribute to the Concentration of Forces. They make all the difference in battle and are considered special when at the reach of only one contender, preferably us.

Capture enemy's resources

Capturing the enemy's resources was a primary Mao Tse Tung's tactic. We may capture both internal and external resources.

Internal resources concern everything needed to go to market, from tangible raw materials and supply chains to intangible resources. Plundering resources is a risky business, subject to regulatory concerns and the law. We must keep in mind that military affairs are much less bound by the law, even if there are international conventions, courts, and organizations concerning these matters.

I have seen movements involving the financial sector diminish or even block access to debt, using the courts; they may even involve corruption. Still, there are safe examples in the capturing of internal resources, namely intangible ones, and there is no place for espionage here. We may deploy intelligence to learn about competitors, which is called competitor intelligence, always abiding by ethics and the law. However, we should be aware that the law differs from country to country and that espionage itself may have several entirely different definitions in different cultural and legal realities.

A classic acquisition of intangible resources comes in the form of individuals. In 2007, a report referred to Deloitte as having a significant espionage procedure against its competitors by hiring people with covert intelligence skills and competitors' ex-employees.[312] Not pretty, but part of the game. And, as already mentioned, some countries tolerate intelligence practices better than others.

Another possibility is buying a company altogether, including its human resources, because the acquired intangible resources are more effective than with separated companies after sharing their secrets. Reducing competition is another option for mergers and acquisitions, which regulators do not particularly appreciate. The example of Unilever buying Dollar Shave Club, a small company of a little more than a projected turnover of $200m at the time, for $1bn, can only be justified for the potential impact of its knowledge in Unilever's other operations. A clear case of intangible resources acquisition.

---

312 https://www.cnbc.com/2016/12/19/accountants-and-spies-the-secret-history-of-deloittes-espionage-practice.html

Capturing the enemy's resources contributes to the Economy of Forces, with implications for momentum, and intelligence, thus positively pushing Freedom of Action. If the resources involved are tangible, adversaries are effectively weakened, resulting in diminishing competition, thus favoring our momentum, that is, the Concentration of Forces.

Throw your troops to prepare to die (throw the army in a desperate position)
In military terms, this is called a burn-the-boats strategy; it's a tactic. From Alexander the Great to Hernán Cortés, and others, stories refer to conquests with no way back. A desperate position sends messages to both our troops and the adversary. Both understand that commitment must be maximum, or the end is near. Still, there are risks. If the clash is too stressful, some forces may just abandon ship depending on financial or emotional ties to the company. But there are solutions.

Once again, we can find an excellent example in China. Haier Group is a Chinese Fortune 500 company and one of the world's leading appliance manufacturers. From washing machines to refrigerators, the apparent innovation in the last decade has been superlative. Innovation is an instance of the third Sun Tzu's tactic, and Haier throws its forces in a desperate position to increase momentum.

In 2013, Haier successfully implemented an open innovation platform, the Haier Open Partnership Ecosystem,[313] which is behind its success. In fact, Haier is an entrepreneurship platform, meaning that anyone can start their own business, where

---
313   Bil Fisher, Umberto Lago and Fang Liu, Reinventing Giants, Jossey Bass, 2013

more than 4000 micro-enterprises form the tenets of its structure. Each micro-enterprise has between 10 to 15 employees on average, each depending on their ideas or operational success. They are all competing internally against each other by areas of expertise. How desperate can this be? When the workforce depends on open innovation, a cutthroat environment is an effective approach involving desperation. Regarding Foch's Economy of forces superior principle, Haier increases of momentum is the critical aspect of throwing its employees in a desperate position, thus increasing the Concentration of Forces. Besides, Haier's model also has flexibility regarding resources, which increases Freedom of Action. Moreover, by having so many entities struggling for their ventures' success with the final consumer in mind, intelligence is also increased, which, as we already know, is the basis of Sun Tzu's approach to strategy. Intelligence adds much to Freedom of Action by knowing where to move and why. Finally, all this knowledge fosters the Economy of Effort, thus contributing to the complete set of Foch's Economic of Forces superior principle.

Open innovation can be an essential contribution to the Economy of Forces, primarily when used like Haier. Desperation, as a Sun Tzu's tactic, surely is not easy to deploy, but it's undoubtedly overwhelming.

NINETEEN
SUN TZU'S DYNAMIC ENGAGEMENT CHECKLIST

Foch's Economy of Forces is a good rule of thumb to measure each tactic's strategic contribution, although it's not a strategy. At first, a strategy is just an idea, which becomes a reality through tactical maneuvers. Still, Foch's system is an excellent means to link tactics with strategic intent and never lose focus on what we are trying to achieve.

Situational awareness, both external and internal, is the basis of everything else, so it's good to check any strategic approach on these grounds.

Planning for any strategic action should build the most appropriate tactical approach, although, according to Sun Tzu, top-down strategic planning is not the way to go. The disposal of each tactic is performed bottom-up, and we can evaluate each move with Foch's superior principle. But that is just the first step of the journey. We still need to combine all frameworks above to define a business strategy.

For Sun Tzu, a real strategy is all about dynamics and not just planning. After conducting good and sound situational awareness, we can start building the sequence of tactical moves. Sun Tzu's scheme is pure science, which is admirable when we recall it was conceived more than 2400 years ago. He postulates[314]:

- define the battlefield, that is, the ground,
- measure it, estimate it, and then compare,
- to finally engage to achieve victory, that is, take your chances.

Nonetheless, according to Sun Tzu, several considerations should be continuously present at the back of our minds during the engagement. Because dynamics is an implicit property of fight, the idea is to conceive the battleground and our tactics on a bedrock of operational motion,[315] with momentum[316] and timing.[317]

The dynamic principles of tactical maneuvering[318] should be part of the all-embracing strategic approach. Therefore, before committing to any particular tactical decision, the leader considers more than the result of any singular tactical approach. A strategy is like a film roll with a sequence of photograms, where the next one always depends on the previous circumstances.

Sun Tzu thus advises in verses changing war methods for unpredictability.[319] Therefore, when possible, a previewed strategy should never repeat the previous tactic's *modus operandi* or

---

314 Griffith, *Sun Tzu The Art of War*, page 88, verses 4.16 to 4.18
315 Griffith, *Sun Tzu The Art of War*, page 134, verse 11.29
316 Griffith, *Sun Tzu The Art of War*, page 92, verse 5.14
317 Griffith, *Sun Tzu The Art of War*, page 92, verse 5.15
318 Griffith, *Sun Tzu The Art of War*, page 106, verse 7.12
319 Griffith, *Sun Tzu The Art of War*, page 100, verse 626, page 101, verse 6.30 and page 137, verse 11.45

sequence. Moreover, Sun Tzu notes that changes procedures aim to create adversary's dispersion, favoring the concentrations of our forces, which is amazingly similar to Foch's superior principle in action. We should always check both.

Timing and speed are crucial, although, after reading Foch, we are also aware that any action entails force dispersion and the subsequent decrease of freedom.

All the above concerns are part of a checklist to be verified when putting up the tactics sequence. The idea is to have an upper-level view of that sequence and verify all referred concerns. Refer to Sun Tzu's "Dynamic Engagement Checklist."

With the principles of Sun Tzu's engagement in mind, Sun Tzu's "Ten Tactics Framework" summarizes the strategy in a series of tactical moves. The objective is to conceive the best sequence of actions to increase our strategic leverage in the market, either by succeeding with clients/consumers/customers, by weakening adversaries directly or indirectly, or by attaining a more comfortable strategic positioning identified with Clausewitz's Trinity analysis. And we measure the chosen sequence of tactics with Foch's "Economy of Forces superior principle."

Now consider the final strategic check before going to battle.

TWENTY
SUN TZU'S TACTICAL HEALTH CHECKS

According to Sun Tzu, before engaging in battle, it's crucial to ensure that everything is prepared and in place. In this regard Sun Tzu enumerates five leadership losing factors and six tactical losing conditions. After going through all previous steps, even if we believe that all requirements for success are in place, at least for everything we can foresee, there is no harm in double-checking. We must be cautious not to delay crucial decisions due to concerns about timing. Still, even the best plan can fail because an infinite set of non-predicable factors may happen, originated by adversaries or by any other entity or element possibly influencing the competitive environment, either directly or indirectly. That said, increased preparation for battle is positive, which justifies this last step.

The Five Command Losing Factors

We test the robustness of our leadership before going to battle with the five "Command Losing factors". Sun Tzu refers to these five factors[320] explaining why they need to be duly scrutinized.[321]

The five traits mentioned by Sun Tzu constitute a leadership audit to validate the merits covered in Sun Tzu's "Leadership Virtues." It's good to check these before and during battle due to their implicit nature. Some traits only reveal themselves through practice and can significatively influence combat decisions. Therefore, it becomes mandatory correcting any dysfunctions at this level. Please keep in mind the difficulty in being self-aware about tacit shortcomings and the risk of having authoritarian leaders completely immune to feedback and unwilling to evolve their leadership competencies. Let's go through all five factors, one by one.

Factor #1 - Recklessness

The first command losing factor is recklessness.[322]

There are two difficulties with this first trait. Who will assess it? Is it possible for the leader to get this type of awareness alone? Griffith enlightens with an exciting citation from Tu Mu (803-852):

> *8.18 Tu Mu: A general who is stupid and courageous is a calamity.*[323]

---

320 Griffith, *Sun Tzu The Art of War*, page 114, verse 8.17
321 Griffith, *Sun Tzu The Art of War*, page 115, verses 8.23 and 8.24
322 Griffith, *Sun Tzu The Art of War*, page 114, verse 8.18
323 Griffith, *Sun Tzu The Art of War*, page 114

The risk posed by this factor thus depends on the leadership culture in place. Hegemonic leadership, where a single leader dominates decision-making, poses a significant risk. It can lead to narrow perspectives and unchallenged errors. In contrast, a balanced approach to leadership is advisable because the leader doesn't act solely on personal compulsion but considers diverse viewpoints. This can mitigate potential disasters and may even steer actions back onto a positive course.

Factor #2 - Cowardice

The second losing factor leading to defeat, according to Sun Tzu, is cowardice.[324] This aspect presents a significant challenge for self-awareness. Griffith, in his interpretation, cites Ho Yen-Hsi from the Sung dynasty, who emphasizes the role of hesitancy in this context.[325]

We can opt for a more constructive way to measure this trait by looking at courage. High-level decisions entail the emotional risk of failure, of frustration. In a turbulent and evolving environment, test and fail have become the norm for successful adaptation. Courage has thus become a primary strategic resource, namely when failure risks social amplification. Maybe courage can be simpler to measure by focusing on the emotional endurance towards loss and risk. Gert Hofstede calls it uncertainty avoidance,[326] and yes, it can be estimated.

---

324 Griffith, *Sun Tzu The Art of War*, page 114, verse 8.19
325 Griffith, *Sun Tzu The Art of War*, page 114, verse 8.19
326 Cultures and Organizations: Software of the Mind, Gert Hofstede, 1996

Factor #3 - Short-temper

The third detrimental characteristic identified by Sun Tzu is short temper.[327] Like cowardice and hesitancy, this trait requires assessment through observing the leader in action. It poses similar challenges in self-assessment, as individuals may not always recognize their own propensity for impatience or anger. Griffith cites Tu Yu (733-812) to emphasize the dangerous nature of this trait.[328]

It seems that a short temper induces mistakes, which will decrease *Freedom of Action*. Like the previous two traits, the leader must put himself in the second position or ask someone to assess his temperament.

Factor #4 - Irascibility

The fourth detrimental factor is irascibility. A leader with a "too delicate sense of honor,"[329] becomes easy manipulable, losing their composure and making foolish, predictable decisions. Griffith, citing Mei Yao-ch'en (1002-1060), offers another insightful citation to exemplify this point.[330]

Yes, some leaders only think about themselves. When managing their own resources, individuals might tolerate or overlook their own shortcomings, such as a lack of foresight or poor decision-making, often labeled as "stupidity." However, this trait becomes less acceptable when leading organizations on behalf of others. Irascibility is like short temper amplified. Once again, inconvenient examples are left out here.

---

327 Griffith, *Sun Tzu The Art of War*, page 114, verse 8.20
328 Griffith, Sun Tzu The Art of War, page 114, verse 8.20
329 Griffith, Sun Tzu The Art of War, page 115, verse 8.21
330 Griffith, Sun Tzu The Art of War, page 115, verse 8.21

Factor #5 - Excessive Compassion

The final harmful trait highlighted by Sun Tzu is excessive compassion.[331] Griffith references Tu Mu (803-852) again to offer a compelling perspective on the risks associated with this trait.[332]

For instance, in a culture where social well-being is highly valued, it's likely that leaders have been implicitly raised with these values at the forefront. Such leaders are often aware of the needs and well-being of the community. The society, in turn, will respond to their decisions, positively or negatively, reflecting these cultural values. Maybe that is why Corporate Social Responsibility (CSR) has been gaining traction these days. A sense of awareness has been flourishing with CSR, compelling companies to look beyond profits.

Sun Tzu is not against compassion in leadership but cautions about excessive compassion because the leader must be prepared to accept casualties along the way.

---

331 Griffith, *Sun Tzu The Art of War*, page 115, verse 8.22
332 Griffith, *Sun Tzu The Art of War*, page 115, verse 8.22

TWENTY-ONE
THE 6 TACTICAL LOSING CONDITIONS

Building on the assessment of leadership qualities, it's wise to meticulously examine tactics for potential errors before engaging in battle. Sun Tzu outlines six conditions that can lead to defeat.[333] Let's review each of these conditions in detail.

Losing condition #1 - Insubordinate troops

The loyalty of troops is an assumption throughout the strategic planning exercise. So, why don't we check it before going to battle?

After every strategic planning, Sun Tzu advises checking for loyalty or any negative emotional state.[334] As soon as failure comes along, people naturally tend to behave differently, revealing courage or cowardice, valid both for warfare and the company's internal disputes.

Insubordination is a factor that may not become fully apparent until the confrontation actually. However, training

---
333 Griffith, *Sun Tzu The Art of War*, page 127, verse 10.16
334 Griffith, *Sun Tzu The Art of War*, page 125, verse 10.8

and simulation exercises can often reveal tendencies towards insubordination. Only startups have nothing to lose when going for disruption. Still, incumbents can count on their command-and-control history to assess insubordination levels. The classic example of resistance to change is the most common cause of insubordination.

Losing condition #2 - Strong troops with weak officers
Sun Tzu states that a combination of weak officers and strong troops results in insubordination.[335] He discusses this in the context of exploring the reasons behind negative emotions in the ranks.

The "assignment of appropriate ranks to officers"[336] is one of the foundational pillars of Sun Tzu's doctrine. Assessing it before engaging in battle makes total sense, which is at the leader's reach. Once again, stamina, particularly in the context of enduring challenging situations, often only truly reveals itself during actual combat or high-pressure scenarios. However, exercises and simulations can be utilized as effective tools to assess its stamina. If it's not feasible to assess stamina through exercises, the alternative approach is to proceed with the operations and hope for the best. In this scenario, evaluation of officers and team members would occur in real-time, during actual operations. Victory depends on it.

---

335 Griffith, *Sun Tzu The Art of War*, page 126, verse 10.11
336 Griffith, *Sun Tzu The Art of War*, page 65, verse 1.8

Losing condition #3 - Valiant officers with ineffective troops

Sun Tzu also makes a harsh assessment regarding troops.[337] If forces are not prepared, we better not go to battle because attrition will only worsen. It's as simple as that. This factor can be assessed in conjunction with the previous one and using the same approach for testing.

Losing condition #4 - Angry and insubordinate officers

Even when officers possess the necessary skills and have been promoted based on merit, Sun Tzu cautions that their negative emotions might adversely influence their performance in combat, resulting in insubordination.[338]

This fourth losing condition is easy to assess because it reflects the direct relationship between the leader and their subordinates. Once again, the past relationships may help, mostly if lived under stressful situations. Like the previous factors, the leader should keep his eyes open and see relationships evolve. Mergers are an excellent example of complete incertitude regarding all these factors because, like a startup, the new interrelationship environment is still unknown, although bearing all traditional incumbent liabilities. The high incidence of failure in mergers could potentially be attributed to this factor.

---

[337] Griffith, *Sun Tzu The Art of War*, page 126, verse 10.12
[338] Griffith, *Sun Tzu The Art of War*, page 127, verse 10.13

Losing condition #5 - Morally weak general without a strict discipline

Sun Tzu returns to the leader's shortcomings.[339]

Maybe a 360° leadership appraisal can do the trick, although the leader should humble enough to accept the procedure. If it's not the case, a crucial losing condition assumption is already revealing itself.

Losing condition #6 - Unable to estimate the enemy's forces

Lastly, the last condition for defeat that Sun Tzu specifically mentions is closely related to the principle of Economy of Forces, which can be compromised by inadequate intelligence.[340]

This final check emphasizes the necessity of having robust intelligence in place to accurately assess the balance of forces. This losing condition, unlike the previous ones, is somewhat easier to evaluate as it relies heavily on thorough planning well before the battle begins.

---

339 Griffith, *Sun Tzu The Art of War*, page 126, verse 10.14
340 Griffith, *Sun Tzu The Art of War*, page 127, verse 10.15 and page 84, verse 3.33

TWENTY-TWO
SUN TZU'S STRATEGY IN ACTION — THE ROUTE MAP

The essence of the proposed interpretation of Sun Tzu's approach is quite simple:

1. Start with abundant intelligence activities because it will fuel the continuous refinement of our strategy, that is, the planned sequence of tactical moves.
2. With a good sense of situational awareness, both internal and external, the next step is to consider tactical options. A varied number of actions can lead or contribute to the same objective.
3. Next comes the choice of the most appropriate tactical sequence, that is, the strategy to attain the objectives at stake. We use Foch's Economy of Forces superior principle to evaluate different tactics and the same for its aggregated outcome. Moreover, we also appraise the strategic leverage created by each tactic towards our adversaries.

4. Select the seemingly most successful tactical sequence.
5. Verify strategy dynamics.
6. Check for common tactical and command pitfalls.

At this point, we have all the pieces to proceed with strategic action. But remember that Sun Tzu only tackles head-to-head conflict, so we still need a way to contextualize it in the global competitive landscape, and Clausewitz's Trinity will do just fine.

This chapter explains, step by step, how to deploy the sequence concepts proposed by both Sun Tzu and Clausewitz to build a sound and enlightened business strategy. We use Clausewitz's Trinity to fathom the significant forces shaping the global strategic landscape and then Sun Tzu's vision for the bottom-up strategic engagement with the appropriate tactics, appealing to Foch's Economy of Force's superior principle for tactical robustness appraisal. It's an architecture of all covered frameworks up to now.

Start with Clausewitz Trinity to define strategic objectives

Strategic objectives are the bootstrap of Sun Tzu's approach and are the outcome of Clausewitz's Trinity analysis. Clausewitz's Trinity framework puts forward the main strategic facets are stake, from which can depict possible strategies. We use it to foresee some possible strategic paths and their corresponding objectives.

Clausewitz's Trinity analysis imparts a high-level appraisal of conflict, with the three pillars of (i) reason, (ii) chance, and (iii) violence in mind. The strategic balance at a governmental level resulting in reason, playing amid companies' equipoise with chance and the violence coming from the actors in the field. By going through all Trinity's subdimensions and taking intermediate conclusions for each, we arrive at the principal strategic facets from which we may discern some viable and enlightened strategy.

The question to put forward now is: "What do we really want?"

Using Sun Tzu's orientation, we now mind how to get it done while assessing if we are up to the challenge. Needless to say, if the chosen objectives are not feasible, for any reason whatsoever, new ones should be advanced, which can happen along the course of action. We may stumble on new knowledge, either because we discover some information or due to some evolution in Clausewitz's Trinity dimensions.

Any strategic approach should be evolutive, at least as much as the competitive environment itself; a challenge these days. Even with the right intelligence procedures and scenario planning in place, nothing can prepare us for the environmental volatility that seems to be accelerating. Therefore, the best possible insurance to handle the competitive environment's volatility is strategic agility, which means agile tactical capabilities, we cover next. That is the power of sun Tzu's bottom-up approach. In any case, strategic agility should begin at a cognitive level, where understanding, abstractions, and ideas apprehend the complexity and craziness we are currently living in.

Explore Situational Awareness for Tactical Planning

We begin with situational awareness,[341] as Sun Tzu emphasizes that intelligence primarily guides tactics,[342] establishing a markedly different approach from traditional business strategy. Therefore, tactics are based on a thorough comprehension of the

---
341 Griffith, *Sun Tzu The Art of War*, page 84, verses 3.31 and 3.33
342 Griffith, *Sun Tzu The Art of War*, page 139, verse 11.56

adversaries' intentions and the analysis of their tactical formations in the field.[343] Addressing the enemy's desires might also involve disinformation when necessary.

At this point, we appeal to the first three of Sun Tzu's frameworks in a row. We frame situational awareness with Sun Tzu's "Six Factors Situational Awareness framework". It's a 360º vision, looking both to the inside at the outside, including the contenders and the market. It includes both internal and external analysis, and, to prepare it, we should include the two previous frameworks as follows:

i. Internal situational awareness

For internal situational awareness, we start with Sun Tzu's "Command and Control Leadership Virtues"; this framework focuses on leadership traits, which is somehow refreshing for internal business strategic analysis. For Sun Tzu, it's mandatory to start here. We will incorporate other internal competencies in the third framework below.

ii. External situational awareness

For the external situational awareness, we start by looking at the battlefield conditions in the form of combat grounds, deploying Sun Tzu's "Nine Combat Grounds framework"; this approach may unveil generic opportunities that become exploitable when studying the tactical alternative scenarios later on.

---

[343] Griffith, *Sun Tzu The Art of War*, page 140, verse 11.60

iii. Complete situational awareness
Then we go through the details of each of the six factors of the third framework, benefiting from the analysis performed with the first two:
    a. internal capabilities and competencies (doctrine and resources),
    b. our adversaries,
    c. and the business environment (weather and terrain).

Thus, this framework includes competitor intelligence, an essential and traditional facet of external analysis, even encompassing frameworks like the well-known frameworks (i) Strengths, Weaknesses, Opportunities and Threats (SWOT) and (ii) Political, Economical, Social, Technological, Environmental and Legal (PESTLE). These are also included in this first methodological step, although incorporating other unusual aspects for strategic analysis, like leadership and trust.

With situational awareness in place, we proceed with strategy definition through a set of tactical moves. The various tactical possibilities should be explored in detail, searching for business opportunities, which we tackle next.

Explore Sun Tzu's tactics

Recognizing opportunities is very difficult without any preparation. So, we usually get inspired with tools that have been evolving through the years, in line with the business environments. For instance, topics like innovation and technology, the latter in so many flavors, have been recently influencing current doctrines.

With Sun Tzu's method, we are free to consider any type of technology, business model, or anything else, as long as we have tactical capabilities to exploit it. Indeed, one of the most intriguing aspects of this doctrine is the application of a diverse array of tactics, some specifically designed to exploit the weaknesses of adversaries. Additionally, on the list of Sun Tzu's tactics, we find that the first two target political level, well into Clausewitz's type of rationale. Although a bit Machiavellian, we have to agree that this is an entirely different way of dealing with opportunities because it does not even relate to business models, innovation, or classic approaches coming from value propositions and other market moves. No, this is entirely different and possibly mind-blowing because the contribution to our strategic intentions may come from unusual tactics like information warfare, regulatory level moves, and even economic warfare, if our organization can play those games.

Sun Tzu offers ten different types of tactics to explore, two at a purely strategic level, five at battleground level, and three support ones. They are summarized in Sun Tzu's "Ten Tactics framework", along with some questions in line with corresponding sub-dimensions for each tactic. The outcome of this tool is a non-empty set of possible tactics.

Define the strategic route map with a sequence of tactics
Following these tactical considerations, we arrive at what is commonly referred to as sheer strategy, especially in the business context. And we can move fast now. The previous analysis portrayed everything we need to know about the competitive environment, from politics and regulations to competitors and market-level

operations. We should now possess all required information to devise various possible strategies and choose the seemingly best one because this bottom-up approach is an iterative and recurrent process. We accomplish this by scrutinizing multiple tactical options.

To conceive the strategic route map, we will use Sun Tzu's "Strategy Framework" to prepare a possible best sequence of tactics. If short on creativity, we may enter a single tactic to proceed.

With the sequence of tactics in place, we verify strategy dynamics. We use Sun Tzu's "Dynamic Engagement checklist" included in Sun Tzu's "Strategy framework" to revise the proposed sequence of tactical moves with positive dynamics. The checklist first confirms we duly executed internal and external situational awareness and then the adequacy of strategic dynamics. In this regard, we should remember to obfuscate our moves as much as possible for adversaries not to predict the next one. We also verify that we pace our actions according to the perceived tactical needs, not faster nor slower than advisable. Even if this checklist analysis is not easy, we should embrace it to the best of our abilities.

For situational awareness assessment, we revise the respective frameworks, the first three of Sun Tzu's methodology. Sometimes, the best way to assess this type of knowledge comes from poking new information in the field and see if it matches our current assumptions. If not, we should revise everything all over again.

Obfuscation is just a question of good planning. We can grasp tactical patterns only by looking at the proposed sequence of actions. Moreover, we should also recall past strategies and compare them. If we devise a different way to get to the same objective without losing leverage, deploying any innovative route map is undoubtedly advisable.

Timing assessment is more complicated again due to its intangible nature. Sometimes we just have to trust our gut feeling on that matter. Nevertheless, if the first mover's advantage is at stake, we surely want to be leaders, not followers, also having in mind that first moves are always costlier. But is the market ready for it? How many good ideas appeared too soon? To check an idea's feasibility, we may apply crowdsourcing, open innovation or Minimum Viable Products[344] because all work for learning about customers' preferences. In summary, we revise assumptions and take a fresh look at the combined effect of the set of chosen tactics by considering our adversaries' expected reactions and market dynamics.

The tangible outcome of this checklist is a spot-on sequence of tactics almost ready for action. Almost, because now we proceed with strategic leverage measurement with Foch's superior principle.

Test the strategy against Foch's Economy of Forces

We now use Foch's Economy of Forces to measure the strategic strength of the chosen tactical moves. At this point, we should perform internal and external tactical measurements:

---

[344] Minimum Viable Product: Master Early Learning and Develop an MVP with SCRUM, Scott Grossman,

- **Internal** – by looking at the disposition of our forces, we use Foch's Economy of Forces to confirm that each tactical move does not weaken our strategic position because, as our adversaries, when failing in one of the three Foch's principles, defeat is inevitable.
- **External** – by looking at our adversaries, determine the tactical leverage on at least one principle while maintaining our strategic strength. The idea is to build an incrementally stronger position, using the Economy of Forces to measure it.

In the Foch's Economy of Forces framework, each tactic should positively contribute to at least one underlying principle because our victory always comes in the form of someone else's defeat. Indeed, strategy cannot be purely defensive; it also requires proactive moves that may cause some level of dispersion within our own ranks. However, this dispersion should not be viewed as a weakness as long as it leads to a greater dispersion or disarray among our adversaries. Alternatively, if the market responds positively to our strategic moves, any internal dispersion can be offset by the advantages gained, such as occupying key terrain or acquiring additional resources. After the internal and external analysis of each tactic, we should tick the corresponding box.

When finalizing your strategy, it's essential to evaluate the chosen combination of tactics with the end goal in mind. We may temporarily lose strategic leverage in some intermediary move along the way, only to win everything back, and more, with a better positioning later on. It's like in chess: we may sacrifice the queen when going for a checkmate.

The final check entails revising the sequence of tactics and ticking the corresponding checkbox located at the end of the framework. The most important aspect of the analysis here is twofold: (i) maximizing our Economy of Forces' end state, (ii) while ensuring that we do not fail along the way. Keep in mind that necessary attacks also create dispersion, and this momentary loss of freedom always poses a risk.

We are almost there, but there is still a final check to perform before going to action.

Perform a tactical health check

For the final tactical health check, we use Sun Tzu's "Tactical Health check framework", combining the "Five Command Losing Factors" and the "Six Tactical Losing Conditions". If we execute all previous steps correctly, the last health check should not bring any surprise. Only an organization with sound leadership and an adequate human resource climate can successfully achieve all the previous steps. And there is no harm in confirming it.

TWENTY-THREE
PUTTING IT ALL TOGETHER: SUN TZU'S STRATEGIC CHECKLIST

1. What are your strategic objectives?
    - Use the outcome of Clausewitz's Trinity analysis to define strategic objectives

2. What is your Situational Awareness assessment? "Know your enemy and know yourself upfront of everything else" and "determine enemy's plans," so:
    - Use Sun Tzu's "Six Leadership Virtues" to bootstrap internal awareness.
    - Use Sun Tzu's "Nine Combat Grounds framework" to bootstrap external awareness.
    - Use the two previous framework results to develop Sun Tzu's Six "Factors Situational Awareness framework", thus complementing the cognizance of both internal and external factors.

3. Explore your possible tactics using Sun Tzu's "Ten Tactics framework."

4. Use Sun Tzu's "Strategy framework" to prepare a possible sequence of tactics, or the first strategic route map.
    - Then, use its "Dynamic Engagement checklist" to verify the dynamics of the proposed sequence of tactical moves.
    - Revise the sequence of tactics if needed.

5. Use Foch's Economy of Forces framework to assess tactics:
    - Confirm that each tactical move does not weaken our strategic position.
    - Verify that each tactical move weakens our adversary in at least one of Foch's principles.
    - Evaluate the complete set of tactical moves according to the Economy of Forces.

6. Perform a tactical health check using Sun Tzu's "Tactical Health Check framework."
    - use the Five Command Losing Factors.
    - and the Six Tactical Losing Conditions.

7. Engage in Battle.

8. After victory, deploy Machiavel's *Virtù* and Value Capturing Chords covered in Part III.

TWENTY-FOUR
AFTERTHOUGHT

Clausewitz helps to examine the global competitive environment, and Sun Tzu provides a unique approach to prepare for battle, focusing on the tactical details that win wars. In this Part, we proposed an actionable a streamlined version of Sun Tzu's ideas to be easily actionable with a set of frameworks to methodize strategic thinking on top of profound intelligence while inspiring agile tactical solutions to win. If there is a possible victory, we will have it. If there is none, we will spare our resources and choose the right battles later on.

What then? How to better exploit victory?

We felt the need to apply the teachings of Machiavelli as an expert on the matter. In his book *The Prince*, Machiavelli delves into the delicate balance between all stakeholders sharing the same strategic space, or ground, as Sun Tzu defines.

PART III
CAPITALIZING ON MACHIAVELLI'S *VIRTÙ*

Everybody wants to win, but victory should not be an end in itself. History can be enlightening! Napoleon learned the hard way that Moscow's conquest only contributed to his resounding final defeat. So, what should be the meaning of victory?

Vegetius[345] defended the preparation of war to attain peace. As did Machiavelli, referring that a leader should work "even harder in times of peace than in wartime."[346]

Still, making the best use of the advantage granted by losers' capitulation is an entirely different challenge from the fight that led to victory in the first place, a challenge underneath any conquest's benefits. A prince "won't idle away in times of peace."[347]

Avoiding aggression indeed is alluring, although clearly just part of the challenge because peace, as Sir Michael Howard so

---

345 Publius Flavius Vegetius Renatus, Concerning Military Matters, Epithoma Rei Militaris. Utrecht, 1473
346 Niccoló Machiavelli, The Prince, Early Modern Texts, Jonathan Bennet, 2017 https://www.earlymoderntexts.com/assets/pdfs/machiavelli1532part1.pdf, page 32
347 Machiavelli, *The Prince*, 2017, page 32

well remarks, "is certainly a far more complex affair than war."[348] Howard was an English military historian and a leading interpreter of Clausewitz's writings. The truth is that, nowadays, most go to war while yearning for peace. Howard brilliantly quotes the nineteenth-century jurist Henry Maine at the beginning of his book:

> *War appears to be as old as mankind, but peace is a modern invention.*[349]

Yes, we all want to profit from peace. Still, what is peace, really? Is it a state of affairs where nothing negative happens, like paradise?

According to William Lind, one of the first proponents of the Fourth Generation Warfare theory,[350] since the Cold War, we have been living in a permanent state of conflict involving all society's living forces, including information and economic warfare on top of the more conventional military forces lineup. Two centuries ago, Clausewitz enlightened the blurring lines between war and politics, which have become a straightforward common practice since then. What is new now is the enduring significance of conflict where civilians have become combatants by nature, meaning all of us. In the new world order, even knowledge, know-how, and intellectual property are now part of the lot and have become critical success factors for all stakeholders, from state-level affairs and instrumental corporations to the smallest actors

---

348 Sir Michael Howard, *The Invention of Peace and the Reinvention of War: Reflections on War and International Order*, Profile Books Ltd, 2nd ed., 2002
349 Michael Howard, The Invention of Peace and the Reinvention of War, (London, Profile Books Ltd, 2002)
350 William S Lind, Keith Nightengale, John F. Schmitt, Joseph W. Sutton and Gary I. Wilson., "The Changing Face of War: Into the Fourth Generation", Marine Corps Gazette, 1989,

in any economy. Thus, it's only prudent to assume the continuing growth of today's environmental complexity, both for geopolitics and economic warfare. Only monopolists may live a false sense of peacefulness because, even without palpable competitors, monopolists will remain preferred targets of state-level strategic moves, not only with consumer surplus in sight. The 4th Generation Warfare promises to maintain a constant and enduring pressure, as proven by Europe's lawsuits against the United States' Big Techs[351] and Chinese unrest against its own.[352]

Victory precedes profitability, and it's only natural to expect milking the cash cows while maintaining marginal costs as low as possible. However, we still should expect to deal with conflict while securing victory and intending to escalate any confrontation. Like the Cash Cow after the Star,[353] we can conceive it as exploitation after exploration. Managing victory requires an entirely different leadership attitude that impacts the management model and all stakeholders' relationships. Who better than Niccolò Machiavelli to inspire our endeavor?!

The Prince is a treasure of teachings in the art of attaining leadership virtue, or *Virtù*, with one and only one thing in mind: that of securing power after victory. The maintenance of state. We propose applying the concept with an enlarged scope, not only to the leader itself but also to any stakeholder leading through influence, that is, to organizations.

Enter Machiavelli's mind.

---

351 Big Fines and Strict Rules Unveiled Against 'Big Tech' in Europe, Adam Satariano, New York Times, 15 December 2020
352 China orders Alibaba founder Jack Ma to pare down fintech empire, Rupert Neate, The Guardian, 28 December 2020
353 Bruce Henderson, Henderson on Corporate Strategy, (Harper Collins, 1979)

According to the master, destroying the opponent's forces or occupying the ground is not enough. Winning the population's minds is imperative to create the best conditions to exploit the triumph and avoid further aggressions, because "however you look at it, military occupation is as useless as colonization is useful."[354] Besides, "it costs more to have an armed garrison than to have colonies."[355]

That is what Machiavelli's virtue is all about. Still, there is more in *The Prince* than what meets the eye at first glance. More than leadership and virtue by nature, Machiavelli yearns for the best conditions to achieve conquests' stability, which depends on many factors grasped by the tool we propose in the current Part.

The more secure our triumph, the easier it will be to capitalize on its gains. Security and stability also entail less consumption of resources and fewer concerns all over. Thus, we should look for ways to sustain the victories achieved, occupying the land in the most effective way possible, referred to by Machiavelli as colonization. For companies, that means maximizing gains (both tangible and intangible) because capturing value will always be a significant ambition and ultimate goal.

Consequently, after duly considering *Virtù*, we focus its impact on relations between all people involved, which are at the center of gravity of Machiavelli's acumen. In the end, if we gather the favors of everybody involved, we will be granted for good. Everybody meaning the consumers, customers, and clients, but also the opponents, the partners and the allies. We are talking about the increasing intensity of social relations among all these categories of people, growing due to the increasingly present

---
354 Machiavelli, *The Prince*, 2017, page 5
355 Machiavelli, *The Prince*, 2017, page 5

impact of social networks mixed with the media in a ubiquitous communication environment and pushed today by mobile communications. We consider people to govern everything, including nations, states, companies, regulation, justice, and so on, therefore, conscious that, in the end, the human factor is the crux of everything.

Consequently, there is an urgent need to find solutions for strategic stability and sustainability, always considering people to be the essential element, and that the real victory is the conquest of all those hearts. Managing the stability and sustainability of accomplishments through the human element is the art upon which business profitability depends. That is precisely what we learn from Machiavelli's masterpiece to identify the conditions for occupying the economic space to maximize business profitability. Besides, because Machiavelli gives extreme importance to leaders' behavior, we will also check organization's demeanor according to the dimensions mentioned by this inescapable author and part of the tool conceived to assess and manage wishes of both friend and foe, because, in Machiavelli's words, "the means will always be considered honorable, and he will be praised by everybody."[356] Some call it manipulation.

---

356 Machiavelli, *The Prince*, 2017, page 38

TWENTY-FIVE
VIRTÙ – THE SIX PRINCE'S QUALITIES

Virtù is the cornerstone of Machiavelli's leadership.[357] However, like most substantial and exciting concepts, Machiavelli's *Virtù* is surprisingly different from the commonly accepted meaning disclosed by the word *virtue*, hence using Machiavelli's Italian word *Virtù* to mark the difference because Machiavelli professes that "a prince must learn how to act immorally."[358] Therefore, *Virtù* is everything but acting virtuously and may include immorality if needed. Although not advising misconduct or wrongdoing, mastering *Virtù*'s details is imperative to inherit in full the master's lessons. Moreover, *Virtù* will be the pillar for capitalizing on victory, which is the purpose of this Part and discussed in the next chapter, proposing a tool to wrap up the strategic approach.

Machiavelli acknowledges that leading in war is inherently different when compared to peacetime governance. In the previous Part, we relied on Sun Tzu's leadership teachings to wage war.

---
357 Machiavelli, *The Prince*, 2017, page 13
358 Machiavelli, *The Prince*, 2017, page 33

Having attained victory, we now turn to Machiavelli's guidance for capitalizing during peace.

The duplicity of Machiavelli's *Virtù* concept should not come as strange because the master was everything but naïve. The pejorative definition of *Machiavellian* indeed did not happen by chance.

Thus, it's only reasonable to find *Virtù* encompassing opposite connotations within its substantial meaning. In this regard, Machiavelli never wrote about *the ends justifying the means*, although a couple of passages assume it.[359] Will "any means" be honorable? How can wrongdoing be considered full of virtue, with the pretext of being required to acquire power? Well, they do not. And yet, immortality part of *Virtù*, hence proving the above-referred antagonist connotations incorporated in this concept.

Moreover, Machiavelli goes as further as mentioning *Virtù*'s illusory display about its innate qualities,[360] which would be questionable for righteous conduct, to say the least.

The only thing that comes to mind is "wow." When weighing means versus ends, the latter seems to triumph after all, and Machiavelli somehow justifies it by considering ordinary people entirely unworthy.[361] They are the rightful recipient of a leader's deeds.

Machiavelli's view on ordinary people thus seems to erode the negative aspects of *Virtù*. Keeping everybody captivated is the crux of Machiavelli's leadership lessons.[362]

---

359 Machiavelli, *The Prince*, 2017, page 38
360 Machiavelli, *The Prince*, 2017, page 37
361 Machiavelli, *The Prince*, 2017, page38 and page 36
362 Machiavelli, *The Prince*, 2017, page 40

In a nutshell, considering his people and his contenders' nature, the leader should continuously act to win their hearts, whatever it takes. Literally. Moreover, the leader should avoid hate at all costs.[363] Machiavelli dedicates the whole nineteenth chapter to this subject and explains why avoiding hate is a good foundation to lead.[364]

In chapter 15 of *The Prince*, Machiavelli enumerates eleven qualities, not always moral, that a leader must follow to keep his power. A leader's deeds should abide by these qualities, according to necessity. Therefore, the rest of this chapter discusses these qualities to propose a six-dimension tool to assess leadership for two distinct types of entities: individuals and organizations; the same with subjects, thus widening this cause-effect relationship exercise into a two-by-two matrix appraisal.

The organization influences people, being it inside or outside its boundaries, and organizations can take many forms. We will be particularly interested in the relationship between for-profit companies and external individuals, which will be under the spotlight because that is the crux of value capture. However, relationships with other companies are also relevant, either with competitors, partners, or different rapports.

On the other hand, people's relationships are inherent to Machiavelli's acumen, for example, that of the individual leader influencing everybody else. We can also find inspiration for persuading companies as well as individuals, although this will be out of the scope for the current analysis.

---

[363] Machiavelli, *The Prince*, 2017, page 46
[364] Machiavelli, *The Prince*, 2017, page 40

Quality #1: Free-spending and generous

Machiavelli devotes the entire sixteenth chapter to discuss the advantages and risks of both open-handiness and generosity. He considers both dimensions separately, although it's simpler for us to combine them both, for they are two faces of the same coin.

Perceiving free-spending and generosity benefits is merely common sense. The idea is to choose a course of action inspiring acknowledgment, recognition, gratitude, and even admiration. It seems easy, right? Not so fast. Machiavelli devotes a good part of the same chapter to its perils.[365]

Moreover, and even worse than the innate growing scarcity of this quality's actions, at the end of the chapter, Machiavelli concludes that miserliness is preferred because it brings criticism without hatred, whereas open-handedness brings criticism and hatred.[366] Thus, it seems that generosity can have precisely the opposite effect when misused and cause hatred instead of love. Actions of generosity should then be bestowed with care, always with scarcity in mind. Assuming that abundance is the opposite of value, all spending and generous deeds should consider more than the depletion of resources mentioned by Machiavelli. The decreasing importance of each additional action is also part of the whole. So, generosity is good, but these two characteristics have profound implications on its handling.

Additionally, there is a significant difference between tangible and intangible rewards. Whereas tangible resources are consumed, intangible ones are abundantly available at the source. Therefore, spending tangible resources entails immediately discerning the natural value of scarcity, money being the first

---
365 Machiavelli, *The Prince*, 2017, page 35
366 Machiavelli, *The Prince*, 2017, page 35

obvious example. On the contrary, intangible resources' valuation is inherently related to its visible scarcity, where only the act of spending counts.

Outcome #1 for Organizations

For organizations, this trait is straightforward. We can offer either tangible or intangible artifacts, like freemium for example. Creating value with zero-marginal cost knowledge has also been a preferred vehicle since the coming of the Web. More recently, cost value drivers have also matured in multiple formats, including price transparency and consumption-based pricing, for instance, and they can all be contemplated for inclusion when exerting this quality.

Outcome #1 for Individuals

With the individual in mind, intangible resources make more sense when striving for this quality. The sky is the limit here, although with ethical considerations upfront. It's not because Machiavelli may advise immorality that we are getting rid of our values and beliefs, even if it entails the sure cost of failure. Intangible resources here are communication, content, and actions adding value to recipients. Long story short, the bedrock of manipulation, hence the ethical concerns.

Quality #2: Merciful

Machiavelli devotes the entire seventeenth chapter to discuss cruelty, setting its tone asking if "it better to be loved than feared or better to be feared than loved."[367]

---

367   Machiavelli, The Prince, 2017, page 36

And why cruelty? Because it's the opposite of merciful, meaning that mercy is the same as the absence of evilness in a heartless and atrocious environment. And is cruelty deserved in the first place? How effective is it for *Virtù*?

As we've said, Machiavelli holds ordinary people in low regard,[368] meaning that, for Machiavelli, ordinary people's loyalty is a direct consequence of fulfilling their wants and needs, hence the necessary generosity discussed in the previous dimension. Still, generosity can come in many forms, and mercifulness may indeed lay the foundations for love.[369]

Generally, people cannot be trusted unequivocally, and, even if it's not the case, assuming distrust does not hurt anyway.[370] So, we cannot assume trust to be secure, and that is where the cruelty-merciful tension comes along. Fear is more substantial and should be unleashed.[371]

Nevertheless, cruelty alone works best on the battlefield, not in peacetime. Thus, mercifulness should happen in a fearful background, without provoking hate. Otherwise, love will vanish. People's minds are essential, and that is the way to go.

Outcome #2 for Organizations

Within organizations, even silence can be taken as a punishment. Fearful environments are naturally prone to what we might call a mercy ploy, and that is how brainwash is most effective. Brainwash recalls the ultimate effect of manipulation, which is the seeming cornerstone of *Virtù*.

---

368 Machiavelli, The Prince, 2017, page 36 and page 38
369 Machiavelli, *The Prince*, 2017, page 35
370 Machiavelli, The Prince, 2017, page 36
371 Machiavelli, *The Prince*, 2017, page 26 and page 36

We are particularly interested in the relationship between the organization and people outside its boundaries. Not comfortable in this case because we are taking the negative side of this quality's coin, that is, cruelty to lay the ground for mercy. However, we have to, because without it, the customer, consumer or client, would have to stumble by chance on some disadvantageous positioning to see himself granted the pardon that will be perceived as mercy. Too complex. It's an emotional issue, and there are easy ways to get through:

- Sometimes, the external stakeholder feels trapped in a relationship with the organization, where project-level creeping commitments, servicing traps, or exit fees are most honorable examples. Even if these traps are interesting for capturing value, pardoning even a part will be understood as mercy and favor the quality at stake.
- Unexpectedly helping the external stakeholder also works. Personal or contextual knowledge can do wonders, especially in urgent situations. That has been a preferred use of AI and Big Data nowadays.

The previous reasoning can be extended to convenience, also with knowledge systems taking the stage, especially in the emergent online to off-line environment (O2O).

Outcome #2 for Individuals

For individuals, this trait is challenging to play with, but there is hope. The first evident attitude is to forgive in case of tension. To revenge is human and to forgive is divine, they say. However, we have to wait for that moment of pressure to appear. Or we may not. We can tension with, for example, the good-cop bad-cop approach. How Machiavellian is that? It's also an emotional issue again, and in the time of social networking, disinformation, counter-information, and useful-idiots, anything goes. Once again, ethics also comes to mind, for there should be a limit to our action's scope.

Quality #3: Word-keeping and socially chaste

The need for word-keeping is another well cherished Machiavelli's quality trait, for it's the last one he consecrates a whole chapter. Although, Machiavelli distinguishes two traits that we will consider in the same dimension, word-keeping[372] and chaste.[373]

Machiavelli does not explain the meaning of chaste in more detail. Our interpretation is the following. In Machiavelli's view, being chaste is seemingly the opposite of promiscuous, and we fathom it in the context of social relations. That is why both traits are treated here as forming a single dimension because no one can betray their circle of confidence while simultaneously keeping his word.

Maintaining one's word appears contradictory to *Virtù*, as the latter doesn't necessarily involve truthfulness but rather its semblance when it counts. However, a leader can justify "legitimate reasons for not keeping his promises."[374] So, Machiavelli advises saying whatever needs to be told, while never being caught

---

[372] Machiavelli, *The Prince*, 2017, page 33
[373] Machiavelli, *The Prince*, 2017, page 33
[374] Machiavelli, *The Prince*, 2017, page 37

with justified inconsistencies along the way. He uses a compelling allegory, that of the fox and the lion.[375]

For word-keeping, the leader "shouldn't keep his word when that could be used against him."[376] Besides, people often merit this by being egregiously unreliable and failing to keep their promises, thereby not warranting the adherence to word-keeping in the first place.[377]

And yet, we must keep our word, rather, we have to appear keeping it, and Machiavelli forges an ingenious solution. Instead of appearing to be word-keeping, the leader only has "to appear to be merciful, trustworthy, friendly, straightforward and believing,"[378] which is genuinely Machiavellian.

Like a fox devising the right path, it's all about communication and impressing for leadership as the lion. Besides, we already discussed Machiavellian mercy, which we can use to impress and discuss the last three qualities, friendliness, straightforward, and belief, just below.

For Machiavelli, word-keeping means communication for the leader's own advantage at all times while disregarding the coherency of rhetoric in time.

Outcome #3 of Organizations

Memory does not last forever. What is the recipient prepared to hear so we can get the most out of him? We should aspire to include all the five mentioned qualities in every communication act, and be impressive for the recipient's emotions. So much for

---

[375] Machiavelli, *The Prince*, 2017, page 37
[376] Machiavelli, *The Prince*, 2017, page 37
[377] Machiavelli, *The Prince*, 2017, page 38
[378] Machiavelli, *The Prince*, 2017, page 38

keeping one's word when what counts is the manipulative effect. But it is what it is, and these are Machiavelli's teachings. That should be true for all stakeholders, both internal and external, either individuals or organizations.

Outcome #3 for Individuals
For the individual, it's similar. And it works. It works so well that this is the basis of populism nowadays. Some leaders know how to seem right, even when not. It has been amazingly effective even in situations where lies are self-evident, although totally disregarded by the recipients because seeming right is so strong that it overcomes everything else. Although that is an extreme case, and it does not work with everybody because broadcasting only reaches people's typical idiosyncrasies. In one-to-one communication, content can be adapted, being able to go as far as hypnosis. Not that Machiavelli advocates it, but manipulation can also go this far. Or neurolinguistics, for that matter. Rinse every action with ethics.

Quality #4: Friendly
Friendliness is also a most significant quality for Machiavelli for its direct effect on positive emotions,[379] drawn from love, the crux of virtuous leadership.

After discussing mercifulness, benevolence entails a conspicuous relation with the act of communication. It's the opposite of arrogance.[380]

Being friendly provides a direct relationship with *Virtù*'s objective, "avoiding anything that will bring hatred or con-

---
379   Machiavelli, The Prince, 2017, page 4
380   Machiavelli, The Prince, 2017, page 33

tempt"[381] as a bedrock for being loved. Surprisingly, for Machiavelli, friendliness goes hand in hand with fear.[382] Still, being loved is a most effective way to secure power.[383]

Besides, Machiavelli provides a significant and surprising clue regarding friendliness: men should be "either well-treated ·so that they won't want revenge· or utterly crushed so that they won't be capable of it."[384]

Yes, it's all about communication when exercising power. Subjects should perceive positive communication, at all costs.

Outcome #4 for Organizations

For organizations, being friendly is, for instance, conveying bad news with a smile and making people happy. What can organizations do to earn it? People react to change and abide by habit. Meaning that if offerings become a habit, the expectation of reward jeopardizes its surprise, thus erasing meaningfulness. Quite the opposite, in this case it's the lack of expected reward that may serve as punishment. Therefore, we can find a solution amid irregularity and astonishment. For example, getting a merited flight upgrade is good, but getting unexpectedly upgraded can be a reason for ecstasy.

Outcome #4 for Individuals

For individuals, communication is key in all regards, especially when bad news comes around. On the other hand, because human relationships are like flowers, needing regular watering

---

381 Machiavelli, *The Prince*, 2017, page 39
382 Machiavelli, *The Prince*, 2017, page 36
383 Machiavelli, *The Prince*, 2017, page 21
384 Machiavelli, *The Prince*, 2017, page 5

to strive. The leader should assess the content and the frequency of communication, for there are times where even silence can be deafening.

Quality #5: Decision-making: brave, straightforward, firm, and grave

In the nineteenth chapter, Machiavelli discusses comprehensively the meaning of brave,[385] straightforward,[386] firm,[387] and grave,[388] for they all are sides of the same coin, and that is why we include all in the same dimension. When discussing word-keeping, Machiavelli relies also on these traits to impress for love and admiration.

Besides, "a prince will be held in contempt if he is regarded as variable, frivolous, effeminate and cowardly, irresolute."[389]

During the comprehensive discussion, Machiavelli extensively furnishes examples of the four traits, and all with the same conclusion, that is, each should contribute to love and avoid enmity. The mentioned discussion's comprehensiveness thus impelled the creation of a single dimension, and, in any case, the four traits depict decision making, not communication, because leaders "are judged by their results."[390]

These four qualities mean decision making because our actions also convey meaning, thus impressing any audience.

Starting with grave, the leader should only take care of serious matters, avoiding foolish actions of all sorts. Deeds should matter, be consequential, and be perceived as such. That is why

---

[385] Machiavelli, *The Prince*, 2017, page 33
[386] Machiavelli, *The Prince*, 2017, page 33
[387] Machiavelli, *The Prince*, 2017, page 33
[388] Machiavelli, *The Prince*, 2017, page 33
[389] Machiavelli, The Prince, 2017, page 40
[390] Machiavelli, The Prince, 2017, page 38

decisions should also be at the same time straightforward, firm, and audacious, or at least pretend to be.

Outcome #5 for Organizations

The current dimension adds to friendly communication. It is not only a question of communicating with a smile but the decisions at stake and how they are perceived by the stakeholders, either internal or external.

The challenge in this dimension is beyond decision-making itself, but how to assess the perception of its recipients because the leader seeks the emotional impact. Friendship and admiration may also emerge, even trust. On top of it, with the right communication, the productive feeling may be enhanced by sharing the customer's pride. For the latter, social networks have been handled just fine. Other situations may emerge, as long as they impact receipt's emotions positively.

Outcome #5 for Individuals

Each individual involved in decision-making should carefully evaluate how these decisions are understood by different types of recipients because he way a decision is perceived and understood can significantly influence the emotional response it elicits. In a nutshell, the leader should craft *Virtù* through decisions' emotional repercussions.

Quality #6: Believing

Machiavelli religiously refers to this trait.[391] Remember that, for Machiavelli, it's not a question if the leader believes or not, but weather if communication's recipients perceive it as such.

---

391 Machiavelli, The Prince, 2017, page 33

So, referring to belief, or being devout, Machiavelli argues that "nothing matters more."[392]

The appearance of believing is decisive here, and that is what causes the intended and manipulative emotional response, a last quality to enhance *Virtù* heart-rending ambition.

The recipient must sense belief in whatever course of action is at stake. Moreover, if we get the chance of infecting recipients with belief firsthand, it may spread by itself. That has been the most effective way of spreading disinformation through social networks, where fooled believers become useful idiots, pushing it around in their circle of influence. On average, disinformation is actually easier to spread around than actual real facts because, when fabricating it, we can include whatever we want to inflame the intended emotional response. In contrast, common facts tend to be dull by nature. Yes, for Machiavelli, even disinformation may serve our purposes if need be.

Therefore, the appearance of believing is just the start. In some cases, building belief in our recipients better serves our objectives. In that case, we must discover what works to create network effects and ensure that value creation follows the audience's growth, which may entail designing the communication's apparatus to prescribe comprehension. That is why social network Big Techs have been so successful and impactful at the same time, keeping in mind that influence can be micromanaged towards each recipient and each particular context.

The power of belief thus reveals itself. No wonder why Machiavelli argued that "nothing mattered more."

---

[392] Machiavelli, The Prince, 2017, page 28

Outcome #6 for Organizations

Do decisions and communication nurture belief? This question applies to all recipients, both internal and external. Communication and content are at play to achieve the desired emotional result for conquering everybody's hearts. Any means are possible to influence everybody, individually and as an audience. In some cases, we can go as far as prescribing the communication environment if we have the means to do it.

Outcome #6 for Individuals

For individuals, it's precisely the same as for organizations. The difference lies in the means at our disposal. Can we infect our recipient or audience with the reasonable belief entailing the favorable emotional response towards appreciation, admiration, and devotion? Can we influence the communication apparatus of our recipients with the same objective in mind?

Machiavelli's *Virtù* is the basis of leadership and encompasses eleven qualities. The leader with *Virtù* will comprehensively abide by every quality, practicing each according to his strategic aspirations. This practice entails appearing to possess these qualities while generating the intended emotional responses by its recipients, both for organizations and individuals. The tool sketch in Annex I summarizes *Virtù*'s qualities and can be used for assessing leadership during peacetime.

TWENTY-SIX
THE FOUR BUSINESS DIMENSIONS OF *VIRTÙ*

The Prince offers a leadership lesson of all sorts, namely on how to shepherd for securing power. Machiavelli focuses on different kinds of sovereignties, depending on how the leader acquired his dominance. Each type of state has its own political conditions for ruling, and Machiavelli carefully evaluates the balance of all forces and relationships for each category, that is, inherited or appropriated, the latter seized either by force or occupied by virtue, or mixed. A complete and encompassing scrutiny indeed.

Securing power entails relationships with ordinary people, the army, the nobles, the other states, and all kinds of individuals. Still, in all cases, winning everybody's hearts upfront is the crux of Machiavelli's approach and the lesson we want to draw. We will be interested in cultivating customer goodwill to increase profitability and less in other lessons related to leading our own forces.

Therefore, we explore Machiavelli's teachings, having the customer or consumer in mind, intending to win hearts and increase profitability through value capture. After the victory, we want to wring its leverage.

Why should hearts be won for profitability? If the customer only aims for a single supplier, the latter will tacitly become a monopolist, maximizing its returns by definition. Having the combat ground in people's head, aiming for their particular desires and aspirations, forge that monopoly in each individual's mind. Although, like all relationships, this one is also nuanced by an individual's variety and how distant each person perceives our competition. There is no black and white here, but only shades of grey. So, we fight for each individual's heart the mind, hence increasing returns by being monopolists in each person's perception. This advantage has been called switching cost and is the basis of Value Capturing Chords, the Machiavellian outcome of the current discussion, and a tool for capitalizing the strategy, wringing victory.

As we will see below, Value Capturing Chords mobilize switching costs to extract revenue by using Machiavelli's teachings. For reference, a switching cost is the value tacitly attributed by any entity when switching between suppliers. This value is the highest in the case of the monopolist. And because we live in a shady gray environment, different switching costs will exist for every entity, individual, or organization.

We will have the preference of individuals as long as we keep our price under the threshold of his switching cost, and that is why we try to push the latter as far as possible.

The higher this threshold, the more lucrative becomes our operation. And that is the practical way to capture value.

Switching costs result from the referred wants and desires, which impels scrutinizing Machiavelli's teachings to attain it, or leading with *Virtù*.

In *The Prince*, Machiavelli takes a deductive approach for explaining leadership, starting bottom-up from practical standpoints to establish leadership's theoretical realm. He intentionally divides his book into two parts. Opening with the Kinds of Principality, Machiavelli describes various states, illustrating power balances, guidance, and authoritarian deeds to capture the reader's attention while instilling the seeds of his arguments. *Virtù* is deduced in the second part of the book when covering Other Aspects of Political Power. Still, the deduction of *Virtù*'s theoretical qualities is also chaperoned with examples of ancient Roman, French, and Spanish leaders, to illustrate with practice and reach common sense. Machiavelli's down-to-earth insight is probably his greatest virtue.

Leadership and *Virtù* are the crux of Machiavelli's work, and we will be the bedrock for wringing victory. In the same way, Machiavelli discusses leadership as a means to reach strategic ends. We take the same path in this work. If the objective is to acquire people's sympathy, benignancy, even admiration, and love, what's in it for them? What should be igniting the right desires and emotions?

So, I reversely scrutinized Machiavelli's masterpiece, seeking for all mentioned instruments to attain people's gratitude of all sorts, focusing the particular scope of value capture. In other words, leading people's minds for maximizing profits. Emotions and greed, among others, are dimensions mentioned by Machiavelli. So, we interpret the meaning of deploying *Virtù*'s qualities for capturing value in the current business environment.

Businesses have been preaching customer-first for long, building on the strategic potential of people's rapport, and we only aspire to enhance it. Value capturing should be an enduring objective with profitability in mind, and for-profit organizations should thus include value capturing hooks in their tactics for any strategy whatsoever.

Besides, in the Internet era, Machiavelli's leader can establish one-to-one personalized relationships with all recipients, thus adapting *Virtù* qualities to each recipient's particular context, relying on real-time communication, georeferencing, and AI for ultra-focused targeting.

Machiavelli mentions emotions, convenience, social rewards, and greed. The following sections discuss each of these four dimensions in detail. Each *Virtù* dimension has a set of supporting factors or features, and each one represents a tactical opportunity for companies. Using them all simultaneously indeed is out of the question. Like a piano, we will play a melody that should evolve according to the particular needs of each individual in time.

The strategy should set the scope of tactical possibilities, and our job is to find the best set of factors, or chords, matching the corresponding revenue streams. We will call it Value Capturing Chords, and it's the crux of the next chapter below.

Dimension #1 - Emotions

Seeking an emotional response from individuals is probably the most critical dimension addressed by Machiavelli. *Customer inti-*

macy has been here for decades. Even if the marketing discipline has achieved enormous advances throughout the years, there are still lessons to be drawn from Machiavelli's five centuries-old work.

Machiavelli addresses emotions when referring to friendship, along with the four decision-making qualities of brave, straightforward, firm, and grave. So, we have the more superficial communication facet for igniting emotions together with the more enduring decision-making one, affecting the recipient's life even if just as an observer.

Emotions can be addictive when dopamine is involved, the neurochemical for pleasure. Entertainment, gamification (the application of game elements to other types of activities, like marketing and sales), and humor, extensively rely on emotional responses involving the infamous molecule. Machiavelli mentions entertainment at the end of the twenty-first chapter.

Let's address the supporting factors for emotional response and infer the questions (Q) we can ask for deriving each one.

On top of the list comes **trust**. Machiavelli mentions trust and distrust multiple times when discussing *Virtù* qualities. Trust is fascinating because it can still be decisive even if taken for granted. Once again, trust is not black and white because individuals will tend to choose the entity they trust most, even if they do not entirely trust any of them. The recipient's benefit comes from the value accredited by individuals or organizations to the increased risk of switching to a less reliable option.

- Q1: How can trust flourish?

In the business world, a **brand** is an expression of trust. Brand awareness throughout the years, together with experience, creates an expectation towards the next consumption circumstance. That is precisely what trust is all about, dealing with expectations and the same with a brand. Like trust, the brand can also be taken for granted, still providing the comfort and the safeness of predictability. Therefore, as with trust, the brand's value is found in the perils associated with choosing an unknown or lesser brand. Our challenge is to measure this peril, for this value is different for every individual, as for organizations, because it's the source of our value, as discussed in the next chapter.

- Q2: How can the brand flourish?

Consumers can use a brand for **show-off**, and that, too, produces a significant positive sentiment. It can even be an aspiration. Show-off induces powerful emotions in individuals and deserves special attention. First, showing-off involves the individual to be the source of communication during interaction and not just a recipient. We are interested in the one-to-one interaction here; we discuss social show-off towards an audience in the next *Virtù* qualities dimension. Showing-off goes hand in hand with pride. It's a matter of ego in the end. How Machiavellian is ego polishing? Therefore, we can include in our tactics the capability of knowing how to polish egos to foster pride, and which emotions are valued by individuals. Should they switch to another supplier, we will lose all our leverage.

- Q3: Can we let the individual show off with pride?

Although challenging to address, the **family** drives some of the strongest emotions because it involves entering the individual's sphere. Nevertheless, it's powerful and should be contemplated. The idea is relatively simple. Making an individual's family happy will also make him happy. For some businesses, accessing an individual's family members will be easier than for others, and this tool may be used jointly with other tools, like vouchers or targeted discounts. If the individual values good family emotions, there will be a threshold to be exploited. It will be jeopardized when switching to another supplier without the knowledge or capability to generate the same offerings. We can exploit these emotions.

- Q4: Can the consumer's family be rewarded?

Friendship is essential, and Machiavelli dedicates a whole chapter to it. Unlike family emotions, we can nurture friendship directly, treating the individual as a friend. Still, like with family's feelings, making some individual's friends happy will also make him happy, as long as there is social interaction surrounding that deed. Because this facet is social, we leave its discussion to the next *Virtù*'s qualities dimension. Although, the friendship rapport with an individual, even one-to-one, does wonders for emotional response. Switching to another supplier will be out of the question as long as the savings are smaller than the implicit value attributed to the friendship at stake, the addictive positive emotion we can exploit. Friendship emotions entail bonding and a sense of belonging, and involve oxytocin, a neurochemical not weaker than dopamine. Why not forging both? Once again, how Machiavellian is that?

- Q5: Can friendship be nurtured?

For some individuals, **self-dignity and altruism** can also do wonders. For example, people fighting for the environment are changing their deeds because of it, and not only for show-off, but because of self-dignity. We may help to get it done, and that is a benefit with positive emotions. In the current facet, the emotion happens in the face of the one-to-one relationship, and it may even become a habit. An approach that offers this kind of benefit in a non-linear manner will get the most out of the created value. Non-linear as in airlines' miles, i.e., the more you consume, the greater your earnings. And that is the value we can get out of it, maybe slim, but it's what it's. If the individual aims are switching to another supplier, and even if the new supplier copies the method, the newcomer will have to start from scratch.

The particular case of dignity towards others is a social factor covered in the next *Virtù* business dimension.

- Q6: How can altruism and self-dignity be nurtured?
- Q7: How to foster excellence?

Finally, some of the facets covered in this dimension also entail a social angle. Socially induced emotions are compelling and merit a dimension on their own, which is next covered.

Dimension #2 - Social rewards

Social rewards induce an emotional response and can be substantial, depending on cultural and individual characteristics. Socializing means bonding. Even in more individualistic countries like the United States,[393] social rewards have been doing wonders in influencing people, not always with the best intentions.

Avoiding contempt and hatred is central in Machiavelli's teachings, and friendship is beneficial if exercised at the social level. All the *Virtù* qualities have that much in common. For Machiavelli, influencing is everything, and anything goes. Friendship, mercifulness, trustworthiness, and generosity, all point out in the same direction, and Machiavelli activates whatever means were available at the time, either communicating, making decisions, or organizing social events. Today we have social networking and platforms cultivating social interaction and corresponding emotions all over in an inescapable trend. Super Apps in the East have been particularly prominent in this regard and may even constitute an example to follow in the West. In any case, social networking is here to stay, and we should take advantage of it.

Social networking is all about network effects, and these are not easy to bootstrap. Although, once in motion, they can be easier to nurture because individuals are also active participants. Their stamina brings inertia to keep the wheel spinning and fuels the network. That is why effects are amplified with social magnitude, for good and the bad. We want to wring the value created by social emotions in a Machiavellian way.

---

393 According to the Gert Hofstede classification in the already referred five-dimensional model.

The first reward in social networking is **visibility** in the face of an audience. It's more broadcast than anything else because visibility does not entail actual interaction with the other recipients. Yet, it can have a lot of value and produce an interesting emotional response. Moreover, visibility can vary depending on the interpretation of happenings on the target's side. The idea is to go from visibility to **prestige** and, once again, exploit this value somehow. It's a switching cost an individual should want to endure to benefit from the social emotions. It's Machiavellian indeed.

- Q8: Is there a social stage to offer?

- Q9: Can prestige be nourished?

- Q10: Can accomplishments or behavior be nurtured for admiration?

Still, social networking is most useful for many-to-many interactions between individuals in a **community**. That has been its development rationale in the first place, back when the Internet had no Web.[394] The many-to-many communication feature has been doing wonders worldwide and using it for advantage is of utmost importance. The emotional impact can be immense, seeing the relationship's bedrock where interactions take place. But there is a catch. Despite the direct interplay between individuals, social networking coverage is still key, i.e., the more recipients, the better. Still, this is only true if the value each node's worth with the community's size, which is not always the case. So, we should

---
394 We are referring to the Usenet Newsgroups early 80's. For the record, the Web appeared in 1994 and the Internet in 1969.

manage the community with the ascending value of networking effects in mind and rely on viral approaches to enlarge its scope. In proportion to communities' magnitude, we want to foster benefit for everyone, for Machiavellian exploitation.

- Q11: Can social networking be nurtured with content?

- Q12: How do we nurture socialization and entertainment with courtesy and respect?

- Q13: Is the community's value increasing with size?

One thing is to participate in **social networking** through simple consumption or convey arbitrary content, and another is to contribute to the network. Since the beginning of social networking around four decades ago, **crowdsourcing** has been a significant contributor to value, relationships, and visibility. With crowdsourcing, ideas, problem-solving, and recognition, among other possibilities, touch others with fulfilling reward, full of emotions on both sides. All these emotions exploitable for profit.

- Q14: Can the recipient gain visibility provided by social networking communication and content, including crowdsourcing?

Another decisive and particularly Machiavellian factor is **shame**. Even if this is not a social reward, shame happens in a social environment and can be exploited. The idea is to create conditions for individuals to feel ashamed when switching to another organization. Remorse of scandal is emotionally intense. These might not be easy to instill, although powerful if settled. Once again, we can exploit this switching cost for value capturing.

- Q15: Will the user feel ashamed when electing another organization?

Dimension #3 - Convenience

Convenience is huge for being the bedrock of all living entities, a strong judgment justified with an inescapable law of the universe, that is, the least action principle. Everybody is "lazy" by nature because energy has to be spared for important or strategic matters, like surviving or creating. Even our brain is wired for energy-saving by adopting routines for more automatic, less conscious, and less energy-consuming activities.[395] Routines are so effective and permit playing the piano with no effort at all, with consciousness elsewhere, for example, having a conversation simultaneously. Who hasn't experienced, while driving, to arrive at the usual but wrong destination because a phone call dominated consciousness? Therefore, it's only natural to find all recipients, either individuals or organizations, prone to make their lives easier in all respects. Convenience is compelling.

Machiavelli addresses mercy, which is a kind of compassion for anything disturbing. The more disturbing the better, because of its emotional nature. Thus, convenience is a kind of mercy. Better yet, if people feel discomfort for opting for anyone else, they will tend to avoid it, and the value attributed to convenience

---
[395] Herbert Simon's bounded rationality.

is that of the discomfort they will be escaping. That is the power of mercy in action, and we are going to exploit it for profit in a Machiavellian way.

Regarding convenience features:

Avoiding search costs is probably the most common facet of convenience, and search costs are quite encompassing. First, the individual must know what to look for, which is not always easy. Most products are a bundle of features, sometimes with intangible layers like service and knowledge included, and are difficult to compare. Occasionally, individuals search for intangible elements, challenging to externalize, thus incurring more significant hardship, sometimes even discomfort, depending on the need or urgency involved. To master this facet for profit, we need the knowledge and capability to help both individuals and organizations while conveying a sense of assistance. The value of this type of Machiavellian mercy lies in the effort any entity must endure to search with complete self-reliance. Its benefit can be significant for value capturing. Isn't that how google creates value and has become one of the wealthiest companies on earth in the first place?

- Q16: the offerings decrease search costs?

With the internet era, personalization has become more common than ever before. Without communication technology, engaging in a personal conversation with any individual was expensive. Before the internet, the only way to reach many relied on broadcast, and the latter is impossible to personalize. Today, the marginal cost of personalization using communication technologies is negligible, with Big Data Analytics and Artificial Intelligence commoditizing the personalized and contextual touch. Personalization creates clear convenience because individuals see their needs fulfilled even before getting aware of their existence in the first place. Isn't it wonderful? Its value can be measured by the effort and risk when an individual has to find a new supplier and proceed with the transaction elsewhere. Even beyond that, the individual can get the habit of good surprises. What if the new supplier is unable to match the offer for lacking the required embedded personalized knowledge? Even if the new supplier has the technology, he misses the tacit interaction sourcing the knowledge necessary for good personalization. So, the value to capture comes from the sense of lost personalization when the recipient considers switching to another supplier.

Moreover, personalization is usually employed with discounts, which is part of the greed dimension below, and for reasons discussed in the next chapter.

- Q17: How personalized are offerings and communication?

And then we arrive at **habit**, which is one of the most substantial facets of influence to our advantage. Habit is the very embodiment of human nature of the inescapable principle of least action. Its routines become a safe place to live in for everybody because a lot of energy is required to switch routines. For example, have you ever tried to drive on the other side of the road? You can do it, but with a lot of effort and constant consciousness, especially during turns and roundabouts. Eventually, in time, the new routines will settle. You can drive again somehow mechanically on the other side of the road, following a learning curve pattern specific to every individual associated with age. It's also not easy to unlearn already established routines, which is sometimes required to settle the new ones. We can also call this an implicit learning curve trap. It has a lot of value because individuals tend to direct their energy for rewarding or needed activities instead of jeopardizing it to install new and unnecessary routines. Habit's worth for revenue contribution comes from the individual's implicit cost to learn the new practice. It's the opposite of convenience and entails a subjective appraisal embedding the willingness to engage in learning activities. In a world full of opportunities, including entertainment, an opportunity cost again arises for the time and effort spent to learn anything more, instead of using it for more gratifying activities. So, there is more than the emotional response associated with the learning effort and the sense of losing the opportunity to follow one's wishes. In this regard, an individual's choice is always the most convenient or satisfying, which is our value capturing arena. In the end, habit is a kind of Machiavellian mercy.

- Q18: are individuals used to the product, service, or brand (habit)?

Addiction is a habit fed by need. It involves energy expenditure, both time and effort, for an immediate reward with an immediate positive emotional impression, that is, a pleasurable surge of the already referred dopamine neurotransmitter. Addiction highly boosts the habit's value magnitude, yearning for pleasure on top of it. And yet, there is a catch. Addiction must have a habit as its cornerstone for the established relationship because, if switching to another source involves no additional cost for individuals, capturing value becomes irrelevant. Without habit, individuals can source their needs elsewhere without switching costs, hence without margin for value capturing.

Consequently, the only addiction that counts here is dependency with bold habit. Is addiction Machiavellian enough?

- Q19: Can habit become addictive?

Convenience can also mean exclusively fulfilling one's needs, that is, offering a value proposition that no one can copy. It seems that information about everything is abundantly available in the post-web era, and any value proposition will become unveiled and copied on the spot. Still, that is not always the case, and Big Techs are here to prove it. There is a way out, and the answer lies, again, in network effects. On the supply side, that is.

We already discussed network effects above. Only this time, we target the marketplace's supply side. With platforms, an ecosystem of suppliers can offer an unsurmountable value proposition. A **marketplace** conveys a comprehensive and highly convenient offering by extraordinarily diminishing search costs for consumers. Moreover, the emotions associated with fulfilling an individual's needs also add value to capturing. The option to switch to another ecosystem will be measured by the loss of convenience compared to the savings when using it if that alternative ecosystem exists.

The answer is network effects. A marketplace built over a network effects bedrock will provide the uniqueness needed for monetization. The relationship with the individual is indirect because he chooses to use the marketplace in a kind of Machiavellian mercy.

- Q20: Can we offer a marketplace ecosystem?

We continue the path of network effects with another unusual and often disregarded option, that of the demand side, although hidden in this case: **contextual knowledge**. It's hidden because we can implicitly learn from consumers and help every individual with this newly acquired knowledge.

In the previous dimension, we discussed network effects on the demand side, dealing with relationships and emotions. Now, we want to explore network effects with hidden or implicit consequences on context. The idea is to use Big Data analytics again, and possibly AI, to offer convenience because the individual is joining the crowd, even without being aware of it. This form of explicit knowledge is an exclusive convenience, sourced by implicit network effects on the demand side. Implicit as in proprietary, which is crucial for exploiting its value. Knowledge includes everything we know about the market and the individual, thus being contextual on top of personalized.

Like GPS telemetry and IoT, emerging technologies are becoming increasingly integrated into everyday devices, starting with our mobile phones. These advancements are proving to be highly beneficial for many companies, with Big Tech leading the way. Can the value proposition be copied? Maybe it can, but without profitable success because of the non-linear property of network effects. **Context** is also a kind of Machiavellian mercy due to the enormous potential to save an individual's effort and add positive emotions, even surprise. Its value relies on convenience loss due to offerings embedding contextual knowledge.

- Q21: Is contextual knowledge part of the offering?

Service convenience, relying on renting to replace other types of transactions, including acquisition or licensing. Renting instead of buying is a kind of mercy, but what counts for this facet of convenience is the annoyance of switching elsewhere, with the risk and effort it may cause. If service convenience is cumulative for some reason, individuals or organizations may indeed feel trapped because the service must start from scratch, and previous investments will be discarded as sunk costs. It's like the case of projects when they cannot be stopped. The go decision, for the latter, acquires the name of creeping commitment.

- Q22: Can service convenience be included?

Here is a final word for discussing the ecosystem trap. **Industry standards** have been an ordinary and most compelling example, particularly when technology is involved. Standards enhance ease-of-use for consumers, but in some design ways, diminish choice for product designers. Not being a punishment on its own, trying to move out of an ecosystem can have many costs, even without network effects involved. Web3 will probably have this kind of impact on convenience, and wringing the ecosystem's positioning should become part of revenue-maximizing tactics.

- Q23: Are standards, regulations or laws, valuable?

Dimension #4 - Greed

Machiavelli unquestionably considers people as greedy. Ungrateful, fickle, deceptive, cowardly, and greedy, to be more precise. Greed means making choices that maximize monetary value in all regards.

> *As long as you are doing them good, they are entirely yours: they'll offer you their blood, their property, their lives, and their children,*[396]

The previous quote means fulfilling people's wishes, and greed serves just fine. Machiavelli exploits this greed and consecrates a whole chapter to free-spending and generosity. Services for free have become quite common since the internet era, which is the case, for example, of e-mails and entry-level services for most suppliers. It has been called freemium.

However, creating value with nothing in return is the opposite of wringing any strategic positioning and is undoubtedly not a hook for greed. The solution may come from managing expec-

---

[396] Machiavelli, The Prince, 2017, page 17

tations because prospects have an emotional impact, like awaited discounts. It's Machiavellian free-spending generosity in action to create exploitable emotional leverage.

Besides, Machiavellian mercy can also take place. If switching sources incur a cost increase for the individual, that same cost will be the implicit value of not switching at all, and we can capture it.

The idea is to apply Machiavelli's *Virtù* to set the stage for wringing the greed of individuals and organizations. The fourth *Virtù* dimension is greed and relates to generosity, mercy, and decision-making qualities. An interpretation of this dimension's facets follows:

Offering **discounts** is the first prominent facet of this dimension, but not any kind of deal. If all suppliers start competing on discounts, broadcasting offerings with no criteria will decrease profitability for everybody. **Discounts** have to be **non-linear**, thus inducing additional consumption through loyalty.

It's called the loyalty effect and has been extensively studied for more than two decades. Some think about it as a strategy, but it's not. The loyalty effect is a tactic for value capturing and is, at the same time, a price discovery technique, which we will discuss in more detail in the next chapter. So, yearning to amass funds, with loyalty effect's discounts, individuals will disburse even more, at least with us.

- Q24: Can we offer non-linear discounts?

Offering **cashback** is a natural evolution of discounts. Where discounts cash the advantage on new transactions, and vouchers have limited applicability by definition, cashback expands discount's value in the form of fiduciary money, which can be used according to each individual's wishes. All the previous reasoning about the loyalty effect also applies here. We gain an individual's preference based on his greed because the more the consumption, the more significant the cashback. With discounts, non-linearity is critical to avoid unwanted price wars.

- Q25: Is there an opportunity for non-linear cashback?

Other cost value schemes have been proposed on top of discounts and cashback, although not all are interesting. Even if cost value appeals to greed, we can only wring Machiavellian ones, that is, those inducing individuals' attachment. Thus, greed must create some switching cost when opting to another source with some sort of punishment, monetary in this case, thereby setting the stage for mercifulness for discarding malleolus switch intentions. Non-linear cost value schemes serve just fine. So, which has been proposed? Group-based vouchers are a good example. Grouping on the demand side increases bargaining power, decreasing buyers' prices, and inducing a network effect for the whole group that counts as a value because it always entails a switching cost.

Why? Because organizing the group for buying from a different supplier will call for managing and coordinating efforts for the various decisions required to make it happen. That is the value we should expect to capture. It's called **buyer aggregation**.

- Q26: Can we offer cost value, like buyer aggregation?

Another prominent greed facet is that of credit, which has long been a heavily exploited tactic. Credit involves emotions because individuals will be fulfilling their wishes immediately, which creates dopamine, the very neurochemical behind addiction. Credit has been quite adequate for gluing with individuals, for the easiness to personalize transactions. Even banks have been extensively investing in AI to finetune scoring. The financial industry has been on top of the loyalty-effect benefits since it was first discovered. So, credit involves forced loyalty, which can also generate value we can capture. The consequence is similar to non-linear discounts. It's Machiavellian generosity in action.

Still, credit can be relieved, and someone conceived **exit fees** to increase the forced liaison's leverage. It's called the exit trap and is Machiavellian mercifulness. Like in other merciful situations, the individual will not feel the fee's monetary punishment if not switching to another source. Fees do not apply solely to credit, but any other dimension or facet for that matter.

- Q27: Can an exit fee be naturally imposed?

Combining *Virtù* qualities

The four Machiavellian dimensions for applying *Virtù*, and capture value, aggregate Machiavelli's teachings, as seen from the recipient's perspective. Machiavelli talks about princes, which we interpret as leaders, dealing with people of all sorts to acquire and preserve power. All types, meaning ordinary people, nobles, and even contenders, like adversaries and enemies.

As already referred, Machiavelli has very low regard for human nature, and we do not pretend to filter anything from it. For Machiavelli, individuals are recipients of the leader's deeds, including communications and decisions. So, by building Machiavelli's harsh view on people, we reverse the path and collect the roots of the intended effect of his *Virtù* on the respective audience, hence the above-discussed dimensions. The facets of the four dimensions are yet another challenge to accommodate Machiavelli's instruments to the current business environment, which means that other aspects, coming from possibly innovative ways to undertake the market, may be added at will, as long as they abide both to Machiavelli's dimensions and provide means to capture value, entailing some kind of switching cost for individuals.

Moreover, following the piano keys allegory, we should devise the right and most practical combination of Machiavellian *Virtù* dimensions and their facets, like chords, for each business strategy. Besides, like melodies, these combinations evolve in time, and in the current business environment, they can also be personalized and contextualized for each individual. On these grounds, value capturing is highly granular and agile, following business strategy's nuances.

Let's overview an example. A personalized payment system can be a good illustration of the above combination of Machiavellian *Virtù* dimensions. First, payment instruments are convenient by nature and induce habit, also assembling network effects. Because loyalty schemes are personalized, they also fulfill Machiavellian greed. We can also associate brand and trust with loyalty, thus encompassing the Machiavellian emotional dimension as well. The challenge relies on measuring and capturing the value related to the Machiavellian consequence of all these facets, and we can find the answer on Value Capturing Chords, presented and discussed in the next chapter.

TWENTY-SEVEN
VALUE CAPTURING CHORDS

We now focus on how to capture the value of SunTzu's strategy, unleashing Machiavelli *Virtù*'s dimensions and its various facets. Value Capturing Chords (VCC) are *Virtù* deeds with revenue maximization in mind. We call them chords because they encompass an arbitrary set of elements we can play, like sets of piano keys, to formulate a melody for wringing strategic positioning out of buyer's pockets, thus maximizing revenue.

After discussing the ingredients of Machiavellian *Virtù* and the four dimensions reflected in the current business environment, we already know the tools for creating exploitable value in recipients' minds following the business strategy. We are also aware that these tactics are personalized, contextualized, and evolving in time, which is a challenge on its own. So, how can we measure the value created and proceed with the wringing strategy? The answer comes from price discrimination and price matching, following the switching costs created by Machiavelli's *Virtù*. Welcome to the beautiful world of Value Capturing Chords.

We discuss next each of the three ingredients and propose an actionable tool in the form of a framework.

Towards price discrimination

Price discrimination is mandatory because individuals diverge from each other, valuing different tangible and intangible attributes for any potential transaction. Less visible aspects like attentiveness about possible alternatives, or even willingness to explore substitutes, contribute to the implicit individual's valuation. A decision to buy only happens if the asked price falls below the referred encompassing valuation. There are two distinct possibilities for that choice, absolute and relative, depending on the market structure.

First, the transaction may happen with a monopolist supplier, or at least with the sense of having a single source available, a perception coming from sheer differentiation, or by a pressing and urgent need when there is no time to search or embrace alternatives. In this case, the ceiling for the individual's pricing is its absolute valuation. Is it worth paying for the gross benefit we aspire to acquire?

The existence of possible competitors is the other possible circumstance. In this case, the individual decides among the various offered options, and it all depends on how close they are from the buyer's point of view. In the extreme case of perfect competition, where the possibilities are commodities, all contenders are known, and all easily accessible, so the decision is a no-brainer. The individual will choose the cheapest option. Although that is hardly the case in the real world, maybe never. So, a comparison will take place to select the best choice, in a two-dimensional space, that of products versus sources. The product's dimension examines their similarity, fitting their features to the wants and needs underpinning the search and desire. Machiavellian emotional, social, convenience, and greed's dimensions are involved in the evaluation, and the choice will reflect the best compromise, maximizing the different possibilities against available funds.

The second dimension for choice occurs when more than one source measures all available suppliers' proximity. Proximity is the hardship for the individual to choose, that is, a nearer option. The more convenient alternative in Machiavelli's terms above will be cheaper in terms of effort for that individual. Meaning that, if nearer in the recipient's mind, we can capture more value. The value conquered threshold is exactly our relative distance regarding the nearest competitor in the individual's mind. In other words, the value we can capture equals the switching cost involved when opting to the next closest source.

Because we can only extract the value sensed by an individual at each moment in time, and that has proven to be particularly difficult, businesses have relied on discounts, vouchers, and yield management, among others. We want to address the reasoning related to these techniques and use it to wring value, ultimately giving place to Value Capturing Chords.

We assume that the price of a transaction encompasses the ensemble of all its tangible and intangible elements. The buyer is willing to proceed as long as the price is below the threshold of its valuation. Economists refer to the difference between both valuations as consumer surplus. So, we have two challenges. The first one is increasing exploitable value using Machiavellian *Virtù* dimensions. The second one is price discrimination and matching to find the exact value everyone is willing to pay at each moment in time. So, the tactics of value capturing involve (i) playing in Machiavelli's dimensions to gain maximum leverage, according to the strategy at large, (ii) followed by price discrimination and matching techniques to extract the most from each individual's pocket at each moment in time. That is why price discrimination is mandatory and should follow this two-step procedure. It's good yield management in action, and in the next subsection, we discuss how to price discriminate and match buyer willingness to pay. Combining both steps to define Value Capturing Chords will then end the chapter.

On price discrimination and price matching

Traditionally, there have been two forms of price discrimination.

Skimming

First-order price discrimination is performed in time, varying the price of an item towards an audience of buyers. Skimming, for example, starts high, selling to everybody willing to pay that exorbitant price. When sales begin to decrease because the buyer universe at that price level is getting exhausted, it's time to lower prices, thus matching it to the next and less opulent buyers. The procedure continues until the lowest level of willingness to pay is achieved. This way, we avoid cannibalizing those willing to pay more by not cutting prices before allowing them to buy it beforehand. Thus, skimming is price discriminates and matching at the same time because the individual is naturally unveiling his willingness to pay when making the buying decision. But there is a catch. What if the competitors start decreasing prices faster, thus jeopardizing the procedure and grabbing the market upfront? The solution is second-order price discrimination.

Versioning

Second-order price discrimination is also called versioning. In this scheme, we intentionally fabricate different product versions, attributing each one a distinct price. However, the layout of versions should impel the buyer to go for the higher priced ones. In the end, each buyer will choose the version that fits their pocket, once again, including all tangible and intangible elements of value composing the purchase. Not only this protects our offerings against competitor's cannibalization, but it also entails implicit price matching again.

Bundling

Moreover, there is another way to produce versions by bundling previously separated products of features. Bundling is attractive because it also generates additional demand on its own, for individuals not resisting a bargain (Machiavellian greed). It's beneficial when the bundling of marginal costs is negligible compared with the price of each particular bundled element. In this case, its marginal cost is tiny, with zero becoming quite common on the Web.

Other facets of price matching

The two price discrimination techniques, skimming and versioning, comprise price matching, which is excellent, although we can also explore other price-matching policies. Auctions, which have been gaining traction in e-business, are the first example.

Auctions can also be reversed, increasing the bargaining power of buyers when suppliers struggle to win the transaction. However, auctions best fit commodities, so all contenders become close to buyers and also to each other, hence drastically reducing value capturing. Therefore, auctions are not adequate to capture Machiavellian value and are best used, for example, to stock out goods when it makes sense.

Offering vouchers is another price-matching possibility and is useful when vouchers are hard to get. Hardship in getting vouchers measures a buyer's price sensitivity and willingness to economize.

Combining price discrimination and price matching has been called yield management. Today, with Big Data analytics, we have ways to deal effectively with the market. For example, Conjoint Analysis helps to define the offerings, and Choice-based Models also help in pricing. For personalization and vouchers, we have Cognitive Filtering. And there are others like Time Series Analysis.

Moreover, Big Data deals with unstructured data and can characterize an individual's nuances, as long as we can get data on their behavior and interactions. We should still deploy all these procedures with value capturing, price discrimination, and price matching in mind, or, in other words, playing Value Capturing Chords.

We next overview in detail options for revenue models combined with price discrimination and price matching, the ingredients for wringing Machiavellian value.

Revenue models (RM)

Price discrimination is only part of the story. First, we need revenue streams in place. What is the possible revenue model for our offerings? How is the buyer willing to pay? According to the revenue model, we will finetune price discrimination, together with price matching, to define everyone's right price at each moment in time.

We review next to the most common revenue models, including revenue streams and price discrimination options, which we will use to compose Value Capturing Chords below.

- RM1: **Licensing or rental** is the simplest revenue model. Not much to say, except that we can combine it with price discrimination, like versioning for price matching. Licensing has the advantage of linking well to Machiavellian habit.
- RM2: **Membership licensing** is similar to simple licensing and can be used to price-match, although with the added benefit of materializing demand-side network effects, thus involving a Machiavellian switching cost.
- RM3: In **Versioning**, we first conceive the best possible offering, which will be premium. Then, we degrade it intentionally to create other lower-priced versions. We may use Big Data analytics techniques, like Time Series Analysis, Conjoint Analysis, and Choice Models, to develop the versions and prices adapted to the market at stake. Versioning may be combined with other price matching approaches. Each version can be skimmed to

accommodate yield management or only using vouchers for more focused individualized price matching.

- RM4: **Versioning based bundling** - In this case, we apply the same versioning reasoning, although added with a personalized dimension bundling the significant components. We may use Big Data analytics like Cognitive Filtering to define individualized bundles, including recommendations.
- RM5: **Personalized pricing** - It works for each transaction. We may guess the right price, using Big Data analytics' choice models, for example.
- RM6: **Skimming** as time-based price discrimination - We can do it for any version (RM3) or aggregated offering with bundling (RM4). The period and life cycle will depend on the market and offering's characteristics. We may use Big Data analytics, like Time Series Analysis, to decide when to decrease pricing and how much. Choice Models may also help to sense the market.
- RM7: **Congestion pricing** - is the opposite of skimming because it works upwards instead of downwards, and its most notable example is that of Uber in peak hours. Congestion pricing exploits demand spikes with claims for regulating both supply and demand. Where regulating demand is straightforward, supply depends on its possible elasticity and only works when suppliers receive their share of value capturing. All things considered, congestion pricing is always a way to wring supply-demand unbalances.

- RM8: **Deadline or urgency** in time-based price discrimination - This one is pretty Machiavellian. Sensing urgency and lack of options bring the transaction closer to Monopoly, with all other options becoming more distant. It's entirely dependent on context, and we may take advantage to capture more value out of buyer's pockets. The revenue model should reflect an acceptable option for a pricing increase. For example, airlines use many different fares and simulate their availability or unavailability according to the market's patterns and evolution, following the balance of supply and demand. For airlines, fares are versions used for acceptably increasing prices. Another way to increase prices is to offer discounts upfront and stop when recipients can accommodate the target price.
- RM9: **Group-based pricing** are group discounts, also called buyer aggregation, when offering cost value. However, they are less attractive because this revenue model entails increasing buyer's bargaining power with negative natural impacts on value capture. However, group-based pricing also entails network effects on the demand side (consumer), which can be exploited to extract value by combining this revenue model with other price discriminating revenue models, like versioning or bundling, depending on the *Virtù*'s dimensions end features embarked in the offerings.
- RM10: **Broadcasted discounts** are not interesting because competitors can learn about their usage with

simple competitive intelligence techniques, leading to uninteresting price wars. This revenue model should only be used to annoy competitors or get rid of unwanted stocks. Still, we can also use it for Machiavellian open-handedness and generosity.

- RM11: **PWYW (Pay What You Want)** are discounts on steroids. The buyer literally pays according to his wishes. It's a price matching technique, only effective if the buyer is convinced to pay a fair amount for the transaction as an effect of Machiavellian *Virtù*. Still, most businesses relying on PWYW for payments have just failed. It's best used sporadically and in peculiar situations appealing to people's values, inner feelings, and beliefs. As a matter of fact, it's highly used by scammers, luring people towards some kind of investment, although false. It has been called the advance-fee scam, with the Nigerian scam letters being a most notorious example. Like many things in life, including love, Machiavellian *Virtù* also has a perverse side.
- RM12: **Personalized discounts** are exciting because they entail personalized price matching, thus grabbing the most out of each transaction, depending on the accumulated knowledge about the buyer and the market. Vouchers and loyalty schemes have been extensively used in revenue models, combined with other revenue models liver versioning or skimming.
- RM13: **Loyalty coupons** are a form of personalized discounts, although we consider them separately due to the network effects on the supply side for this revenue model. Whereas personalized discounts are

one-to-one, loyalty coupons can span complete business environments, like the Nectar card in the UK with an ecosystem of almost thirty companies.

- The particular case of crypto-tokens is worth mentioning here. Diving in the crypto world is to tackle strong ecosystems, meaning to foster network effects with all their switching cost potential, which is pretty Machiavellian. It can thus serve to support *Virtù* options for network effects and also serve as a price matching mechanism at the same time.
- RM14: **Auctions** are self-explanatory. On the one side, they work best with commodities, which is not interesting because it hinders value capturing intangible *Virtù*'s facets other than convenience. Still, if we can differentiate somehow, auctions can fulfill the price matching objective, but with a catch, because it depends on the targeted audience. With few recipients, it will generate much consumer surplus, which is not suitable for value capturing. Auctions are thus to be deployed with care.
- RM15: **Reverse auctions** are also self-explanatory and are even less attractive than auctions because they give the buyer too much bargaining power, hence reducing value capturing to the limit. The only escape is to strongly use Machiavelli's dimensions, although, in this case, the offering becomes differentiated and unsuitable for this revenue model. Request for Quotations is a kind of reverse auction. We should always try to stay away from reverse auctions as much as possible.

The list of fifteen revenue models, price discrimination, and price matching techniques above does not intend to be exhaustive. Still, it illustrates the most common ingredients for Value Capturing Chord pricing dimension.

Having covered both dimensions, we now proceed to explain how to layout Value Capturing Chords.

Playing melodies with Value Capturing Chords

Value Capturing Chords are the crux of the Machiavellian way to wring a winning strategy, attacking buyer's pockets. Yes, strategy creates value, with the value proposition laying the foundation for profitability. As already referred, creating value is not enough because revenue is part of the business intention, thus including revenue models in business models. Finetuning the value proposition, the revenue streams, and eve the revenue model business models is not enough because value capturing depends on the competition. For example, the same value proposition will generate more returns for a monopolist than for any contender in a market with string competition. So, Value Capturing Chords provide a practical way to include value capturing elements in business strategy, providing the complete revenue model solution for profit maximization.

A Value Capturing Chord plays simultaneous keys from the two above dimensions:

- Machiavellian *Virtú* facets to win hearts, we call switching costs, and
- revenue models with adapted price discrimination and matching alternatives.

The explanation is best understood with the framework in Appendix I.

1. The first column lists all Machiavelli *Virtù* facets at the left, inducing switching costs for non-monopoly environments or simpler emotional, social, convenience, and greed attachments for monopolistic relationships. Our first job is to select all facets that match the business model and deploy them with the corresponding revenue model. The twenty-six questions help to identify the possible Machiavellian *Virtù* dimensions and facets.
2. We proceed exactly in the same way with the other column, at the right, which should list all possible revenue models, this time with price matching and price discrimination techniques. With the business model in mind, we note all fitting revenue models in all their dimensions, including buyers.
3. The two lists should be revisited and added with any other less usual practice, both on getting consumers' or clients' attachment and other possible price-dealing factors or even innovative revenue models.
4. With the subsets of possible actionable elements for both VCC dimensions and retaking the business model, we select the combinations that do work. A combination is an arbitrary set of features coming from both dimensions. The minimal combination is that of a single *Virtù* facet and a revenue stream. The case of not paying consumers is considered an absent revenue stream because cost value is still being offered with

Machiavellian generosity, which is, for example, Google consumers' case for their serach engine.

We may add more facets for each actionable combination, that is, supplementary revenue models, price discrimination, and price matching.

The last step is defining the VCC melody as a sequence of chords for each segment of customers or consumers. A segment may include just one individual for utter personalization. There will probably be a major chord for the business' bedrock on each segment, which we can extend for certain campaigns. So, there is a melody for each segment, and the business will play them all simultaneously, which will be an exciting challenge. Fortunately, it's not difficult to have confidential conversations with all recipients in the current communication environment while making them feel unique with personalized offerings and discounts, that is, Machiavellian emotions and greed at work.

Even if Value Capturing Chords' alignment is ensured in the above-described methodology, we still must ensure that the business models follow the strategy, meaning that Value Capturing Chords also need strategic calibration, discussed in the next and subsection for defining the concept. The last section of this chapter discusses their importance in strategic sustainability.

Aligning Value Capturing Chords with Strategy

In the previous section, we aligned Clausewitz's Trinity with Sun Tzu's battleground strategy. We now proceed with aligning strategy with Machiavellian *Virtù* and Value Capturing Chords.

This is important because strategy goes both ways, conceived top-down and executed bottom-up. Therefore it's crucial to have a thorough understanding of what is possible on the battleground during strategic planning. This means we should complement Sun Tzu's tactics with a focus on value-capturing strategies.

After the higher-level Trinity analysis, we compose strategy with tactical moves, including *Virtù* dimensions. More than alignment, influence also goes both ways, which will be crucial to define the different VCC tracks per consumer segment and its melodies. Each VCC track is a sequence of deeds, just like Sun Tzu's strategy is a sequence of tactics. Mutual influence and alignment are thus mandatory.

Starting from the beginning, we ask the following question: where is Machiavelli's *Virtù* influencing Sun Tzu's strategy? The answer comes from examining situational awareness when exploring Sun Tzu's tactics and before defining any strategy. *Virtù* is a way to influence individuals to our advantage. It's a way to create switching costs when facing the competition and a way to win buyer's hearts when not.

Sun Tzu's tactics produce business models when attacking the market, including value propositions, one per segment. Value propositions are just the first inspiration for value capturing. They are necessary because we will capture a part of its value, so the more valuable the better. The rest is left as consumer surplus, either because we could not capture it or because the competition was close enough to reduce it in buyers' minds.

Because value capturing is accomplished with Machiavellian *Virtù*, and both consumers and clients positively deem its dimensions, we will include it in the value proposition, thus becoming an integral part of the business model. In this way, *Virtù* also becomes intrinsic to Sun Tzu's tactics.

How do we do it? We go through all *Virtù* features, one by one, and:

1. Measure its value creation potential.
2. Delineate the possible composition of elements fitting the business model, representing the first step for defining chords.
3. Design the first sequence of half-chords (VCC's *Virtù* part) to be the melody›s baseline, thus influencing Sun Tzu's strategic sequence of tactics.
4. Evaluate the results with Foch's Economy of Forces superior principle and use this rule of thumb to reinforce *Virtù*'s moves and help choose the best chord sequence again.

A notable property of *Virtù* is its impact on Foch's Economy of Forces. That is why *Virtù* dimensions and features must be part of the tactical roll-out, that is, strategy. Machiavellian *Virtù* involves communicating with the market, and there is a significant difference between broadcast, personalized interaction, and social networking. Recall that tactical moves should maintain the integrity of all three principles composing Foch's Economy of Forces superior principle while trying to compromise our adversaries in at least one. Because we are fighting for a person's mind, communication, in all its facets, will be critical, including decisions, their visibility, frequency, and content.

First, **broadcast** is easier and cheaper but strategically weaker than interaction. **Interaction** is personalized and can, therefore, go straight to the recipient's heart. The first of Foch's principles, the Concentration of Forces, is much healthier for interaction. Besides, as broadcast is immediately visible by the competition, we weaken in the second of Foch's principles, the Freedom of Action. But with interaction, its knowledge highly increases our third Foch's principle, the Economy of Effort. Thus, interaction is better at getting at our recipients' hearts, but with a cost, both on the needed resources to generate knowledge and fighting for the recipient's attention.

Social networking involves interaction between individuals, so it's as cheap as broadcast, possibly even less expensive. And due to network effects, social networking is much more effective in all regards. Therefore, social networking has a superior Concentration of Effort and is even better in Freedom of Action. After successfully unleased, we are winning attention, and our adversaries will lose traction in recipients' minds, thus seeing this second Foch's principle compromised. The trick in activating social networking is to find viral content. That is the power of the knowledge behind the Economy of Effort, the third Foch's pillar. Unfortunately, human nature seems to be much more prone to shock and awe than anything else. That is why bad news, even fabricated news, seems to travel faster, like foolish, thus influential, conspiracy theories. They say that all is fair in war and love. All in all, social networking's ultimate strategic contribution is beyond doubt.

Nevertheless, broadcast still has its place in the communication strategy. All communication has a source. Recognizing the source will entail emotional impact for recipients, including trust, a genuinely Machiavellian attribute. With the right content, broadcast can amplify audience reach, raising awareness and sparking other viral threads. And it's cheap.

We are fighting for minds. Some call this Information Warfare, and others go even further with Perception Management. We are fighting for attention and fighting for emotional attachment. In a truly Machiavellian approach, winning minds is the crux of value capturing, including emotional, social, convenient, and greedy deeds in the tactical storyline. Besides, *Virtù* should be present during strategy development to install the dimensions to be exploited after victory. Otherwise, it will be too late.

Business innovation has been considerably increasing intangible layers in the value proposition. That is why Design Thinking was conceived in the first place, addressing the pains and gains in the customer journey while encompassing social and emotional elements. An insightful approach indeed, although elements like emotions are beyond simple value creation because they also play their part in value capturing. Maybe design thinking just addressing the customer journey to formulate the value proposition is naïve. Emotional, social, convenience, and greed should be exploited in a truly Machiavellian approach with profit in mind. The recipient perceives it as value creation, in what is also a Machiavellian hook to squeeze value out of his pocket.

Finally, remember that aligning *Virtù* with strategy and producing the first part of the Value Capturing Chords is just the first part of the job. After victory, we still have to devise the second half of the VCC chords and play its melodies, thus pushing value capturing to the limit by squeezing buyer's pockets. How Machiavellian is that?

Why profitability is a consequence of strategic sustainability

Victory does not mean profitability, as pyrrhic victories are here to prove it. Moreover, victory may not last because our opponents will continue attacking while hope persists on their side. Sun Tzu grasps the very meaning of competitive advantage when conquering *key ground*, which can be exploited for profit. Machiavelli's teachings explain how to do it with *Virtù*, which is particularly well adapted to the current competitive landscape, weighing on the mind of individuals. Strategic sustainability is thus much more than just keeping the victorious status because of its impact on profitability.

We argue that sustainability happens in an individual's mind. The closer our relationship with an individual, the better, provided that our adversaries stay as far as possible. In this regard, please remember that relative distance in between each individual contender's mind will be the driver for value capturing, as already discussed above. Consequently, tactical moves will create value alongside handicaps and barriers for adversaries, which is the exact definition of Machiavellian *Virtù*.

Increasing our distance to competitors in individual minds strengthens strategic sustainability and has the interesting consequence of heightening profitability because that is the aftermath of rising switching costs.

In summary, championing *Virtù* drives strategic sustainability by creating switching costs in individual's minds, thus driving value capturing, or, in other words, sheer profitability. And following the transitivity of implication principle, a preferred syllogism mine, strategic sustainability thus drives profitability.

Quod Erat Demonstrandum.

ABOUT THE AUTHOR

Paulo Cardoso do Amaral has been an esteemed MBA professor for 28 years, sharing his expertise in prestigious institutions across Lisbon (CatólicaLisbon), Paris (E.N. Ponts et Chaussées), Switzerland (IMD), Brussels (Solvay Business School), Beijing (Tsinghua), Shanghai (Tongji), and Casablanca (E.H. Travaux Publiques). His knowledge domain lies at the intersection of Business Strategy, Competitive Intelligence, Information Warfare, Digital Transformation & Disruption, Digital Innovation, Blockchain & web3, Business Consulting, and Knowledge Management.

In addition to his academic roles, Paulo has dedicated 12 years lecturing at military academies and adjacent intuitions, focusing on Information Warfare and Competitive Intelligence.

He has authored two books: *Knowledge Capital: Evaluating and Managing Intangible Assets*; and *Top Secret: Competitive Intelligence*.

Paulo's professional journey is equally distinguished by his tenure as Chief Information Officer (CIO) for Portugal Telecom and the largest financial group in Portugal, roles he held for 15 years following the completion of his Ph.D. in Information Systems and MBA in International Business. Over the past 14 years, he has held positions as board member for mid-sized companies and has been actively involved in entrepreneurship.

A recognized thought leader in his field, Paulo is a prominent voice in national business and economics media, frequently contributing articles and making appearances on television. For a decade, he also held the position of vice-president of the Portuguese chapter of the Armed Forces Communications and Electronics Association (AFCEA), an organization that honored him with a medal of merit by the USA counterpart.

Paulo's deep-rooted interest in military strategy, cultivated over 30 years, combined with over two decades of teaching business strategy, has culminated in a unique framework that merges military thinking with business strategy, offering a simple yet powerful approach to set up executives for success.

APPENDIX I
FRAMEWORKS

Macro-level strategic assessment with Clausewitz Trinity

Choose one geo-political space for your organization and assess the current situation

For each Trinity's dimension, assess the contenders, their objectives, and probable actions

Conclude with a strategic balance

Geo-political space entities
- Official political level entities
- Companies with political influence
- Other organizations with political influence
- Regulations and unwritten rules with economic impact
- Political/economic alliances
- Political influences coming from the outside
- Law applied to politics
- Media and social networking influences
- Influences from the other two dimensions

Armed Forces' pole
Companies

Other non-profit organizations

Players in the technological & communications' infrastructure

Players in the financial infrastructure

Business level regulators

Players of the legal infrastructure

Players in the energy infrastructure

Players in transportation

Players in the media and social networking

Influences from the other two dimensions

Ground level actors and terrain
People's behavior

Social context

Companies' behavior

Unprofitable organizations behavior

Competitive environment's rules

Special organization behavior (for example, Big Techs and platforms)

Technology, communications, and media available

Energy and transports available

Influences from the other two dimensions

Sun Tzu's Command & Control Ten Leadership Virtues

Or, how to become The Chosen One

For each dimension, identify strengths, weaknesses and next steps

Wisdom
Are you able recognize hints for change, even if faint and new?

Do you act immediately on it?
Strictness
Are your orders consistently followed?

Do rewards and punishments take place?

Are individual's expectations managed?

Are you independent and immune to interference?

Humanity or benevolence
Do you sympathize with others?

Do you revel an appreciation for their capabilities and engagement?

Do you transmit positive emotions? Do you influence?

Courage and engagement
Do you have resolve? Do you hesitate?

Are you doubtful?

Is your courage perceived by others?

Sincerity
Are rewards and punishments consistent?

Are these perceived consistently

Are you perceived as truthful and trustworthy?

Serenity and self-control
Do you get vexed or distressed under fire?

How effective are you in controlling your emotions?

How vulnerable are you to provocations?

Inscrutable- "no one to guess your thoughts, officers included"
Do you keep your intentions to yourself?

Are you unpredictable?

Impartiality
Do you consistently apply the rules and the law?

Ability to learn and adapt
Do you actively seek to learn from the adversary?

Do you test your hypothesis?

Do you cherish failure as a learning process?

Humbleness
Do you acknowledge the existence of unknowns?

Are you ashamed of failing?

How is your communication perceived by others?

The Nine Combat Ground framework

Identify your grounds and explain your choices

dispersive (feudal)	avoid fighting and unify the forces
frontier (shallow penetration)	test and learn engaging few resources and keep forces closely linked
key (equally advantageous)	avoid if already occupied; speed up and take it if free; conquer it if needed
communicating (open, not key)	focus on defense upfront; develop offensive attrition
focal (politically encircled)	political action (alliances, treaties . . .)
serious or deep	similar to open ground but caring about resources (ensure supply chain or plundering)
difficult	press on but be cautious
encircled	strategies needed; block adversaries' points of access; leave escape route; consider its transformation into death ground by blocking egress points
death (desperation)	use for offense if you need that kind of motivation; but avoid attacking adversaries on death grounds

The Six Factors of Situational Awareness framework

Use this framework to organize all dimensions prior to defining strategy

Terrain

In which geographies are we competing or wish to compete?

In which markets/industries? Who are your customers, clients, and consumers?

Which battlegrounds will you be in, including consumers' reach and social networking?

How do you rank in the Competitive Ground framework?

How good and complete are your intelligence sources for the competitive environment's dynamics?

Adversaries

Who are your current contenders?

Who has assets to enter the contest in the considered geographies?

Who are probable newcomers? Which ecosystems are at stake and their strategic balance?

What are adversaries' competencies, tactics, and foreseeable strategy?

How good and complete are your intelligence sources regarding competitors?

How strong the insight generation capability on adversaries and ecosystems?

Weather

Which entities are capable of influencing regulations?

Which companies have significant marketing influence?

Which laws and regulations matter? Are there unwritten rules at stake?

How good and complete are your intelligence sources for what is really happening in the market?

What about intelligence for not publicly available information?

Doctrine & resources

Is the organization fit to purpose? Is it correctly controlled?

Which tangible assets are deployable? What about image, brand, and other intangible resources?

How strong are your competencies and capabilities at stake?

How prepared is the company to take risks, to control risk and to compete?

Command

How well is leadership ranked in the Command & Control Leadership framework and prepared to compete?

Moral influence, that is, trust and the harmony with leadership

How united is everybody between themselves and with leadership?

How trustful are individuals?

Sun Tzu's Ten Tactics framework

Using the outcome of situational awareness, identify possible tactics

Political level

Subdue the enemy without fighting, by attacking his strategy	What are our enemies' strategies? How can we attack their plans? What are enemies' possible tactics? Which are threats? How can we turn them ineffective?
First disrupt alliances	Are there foe alliances (value chains, ecosystems)? How can we disrupt them? How can we lure possible allies away from foes?

Battleground level

Bring the enemy to the field of battle	How can we lure the enemy under our own terms? Can you foster our enemies to jeopardize their resources, creating exploitable weaknesses? How can we avoid our own weaknesses?
Create a position not to be defeated and grab every opportunity	Which opportunities are we expecting to grab? Can these opportunities result in creating entry barriers? Which threats should be avoided? Should we be first or second mover?
Create momentum	What are our strengths? In which opportunities can we concentrate our forces? Which weaknesses are at stake? Which defenses are important?

Conserve your strength and maintain your freedom	Offense: What is the single most important set of projects to consider? Defense: Which enemy strengths are threatful? Which gains should be protected?
Prevent the enemy to concentrate	Which enemy weaknesses can we attack? How can we lure our enemies to disperse his forces and create more weaknesses?

Support level

Use extraordinary (special) forces	Are there intangible assets available? Which resources should we endow?
Capture enemy's resources	Can we grab enemy resources, both tangible and intangible? Deploy a takeover? Grab already created markets or habits?
Throw your troops to prepare to die, that is, throw the army in a desperate position	How are we going to install a sense of urgency in our forces?

Sun Tzu's Strategy

First apply the checklist below

Then, list a sequence of chosen tactics

Sun Tzu's Dynamic Engagement checklist
Internal situational awareness done

External situational awareness done

Do not repeat tactics' modus operandi and sequence

Consider momentum and timing

Consider speed

Consider the dispersion of opponent's forces

General Foch's Economy of Forces Assessment
List all tactics and assess each according to the three principles below:

For each tactic:

> Perform an Internal analysis check to maintain the three intact
>
> Perform an External analysis check, compromising at least one on adversaries
>
> Perform a final comprehensive check

Economy of Forces' Principles
Concentration of forces - I want

Freedom of action - I can

Economy of effort - I know

Tactical Health Check framework

Use the two checklists below, evaluating and proposing possible actions

Five Command Losing Factors
Recklessness

Cowardice

Short temper

Irascibleness

Excessive compassion

Six Tactical Losing Conditions
Insubordinate troops

Strong troops with weak officers

Valiant officers with ineffective troops

Angry and insubordinate officers

Morally weak general without a strict discipline

Unable to estimate enemy forces

Sun Tzu's Strategic Route Map

This is Sun Tzu's methodological checklist to prepare the strategic engagement.

It is also the repository of the other frameworks output for all the necessary steps

1. What is your strategic objective?

    recall Clausewitz' Trinity assessment with "Clausewitz Trinity Analysis"

2. What is your Situational Awareness assessment?

    "Know your enemy and know yourself upfront of everything else" and "determine enemy's plans"
      - Start with "Sun Tzu's Command and Control Leadership Virtues" to bootstrap internal awareness
      - Then with "Sun Tzu's Nine Combat Grounds" to bootstrap external awareness to develop "Sun Tzu's Six Factors Situational Awareness"

3. Explore possible tactics using "Sun Tzu's Ten Tactics" framework.

4. Use "Sun Tzu's Strategy" framework to prepare a possible sequence of tactics, i.e., the first strategic route map

    Then use its "Dynamic Engagement checklist to verify the dynamics of the proposed sequence of tactical moves.

    Revise the sequence of tactics if needed.

5. Use "6 Foch's Economy of Forces" ramework to assess tactics:

    Confirm that each tactical move does not weaken your strategic position.

    Verify that each tactical move weakens your adversary in at least one Foch's principle.

    Evaluate the complete set of tactical moves according to the Economy of Forces.

Switching costs with Machiavelli's *Virtù*

First identify how to build switching costs for customers, clients, consumers, competitors, and allies

Then, for buyers, identify possible revenue modes and price matching techniques

Finally, combine both to create Value Capturing Chords

Emotional switching costs
Trust -
Q1: How can trust flourish?
Brand -
Q2: How can the brand flourish?
Show-off -
Q3: Can we let the individual show-off with pride?
Family -
Q4: Can individual's family be rewarded?
Friendship -
Q5: Can friendship be nurtured?
Self-dignity and altruism -
Q6: How can altruism and self-dignity be nurtured?
Q7: How to foster excellence?

Social generated switching costs
Visibility and prestige -
Q8: Is there a social stage to offer?
Q9: Can prestige be nourished?
Q10: Can accomplishments or behavior be nurtured for admiration?
Community -
Q11: Can social networking be nurtured with content?
Q12: How do we nurture socialization and entertainment with courtesy and respect?
Q13: Is the community's value increasing with size?

Social networking and crowdsourcing -

> Q14: Can the recipient gain visibility provide social networking communication and content, including crowdsourcing?

Convenience generated switching costs
Shame -

> Q15: Will the user feel ashamed when electing another organization?

Search costs -

> Q16: the offerings decrease search costs?

Personalization -

> Q17: How personalized are offerings and communication?

Habit -

> Q18: are individuals used to the product, service, or brand (habit)?
> Q19: Can habit become addictive?

Marketplace -

> Q20: Can we offer a marketplace ecosystem?

Context -

> Q21: Is contextual knowledge part of the offering?

Service Convenience -

> Q22: Can service convenience be included?

Industry standards -

> Q23: Are standards, regulations, or laws, valuable?

Greed
Non-linear Discounts -

> Q24: Can we offer non-linear discounts?

Cashback -

> Q25: Is there an opportunity for non-linear cashback?

Buyer Aggregation -

> Q26: Can we offer cost value, like buyer aggregation?

Exit fees -

> Q27: Can an exit fee be naturally imposed?

Revenue models and price discovery

RM1: Licensing or rental

RM2: Membership Licensing

RM3: Versioning

RM4: Versioning based bundling

RM5: Personalized pricing

RM6: Skimming

RM7: Congestion pricing

RM8: Deadline or urgency

RM9: Group based pricing

RM10: Broadcasted discounts

RM11: PWYW (Pay What You Want)

RM12: Personalized discounts

RM13: Loyalty coupons

RM14: Auctions

RM15: Reverse auctions

Six Prince's qualities checklist

Apply to the dimensions below to the company

Identify possible improvements

Assess your own leadership

Qualities	Dangers to Avoid
Free-spending and generous	diminishing resources; diminishing scarcity; ethics
Merciful (on a cruel background)	hatred; ethics
Word-keeping (impressing with other qualities) and socially chaste	getting exposed
Friendly (decisions and communication's frequency & content)	hatred
Decision-making: audacious, straightforward, firm, and grave	hatred
Appearance of believing; influencing for belief	being caught not believing; unleashing wrong beliefs

Printed in the USA
CPSIA information can be obtained
at www.ICGtesting.com
CBHW021110241024
16330CB00045B/636